Twelve Wings
of the Eagle

**Our Spiritual Evolution through the
Ages of the Zodiac**

Twelve Wings of the Eagle

Our Spiritual Evolution
through the Ages of the Zodiac

Maria Kay Simms

ACS Publications, Inc.
San Diego

International Standard Book Number 0-917086-95-3

Cover Design and Illustrations
by Maria Kay Simms

Printed in the United States of America

Published by ACS Publications, Inc.
P.O. Box 16430
San Diego, CA 92116-0430

Dedicated with love and
thanks to
Mark
. . . for new beginnings

Contents

Author's Notes and Acknowledgments

My thoughts, expressed within this book, are the product of personal reflection, and are influenced by a wide variety of books, classes, lectures and conversations that I've experienced over many years. Some pieces of information about astrology, astronomy, history, numbers and mythology are a composite of so many different sources that no single source can reasonably be given specific credit. In every case where I can identify my statement as being derived from another book, I have credited the author in the endnotes. I have avoided footnoting within the text in order that the reading might flow in the uninterrupted manner of a novel.

My text is interspersed with stories from the Bible and with dialogue--conversations between myself and one other person, or group discussions during a class. These occur in no particular order and are not intended to be a "plot." They are a device to help say what I want to say in a style that flows like a story, rather than a "heavy" textbook. The conversations are fictional, but they are based, in part, on actual conversations and questions, especially involving the following people:

As you will read in the first chapter, my studies that resulted in this book were, in part, motivated by questions about religion from my daughter Shannon Sullivan, who is now a junior in college but who was about 15 at the time. Those of you who are familiar with astrological types will find no surprise in the information that Shannon has Sun in Sagittarius and Moon in Gemini. Thank you, Shannon--this is a time when being inquisitive and a bit provocative really helped Mom!

During the time that I was writing the book I lived in Connecticut, and every Tuesday evening a group of friends met at my home to study Uranian astrology. The class had been ongoing for years with variable numbers in attendance. Five people rarely ever missed a class, and at one time or another each of them read my manuscript and offered comments and helpful criticism. Often, before we got started on our project for the evening, they would ask how my book was progressing and we'd discuss some part of it. One of them, Tom Canfield, even volunteered a good deal of his time to type my first draft and in the process, do some editing. Since Tom is a "walking encyclopedia" of interesting facts about almost everything imaginable, his help was most welcome!

My heartfelt thanks to Tom, and to the other "regulars" in the Uranian workshop who contributed much encouragement and constructive feedback: Egon Eckert, Patti Skiff, Pat Miske and Louise Patrick.

About the Bible stories:

One of the purposes of this book is to show the extensive astrological symbolism contained within scripture; and in particular to put forth my theory that the order of the Great Ages of the precession of the equinoxes is an underlying structure for Genesis. In order to accomplish this I have retold a number of familiar Bible stories. English translations of the Bible vary quite a bit, so at first I compared passages in every Bible I could find at home and in the library to make sure that what I was seeing was really there. After a time I settled on three Bibles to cross-check as I paraphrased each story: The *King James Version,* because it is the most commonly used; the Oxford University Press *New English Bible*; and the Catholic edition of *The New American Bible.* The latter is my favorite because it is clear and easy to read, and because it includes so many informative footnotes. It is the product of a long and impressive list of scholars who translated from the oldest available sources. The result has exceptional clarity. The language is contemporary American while still retaining the beauty of older translations. I cannot, however, in any way slight *The New English Bible.* It, too, is scholarly and clear; and, without its full version of the Apocrypha I would not have my title and my final chapter!

Paraphrased Bible stories are identified in the endnotes by chapter and verse. In the few cases where I have quoted a passage exactly, the specific translation is credited in the endnotes, and the passage (if more than a short phrase) is set apart from the text by indents.

About the book production:

With the exception of the cover painting, which I did the "old-fashioned way" with a paintbrush, this book was entirely produced on a MacIntosh Plus computer with Laserwriter Plus. For those who may be interested in that sort of thing, the manuscript was imported from Word 3.0 to Quark Xpress for page layout. The pencil sketches of astrological symbols were scanned with Thunderscan, saved as Tiff files and adjusted in Xpress. All of the other illustrations were created with Adobe Illustrator.

More Thank Yous:

Several people have made significant contributions to my work. I am deeply appreciative of comments and encouragement from Father Laurence Cassidy, who read early drafts of my manuscript. Jim Jossick offered good advice on style when I was just beginning to write the book and I thank him for that. Also during the early stages of writing this book I received much enthusiastic encouragement from Linda Martin, who accompanied me on a research trip to the New York Public Library, and later located a then hard-to-find copy of *Hamlet's Mill*. Thank you, Linda! Many thanks, also, to Mary Downing, Brita Okin and Arlene Nimark for reading my manuscript and offering criticism and encouragement.

This book is dedicated to my long-time friend, Mark Howard, because it was he who motivated me to start studying astrology 15 years ago. But I thank him also for valuable training on the MacIntosh during the year I spent doing publications for his dinner theaters in Florida.

Many thanks to all of the staff at ACS Publications, especially to my eagle-eyed copyeditor, Mary Effington. Last, but most certainly not least, my deepest thanks for the emotional, physical, intellectual and spiritual assistance of my husband and publisher, Neil F. Michelsen.

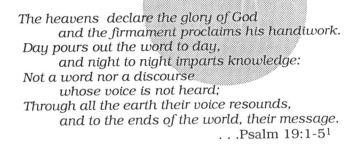

The heavens declare the glory of God
and the firmament proclaims his handiwork.
Day pours out the word to day,
and night to night imparts knowledge:
Not a word nor a discourse
whose voice is not heard;
Through all the earth their voice resounds,
and to the ends of the world, their message.
. . .Psalm 19:1-5[1]

Introduction

What message resounds through all the Earth, proclaimed in the sky above us? What word is poured out by day? What knowledge is communicated by the sky at night? Can we learn about God from the sky?

The attempt to gain knowledge from the sky is as old as the oldest science. The attempt to know God by studying the sky is as ancient as the most ancient of religions. Many thousands of years ago the work began.

Our distant ancestors looked to the heavens with great fear and wonder. The powerful Sun that lighted and warmed the day vanished at night. And the to light the night, but other times as only a slender crescent; and then her face was hidden, leaving all in darkness except the tiny twinkling stars. As the air turned increasingly cold, the Sun came for a shorter time each day until the people feared its loss, and they prayed and danced and sacrificed to entice the great Sun God's return. So began our most ancient of holidays, Winter Solstice, the rebirth of the Sun, still celebrated today by Christians as Christmas, the birth of Christ, the "sun of justice" (Malachi 3:30).

Long ago our foremothers observed the similarity between the repeated phases of the Moon and their own womanly cycles. The cycle of the Moon was found to be predictable, and consequently so was the next time of bleeding. To count the phases of the Moon became the way to measure time, to predict the hunt, and to know the time for planting. For their very livelihood the people came to depend on the Moon. In her cycle conjoined with mysterious woman, who alone produced new life, the Moon became the Goddess.

The scientists of ancient times were those whose keen observations of the movement of the heavenly bodies enabled them to predict cyles. In this way they seemed to exert some hope of control over a vast cosmos within which most people felt no sense of control at all. They became the high priestesses and priests.

For the ancients, astronomy and religion were inseparable--astrology: astra (star) logos (word). The word of the stars.

In modern times the "divine science," astrology, is emerging from a dark age of discreditation at the hands of post 18th century materialist science, and of the primary religion of the Piscean Age, Christianity.

Although in concert on very little else, materialist scientists and fundamentalist Christians cry out in chorus, "Astrology? Mumbo-jumbo, nothing but superstition--dangerous, even." Yet in this present day, thousands are giving astrology another look, a more probing investigation.

The contemporary scientist recognizes intangibles, probes to the "big bang" and cannot explain its cause, then turns to the inner self only to find unknowables as vast as the unexplainable cosmos. It is worthwhile, then, to be open to the investigation of anything that might help to provide answers--even an old "superstition" like astrology. In spite of all attempts to discredit it, astrology has held the imagination of millions throughout the ages.

The contemporary Christian, even if secure in faith, feels justified in interpreting dogma and tradition according to individual conscience. Faith alone does not provide all of the answers, anymore than does pure scientific reason. The truth must lie in a blend of these, and tradition must be probed for its links of reason and faith. Astrology will be recognized to be one of those links.

The Bible reader, if knowledgeable in the language of astrology, will find countless Old Testament references, and also numerous astrological symbols, or teachings related to astrology, esoterically contained within New Testament parables. Why is so much astrology to be found in scripture? What is its true place in our tradition? Can it be possible that the firmament truly does declare the glory and the handiwork of God, if only we can decipher its message?

This book will examine:

      * How the Great Ages of the precession of the equinoxes provide a timeline for history and mythology

      * How the Book of Genesis hermetically contains the order and the symbolism of the Great Ages

      *How the message of the Great Ages suggests a Divine Plan for the evolution of human consciousness

      *How the extreme shifts between world views

*How the extreme shifts between world views emphasizing faith and reason in our present Age of Pisces are symbolized by the Mutable Cross

* How, in our present Age of Pisces, concepts of God are changing, as women and the Goddess and the true significance of the Virgin emerge

* How the mystical meaning of numbers relates to astrology and scripture and the paradox of fate and free will

* How the symbolism of the Great Ages, linked with the prophetic visions of II Esdras, suggests the future course of history and religious thought for the new Age of Aquarius and beyond--to tens of thousands of years into the future!

I had a vision in a dream; I saw, rising from the sea, an eagle with twelve wings . . . I saw the eagle stand erect on its talons, and it spoke aloud to its wings: 'Do not wake at once,' it said; 'sleep in your places, and each wake up in turn . . . "

--II Esdras 11: 1-11[1]

1

In the Beginning

"Twelve wings of the eagle!" I thought with satisfaction as I read the apocryphal book of II Esdras. "It fits so well--like a confirmation of my theory."

But the eagle belongs at the end of my story, and we must begin with the beginning.

"In the beginning," the Bible tells us, "the earth was a formless void. A mighty wind swept over the waters, and God said, 'Let there be light.' "

Genesis, with its familiar and taken-for-granted lines, motivated the Bible study that led me to the twelve wings of the eagle, and to a whole new understanding of zodiacal symbolism in our history and in our scriptures.

It began with my daughter, Shannon, and her indignation over a newspaper article:

"What is the matter with these people who call

themselves 'scientific creationists'? They are actually trying to force the high school science teachers to teach Genesis right along with Darwin. How can they ignore all the scientific proof against Genesis? Are they dumb or just plain crazy?"

"Hold on there," I said, "before you jump to put other people down. Didn't you see *Star Trek II* ? The writers of that movie imagined that advanced scientists could design a massive explosion that would create a whole new living world in just six minutes. God took six whole days!"

"Mother! Be serious! You can't possibly agree with the scientific creationists."

"No, not in the way they're going about it; but in another way, yes, I do think Genesis is true. Don't you remember back when you were studying catechism? You didn't think Genesis made sense then, either, and you challenged the priest about it. What did Father tell you?"

"He said that a 'day' did not necessarily mean twenty-four hours. Our modern methods of keeping time weren't even known way back then. The word 'day' could have symbolized a million years, and the use of the six days of creation followed by a seventh day of rest was similar to the parables that Jesus told, to teach a lesson. In this case, the lesson probably had to do with the sacredness of the holy seventh day, the Sabbath."

"Right! You remember well. Father also said that if we study Genesis for its symbolic meanings, all of the apparent conflict with science can be resolved. Science and religion need not be in conflict at all."

"Well, there's plenty of conflict in this newspaper story. These people seem to take the Bible very literally. They really **believe** that everything started only a few thousand years ago. Why?"

"Maybe one reason the creationists are trying so hard to cling to their literal interpretation of Genesis is because of their fear that the findings of science have reduced their lives to insignificance. It's difficult to cope with the apparent infinity of time and space, or conceive of a God that is large enough for the whole universe. By insisting on six days of creation only a few thousand years ago, they are able to bring God down to a size that will enable them to identify with and personalize Him.[2] After all, how could a God who started the universe with big bang billions of years ago, and who allowed man to evolve unaided from the apes, now take such a personal interest in each detail of our daily lives that we can, in effect, abdicate our personal responsibility for the evolution of our own consciousness by praying to **Him** for our every want, thanking **Him** when things go right, and resignedly telling ourselves that it is **God's Will** when things go wrong?"

"Well," said Shannon, "I have to say that those fears make sense. In spite of the religious education classes you made me take, I'm not yet completely convinced there's a God out there at all. Anyway, no more time to talk about it now. The creationists will make a good clipping to take to social studies. See you after school."

As I watched her leave I thought about my own years of rebellion against the church, of agnosticism, and then of searching. How I have envied, at times, the people who seem so secure and unquestioning in their religious faith. Faith in God is said to be a gift that can't be earned, and that may well be true. I feel secure in my faith now, but oh how many years I searched and questioned and reasoned and was angry before I could accept that gift. Shannon is like me in that--she'll never believe anything just because she's told. But I know that in her own way and in her own time, she will find God. All paths lead to the truth eventually.

It had been many years since I'd read Genesis-- years before my studies in astrology and metaphysics.

Thinking to myself that if all truth has but one source--God--then the truths of Genesis and of science could only **appear**, superficially, to be in contradiction, I found myself opening the family Bible.

Darwin's theory of evolution is still but a theory, not entirely proven, or without "missing links." Yet certainly enough scientific proof has been found for the age of the earth and the development of various species that a literal interpretation of Genesis seems quite impossible. Still, a controversy exists. Christians believe the Bible to be of divine inspiration, and therefore most definitely true. I knew that symbolic, rather than literal, interpretation of scripture was often taught in my church. But beyond the explanation of the "days" of creation that the priest had given Shannon, I hadn't given much thought to Genesis. What does it really say? Surely there must be a link that unites this creation story of the Bible with the discoveries of modern science.

As I read the Bible, my fascination grew. A whole new Genesis had opened up for me, clarified by my understanding of ancient zodiacal and numerological symbolism. The ages! It contains the ages!

My excitement at discovering a structure for Genesis based on the precessional ages was heightened by the fact that all of my free time in recent weeks had been spent in an attempt to write an article on the measurement and history of the ages. I had a theory that the measurement of the ages should be according to the size of the constellations, rather than according to the twelve divisions of about 2000 years per age that was advocated in every book I'd ever read on this subject. History fit better with ages based on constellation size, and I hoped that this new twist on an old subject would be of interest to a publisher.

The precessional ages are not, by far, a new idea. A number of astrology books in print discuss correlations in history, art and mythology with the movement of the point of the vernal equinox around the circle of the zodiac. The "Age of Aquarius" became a familiar term several years back as a popular song in the Broadway musical *Hair.* With a new millenium not far in the future, hopes and dreams of utopian idealism, expressed in writing, are in abundance. Some look to Aquarius as a golden age of love and peace and brotherhood, the confusions of the Piscean Age made clear, its mystical visions revealed as Universal Truth. Others see the coming millenium as the likely time of the Second Coming, with all the sinners punished and Christ to reign over the saved for a thousand years of peace.

But "utopia," or the reign of the Christ, was to be preceded by great upheaval. Dire predictions of war, pestilence, tragedy and tribulation would devastate the planet before the year 2000.

It is my intention to offset a few of these prophecies of doom with the reality that the vernal point will not precess out of the constellation Pisces until about A.D. 2700. **This** age is **far** from over. Our attention would be more productively focused on learning to understand the ideals of Pisces, and how we can improve our world, rather than to suffer like helpless Piscean victims, dreaming that within our own short lifetimes Aquarius will arrive, or Christ will return, and all true believers will be saved.

Now I had a whole new element to add to my theory on the ages: that the authors of Genesis may have known about them and deliberately used them as a structure for the book. After all, Genesis **is** the story of Creation! And the circle of the zodiac, as "the heavens declare," tells a story of the evolution of the soul.

My article had become a book!

My interpretation of the ages of the zodiac through Genesis, Exodus and the Gospels is written in a fictionalized style, with stories from the Bible interspersed with my own commentary, conversations and class discussions. The Bible stories are paraphrased and condensed versions based on my reading of various English translations of the Bible. When I have directly quoted from a particular Bible, the quote is indented, italicized and credited as to the specific translation. In all other cases the Bible sections are paraphrased in my own words, but very closely paralleling actual text.

Readers should be able to enjoy my story even if they have little or no knowledge of the language of astrology. Some points will be missed, however, by those of you who are unfamiliar with astrological terms. For this reason my story of the ages will be preceded by four preliminary chapters. Chapter Two describes the basic astronomy of precession and Chapter Three discusses the meaning of the symbols of the zodiac. Chapter Four is an allegory based on the first chapter of Genesis and Chapter Five is a conversation about the allegory that contains additional introductory material on astrological and number symbolism. These chapters are much slower-paced than the rest of the book, so it was a temptation to start with the adventures of Adam and Eve, and relegate the introductory material to an appendix. However, I believe that these first chapters are important not only because they cover basic symbolism, but also because they establish an underlying philosophy for the book.

Astrologers may be tempted to skim the introductory chapters, but please do note that Chapter 2 contains a theory of the order and measurement of the Great Ages that is different from that which appears in many other books. Also, the metaphysical concepts that are introduced in the first four chapters are basic to an understanding of my interpretation of scripture, and of my correlation of scripture and astrology with the evolution of human consciousness.

2

The Precessional Ages

In order to understand precession we must first understand some basic facts about motion within the universe. Everything in the universe moves. The stars **appear** to be fixed because they are so very far away. The "proper" motion of the stars seems so slight to us that it can only be detected by careful observation at 50- to 100- year intervals.

Although the stars in any given constellation are hundreds of light years away from each other, and at greatly varied distances from Earth, to us they seem to be in family groups. With few exceptions, the stars that belong to each constellation do, in fact, move in the same direction, thus staying "with" the family.

The closest star to Earth is, of course, the sun.

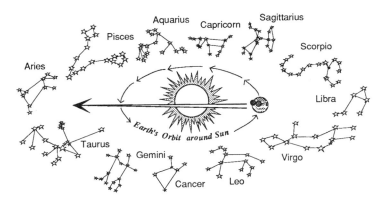

The time that it takes for Earth to orbit the sun is how we determine our calendar year. As Earth circles the sun, it appears from Earth that the sun is "in" (in front of) each of the twelve constellations of the zodiac in succession. This is the counter-clockwise motion of Earth that is called **secondary motion.**

Primary motion is that of Earth's daily rotation on its axis. It is clockwise, and the motion of the sun in a horoscope chart imitates this motion. Imagine that the center of the chart is Earth. You are on Earth, looking south. East is then on your left, and west is on your right. It appears to you that the sun "rises" in the east, reaches its highest point at noon, and sets in the west. Consequently, if you were born at about noon, Sun will be drawn in your chart in the culminating position. It takes approximately two hours for the sun to shift to the next number, so if you were born about 2 PM, Sun will be drawn at about "one o'clock."

Now, if you were able to look right at the sun at exactly the same time every day, it would appear

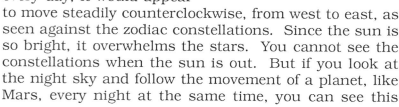

to move steadily counterclockwise, from west to east, as seen against the zodiac constellations. Since the sun is so bright, it overwhelms the stars. You cannot see the constellations when the sun is out. But if you look at the night sky and follow the movement of a planet, like Mars, every night at the same time, you can see this motion.

All of the planets in our solar system appear to us to move in the same plane as the sun does. This **apparent** path of the sun, which is actually the orbit of the Earth **around** the sun, is known as the **ecliptic.** The zodiac is the group of constellations that can be seen right along the ecliptic.

The ecliptic, like a circle, measures 360 degrees. The motion of the sun is approximately one degree for each day of the year. If we could see which constellation appears beyond the sun right at sunrise, we would see that each day the sun rises in one successive degree after the next.

The degree of the ecliptic that rises *with* the sun is called the **Ascendant**, or the "Rising Sign."

A very important measurement used by astronomers and astrologers is the point of the **vernal equinox.** This is the point at which the sun appears to cross the plane of Earth's equator going northward on the first day of spring. It is a point of intersection of the circle, or plane, of the ecliptic (formed by secondary motion) and the circle, or plane, of the equator (formed by primary motion). The opposite point of intersection is called the **autumnal equinox**.

We now come to a third movement of Earth that is not so easily observed as are the primary and secondary motions. It is this third motion that causes the phenomenon that is known as the **precession of the equinoxes.**

Earth is not a perfect sphere. It is slightly flat at the north and south poles and it bulges around the middle. Because of this, its spin on its axis is slightly irregular, much like the spin of a top that is just beginning to slow down.

If you play with a child's top for a while, you can begin to understand precession. Watch the tip ends. The tip that touches the floor seems stationary, but the top tip describes a circle. Then study the center. It wobbles a little.

Earth, in a similar way to the top, wobbles a little. To us, here on our wobbly planet, it looks like the intersections of equator and ecliptic are moving slowly clockwise along the path of the ecliptic.[1] This movement is extremely slow. It takes the vernal point almost 26,000 years to "wobble" past all the constellations of the zodiac, completing an entire circuit of the ecliptic.

Of course, the other stars also seem to be displaced by precession. We now find north by sighting Polaris, the north polar star. But Polaris was not always the "North Star." Back in the time of ancient Egypt, Thuban, in the constellation Draco, was the North Star. And about 11,500 years from now the North Star will be Vega, in the constellation Lyra.

How did the ancients figure this out? Their priests studied the sky very carefully night after night. Many things depended on the accuracy of their observations--success of the planting seasons, and therefore the livelihood of the people; religion, and the power, or perhaps the very lives of the priests. Among the more careful observations were the equinoctial and solstice points.

If over the years you noticed that a certain star that you expected to rise heliacally (meaning just before the sun) on the first day of spring was no longer visible, you could make the assumption that something up there had shifted. Now assuming you are well aware of the twelve constellations along the ecliptic, you now see that only one star of a given constellation is still visible just before sunrise. You would know that in a few years that one, too, would be invisible, and the next constellation in line would rise before the sun. The entire constellation that had risen heliacally for as long as you or anyone else you knew could remember would then be completely invisible (lost in the blinding rays of the sun). What would you make of that?

The ancients decided that a whole new order had arrived. The constellation that now rose **right with the sun,** and was thus invisible, was said to be "sacrificed."[2] At the dawn of the Age of Aries, one of the most popular animals to be offered on the sacrificial altars was the bull or calf, symbol of the "sacrificed" Age of Taurus. The symbol of the Age of Aries was the Ram, and ram or fire deities quickly began to compete with the bull-gods and sacred cows for the devotion of the people. As the new order became more firmly established, those who slipped back into the old ways worshipped a watered-down version of the bull, a **little** bull--**the golden calf.**

By the end of the Age of Aries, the Ram had become a lamb; and as Aries became lost, or sacrificed, in the sunrise and the Age of Pisces dawned, the Christ was understood to be the sacrificial lamb--**the Lamb of God** who gave his own life for the redemption of humanity.

Now just before the Age of Pisces began, a Greek astronomer named Hipparchus studied precession. At that time, the constellation Aries no longer rose before the sun. Perhaps only the first star in the Ram could be seen at vernal equinox, and then, one year, it was invisible. Precessional order is said to be "backwards," so it is the "head" of the constellation that is the last to disappear at the horizon.

Hipparchus and others decided to call the point of the vernal equinox "the first point of Aries." The constellations are irregular in size, so for convenience of measurement of the celestial bodies, the circle of the ecliptic was divided into twelve equal sections of 30 degrees each. The sections were named according to the constellations that appeared approximately within them, and the degrees were numbered in counterclockwise order according to the sun's apparent yearly transit.

The **equal sections of the ecliptic** are what we call the **signs** of the zodiac. At the time of Hipparchus the signs and the constellations coincided with each other. Because of the precession of the equinoxes this is no longer true. On the first day of spring it is now about the fourth degree from the beginning of the constellation Pisces that rises just before the sun. In a few hundred years, Pisces will have completely "disappeared," the constellation Aquarius will rise before the sun, and we will truly be in the Age of Aquarius.

On the timing of the Great Ages there is little agreement. Most books on the subject advocate an equal division of the approximately 26,000-year Great Year cycle into 2000- to 2200-year Great Months, or Ages. Nearly every author agrees that Jesus brought in the Age of Pisces. As the "sacrificial lamb" of the outgoing age, he founded a new religion with disciples who were "fishers of men" and followers who recognized each other by the sign of the Fish.

My initial dissatisfaction with equal division measurement was because history just didn't fit. I could find no significant Aries symbolism for 2000 years before Christ. Not until after 1800 B.C. does Ram symbolism become prominent. Why?

As I looked at a star map, the answer became clear. The constellations are not the same size, so how could the **ages** be the same length? Aries is tiny, compared to Pisces. It would take hundreds of years longer for the equinox to precess through the Fishes than through the Ram!

I searched in vain for a reference that would tell me exactly how many degrees were in each constellation. Astronomers' star maps usually indicate only each 15th degree of the ecliptic. I learned that even though the stars are apparently fixed in position, they do move in space enough that new star maps are prepared at 50- to 100-year intervals. Although the "proper" motion is extremely slow, it obviously would be enough to change the size and shape of constellations slightly over a period of several thousand years.

It would seem that the only way to know exactly when the last star of a constellation rose just before the sun on the day of the vernal equinox, heralding the end of an Age, would be to **be** there--or to have access to a star chart drawn at that time.

Another obstacle to the exact timing of ages is that the rate of precession is slightly accelerating. The mean length of a Great Year is at present 25,920 years.

Finally, I found in Geoffrey Dean's *Recent Advances in Natal Astrology* a list of degrees for unequal sections of the ecliptic, set up by astronomers for the purpose of locating stars.[3] Compared with the star maps, the list matched the constellations if the degrees of the "open spaces" between some of the constellations are added to the nearest small one.

(I place "open" in quotes because obviously the spaces are **not** open. In fact, at least two non-zodiacal constellations appear to intrude within the degree spread assigned to the ecliptic. However all of the astronomy texts seemed to be comfortably in agreement that there are **twelve** zodiac constellations. Apparently the historical and symbolic significance of twelve is acceptable as a precedent to astronomers, so I will not complicate my theory by speculating on the meaning of Ophichus or Cetus.)

At any rate, I decided to use the astronomers' list to work a ratio to a total Great Year cycle of 25,920 years, just to see if the results worked better with past historical evidence. To do this I divided the degrees of a full circle, 360, by the number of degrees for each constellation. The result was then divided into 25,920.

	Degrees	Ratio to 360	Number of years in each age
Libra	18	20	1296
Virgo	46	7.826	3312
Leo	35	10.28	2521
Cancer	21	17.14	1512
Gemini	28	12.857	2016
Taurus	36	10	2592
Aries	24	15	1728
Pisces	38	9.47	2737
Aquarius	25	14.4	1800
Capricorn	28	12.8557	2016
Sagittarius	30	12	2160
Scorpio	31	11.61	2232

In the light of the facts of acceleration of precession and proper motion of the stars, and of the controversy over the actual beginning of the Piscean Age, it makes no sense to try to pinpoint an exact year, or even an exact decade for the division between epochs. A transition period of, at the very least, one hundred years would have to be considered at each division, with an even larger transition period at the divisions between which there are several degrees of "open" space: Leo/Cancer, Gemini/Taurus, Pisces/Aquarius and Capricorn/Sagittarius. Therefore, it seemed only reasonable to round off my figures to the nearest hundred years, and to add or subtract from zero, which may not be exactly the year of the birth of Christ, but is close, and is commonly accepted as the one upon which the calendar is based. My estimate of the approximate beginning of each age is as follows:

Age of Scorpio ....17,000 B.C.
Age of Libra ....15,000 B.C
Age of Virgo ....13,600 B.C.
Age of Leo ....10,000 B.C.

Age of Cancer	7,800 B.C.
Age of Gemini	6,300 B.C.
Age of Taurus	4,300 B.C.
Age of Aries	1,700 B.C.
Age of Pisces	0
Age of Aquarius	2,700 A.D.
Age of Capricorn	4,500 A.D.
Age of Sagittarius	6,500 A.D.
Age of Scorpio	8,600 A.D.

I calculated Scorpio twice because it symbolizes death and rebirth, the beginning and the end of the cycle.

At a meeting of my weekly astrology workshop I shared my ideas, for I knew my class would have questions and comments that would be helpful. As usual, I got plenty of stimulating feedback:

"Guess Scorpio would make sense as the fiducial of the cycle since it has always been the sign associated with destruction, elimination, death--but then the capacity to regenerate, to be reborn."

"But all the books give Aries as number one, the beginning."

"Yes, but how far back do those books go? None before this present age. Is there any good reason for the zodiac to begin with Aries, other than it was the spring constellation 2000 years ago when the Greeks set up the present zodiacal system?"

"So many authors explain Aries/beginning symbolism in terms of spring as the birth of the year. This is fine for the Northern Hemisphere, but what about those that live 'down under'? Their spring comes in Libra. Wonder how they feel about Aries as 'the beginning'?"

"Yes, I've wondered about that, too."

A newcomer to the class directed her question to me, "Why do astrologers still say the astrological new year begins with zero degrees Aries when it doesn't anymore?"

"Actually, it's not just the astrologers," I replied. "Astronomers call the vernal point 0 degrees Aries, too. It's still a convenience of measurement. Any credible astrologer is well aware of the difference between the signs and the constellations. Some astrologers practice what is known as the sidereal school of astrology, and they use the actual positions of the fixed stars as their reference point. However, once they decide on the reference point, they divide the ecliptic into equal divisions, so it's still not a truly constellational astrology. And because it's very hard to pin down precessional movement to any degree of exactness, the beginning of the sidereal zodiac is a matter of disagreement among various groups of practitioners.

"I like the so-called tropical school of astrology better, because its reference point of 0 degrees Aries makes the position of Sun fit the seasons in a clear-cut way. Also, nobody, not astrologer nor astronomer, disagrees about the intersection of equator and ecliptic as defining the equinoctial points. Each year on about March 21, it appears from our vantage point on earth, that the sun crosses the equator moving northward. That moment marks the vernal equinox--a clear-cut mathematical fact.[4]   We call that moment in time zero degrees of Aries. So March 21st of each year is 0 degrees Aries day, and the next 29 degrees or days follow and then we are "in" Taurus, and so on. It's convenient, and astrologers have found the symbolism seems to work well in the interpretation of personality characteristics for those who are born within each 'sign.' "

Another student asked, "Why doesn't the order of the months of the year go along with the signs, then? Why does our year start with Capricorn, and why isn't Sagittarius the twelfth sign?"

"Look at the beginning of December," I pointed out. You've studied languages a little--what does 'dec' come from?"

"Ten!"

"Right! and 'Nov' comes from nine, 'Oct' from eight, and 'Sept' from seven. Obviously at one time these were months seven through ten instead of nine through twelve. I have read that January 1 was adopted as the beginning of the year about 150 years before Christ to coincide with the time that Roman officials took office. Before that, the Roman calendar began with March. Right down to the eighteenth century, however, some church calendars persisted in considering the Annunciation on March 25 to begin the year. The history of the calendar could make a whole book in itself."[5]

"O.K., I guess that's a good-enough answer. But I don't get how you think the Age of Aquarius is so far off when there's been a song about it for years, and there are so many books out now that in one way or another predict that either the world is about to end, or that we'll be in a whole new age by the year 2000."

"Yes, and I've read a bunch of them." I said. "End-time talk and grandiose hopes for the future are pretty understandable when we approach a whole new millenium. We read in the paper every so often, now, that some religious group has set a date for Jesus to return. The members sell or give away everything and confidently wait, and then the day passes. This type of thing went on in the very early years of Christianity, too. The followers of Christ made no plans for the future because they confidently expected that the Second Coming would be any minute. Finally they realized that the wait might be a little longer than they expected. So, they started getting organized, and the church hierarchy began.

"Before the time of Christ, end-time talk was

heavy, too. That's why they so feverishly hoped for a Messiah to save them. Although this type of thinking seems most widespread at around the change of a millenium, other times are not immune. I've read lots of books on prophecy, some recent and some very old. With very few exceptions, the authors all think the end-time Armageddon, the Second Coming, the Age of Aquarius, or whatever, is going to be within their lifetimes. Seems to me to be one more example of human nature wanting to bring the universe and God down to size: 'Look at me! I am **not** a speck. I am **significant**, so **my** lifetime has got to be the most significant period in history.'

"It's no wonder that there's so much end-time literature now. This type of idea is most attractive to people who feel that their world has gone awry, and they have no control over it. The bomb is a big enough threat to make a lot of people feel that way. Other than that, things are really no worse than a lot of other times in history. If you live at the base of an erupting volcano, it's the end of the world; if you live 3,000 miles away and read about it in the newspaper while curled up in a comfortable chair, holding a cool drink, it's only a passing story that may affect you for a moment and then life goes on.

"Anyway, there's nothing in the symbolism of a switch from Pisces to Aquarius that suggests the end of anything, least of all the whole world. We will experience some turmoil that always accompanies the transition of an older order giving way to a new, but I am confident that the year 2000 will come and go, and the world and plenty of its people will still be very much alive."

"I heartily agree," said another class member. "But to get back to the past history of the ages, it seems to me that there ought to be something really dramatic about the end of a whole Great Year cycle and the beginning of a new one--and we know that no major destruction upheaval or last-judgment-type event happened either at the beginning or the end of the Age of Aries. The Exodus and the birth of Christ are important in the course of affecting history, but at the time they happened they were felt in only small parts of the world."

"When was there a major world-wide destruction?"

So went the discussion. At this point I said, "Well, I came across something interesting just the other day as I thumbed through a recently published and very thick book called *The People's Chronology* [6] at a book store. The **glacier** was beginning to recede at just about the time of the last Age of Scorpio. Now, that was definitely a major destruction. There must not have been too many people who survived it. Maybe the survivors in the ancient land of Ur became the legendary Adam and Eve. That fits Libra, the sign of relating. Another whole Great Year cycle back from the last Scorpio age would put us back to about 43,000 B.C. This is about the middle of the time range in which the anthropologists have come up with the so-called 'missing link.' Modern man, *Homo sapiens,* suddenly appeared on the scene, traceable to the area of Ur, and Neanderthal man began to disappear. No one can explain the sudden, dramatic leap in evolution. And another date in the chronology that struck me was 13,600 B.C. as an estimated time of a great flooding all over Earth that was caused by runoffs from the melting of the glaciers. The Noah story seems to fit so well with what we think of Virgo."

"You're right! It sure does. Think of all the systematic detail of the ark building, and the gathering and categorizing of all the animals."

"Well, maybe you have a really original thought with this Scorpio idea. Haven't read it anywhere before in regard to the Great Ages cycle. I **did** read once, that the scorpion was the very first creature ever to emerge out of the waters and live on land. That fits your theory, too!"

For a while after that class I flattered myself that maybe my ideas on constellation size and the Scorpio beginning and end were original. But later I attended two astrology conferences that brought home the realization that quite probably there are no thoughts that have not been thought before. Perhaps it's all in a Universal Mind, and every so often we tap in and something comes through.

At the first conference I found that astrologer Rob Hand was also working on the idea of ages timed by constellation size. He'd run a computer program based on the star maps of Ptolemy, and lectured on historical correlations within the Age of Pisces as the vernal point moved past each star in the constellation. Rob's lecture has since been published in his *Essays on Astrology*. [7]

Later, at another conference, I heard Robert Powell from West Germany point out that the oldest known zodiac of the Babylonians took its reference axis from the two stars Aldebaran and Antares.[8] Aldebaran is known as the "Bull's Eye," as it is right in the center of the constellation Taurus. Exactly opposite in the constellational zodiac is Antares, which is in the middle of Scorpio! These are two of our brightest first magnitude stars, and they lie diametrically opposite each other in the zodiac. Since they divide the zodiacal belt exactly in two, they were chosen as the reference axis for the Babylonian zodiac. So much for my original thinking!

3

The Symbols of the Zodiac

The most familiar order of the zodiac, in counter-clockwise direction, begins with Aries, the sign of the vernal equinox, followed by Taurus, Gemini, Cancer, Leo, Virgo, Libra, Scorpio, Sagittarius, Capricorn, Aquarius and Pisces.

This chapter will begin with a very brief paragraph on the characteristics of each symbol. For readers who are new to astrology: please understand that these phrases are only a small part of what could be said. They are given as only a basis to increase your understanding of future references to the zodiac symbols throughout this book.

I do not like the use of the generic "he" as a personal pronoun and I try to avoid it whenever possible, but "he or she" is unwieldy. Here I have chosen to alternate the use of "he" and "she" according to the traditional masculine/feminine polarity of each sign. Polarities will be explained later in the chapter.

Aries the Ram bends his horns and thrusts forward assertively and often impulsively. Dynamic, forceful and pioneering, Aries is quick to take initiative on a new project, but leaves to others the tedium of follow-through. Aries is active, energetic, ardent, spontaneous and thinks "me first."

Taurus the Bull has the settled persistance to structure and build upon the projects that Arian types have begun. The expertise of Taurus is reflected in the term "bull market," which denotes prosperous growth. Taurus is materialistic, sensual, possessive, stubborn, patient and loves to be comfortable.

Gemini the Twins. As the twins are two, so is duality the nature of Gemini. Mentally quick and restless, two sides are seen to every question; two paths to every destination. Gemini is versatile, flexible, articulate, inquisitive and loves to communicate.

Cancer the Crab is soft and sensitive inside, but is surrounded by a hard, protective shell. The "shel-ter" is home, and home and family are the vital interests. Cancer is emotional, motherly, nurturing, sentimental and remembers everything.

Leo the Lion radiates royal authority and self-confidently expects the spotlight of center stage. Leo is proud, outgoing, demonstrative, generous, grandiose, dominating and dramatic.

Virgo the Virgin, who carries a sheaf of wheat, separates the wheat from the chaff. She skillfully attends to the practical details of daily living. Virgo is discriminating, productive, efficient, critical, analytical, discreet, modest and loves to serve.

Libra the Balance weighs and considers and compromises in order that peace and harmony can prevail.

Libra, the symbol of partnership, is cooperative, fair and deeply appreciative of beauty.

Scorpio the Scorpion has a deadly sting, which more often than not, is turned on self. Complex, passionate and intense, the **scorpion** can live in the lower nature, coarse, sensual and sarcastic; or can rise to fly as the **eagle,** to share strength with brilliant magnetism. The symbol of degeneration and regeneration, death and rebirth, Scorpio is penetrating, secretive and very strong willed.

Sagittarius the Archer enthusiastically shoots arrows of ideas into everyone he meets. With fervent idealism, he shoots his arrows for the highest stars. Sometimes the goal-oriented Archer will focus his enthusiasm on competitive sports or travel, as well as on ideas. Sagittarius is optimistic, truthful, tactless and adventurous.

Capricorn the Goat ambitiously climbs to the top of the mountain. Cooly pragmatic, responsible and organized, she will become the executive or the tyrant of her particular mountain. Capricorn is cautious, conservative, serious, dutiful and status-seeking.

Aquarius the Waterbearer pours out the contents of his urn to benefit the masses. Universalist and humanitarian, he rebels against any elitest figure of authority. Friend of everyone, yet emotionally detached, he is often mis-

understood by those who would like to be close to him. Aquarius is individualistic, independent and nonconforming.

Pisces the Fishes is two fishes, tied together, but swimming in opposite directions. Contradictory in nature, the Pisces often seems to work against herself. Yet at her best, she has an intuitive sense of the synthesis of all contradictions. Sympathetic and compassionate, Pisces can be the saviour or the victim. Pisces is imaginative, often psychic, impressionable and self-sacrificing.

Aries was not always the sign of the vernal equinox, the first sign of the zodiac. In biblical times Taurus the Bull headed the zodiacal parade:

> *Can you bring out the signs of the zodiac in their season or guide Aldebaran and its train?*
> *--Job 38:32* [1]

Aldebaran, the "Bull's Eye," brightest star of Taurus, leads the zodiacal train. When the vernal equinox sun rose in Taurus, the autumnal equinox was in Scorpio, the summer solstice in Leo, and the winter solstice in Aquarius. These four signs were considered to be the "four corners of the earth."

The Bull (Taurus), the Lion (Leo), the Eagle (Scorpio) and the Man (Aquarius) show up in biblical symbolism as the living creatures of Ezekiel's wheels, and in Revelation:

> *Each had four faces: the first face was that of an ox, the second that of a man, the third that of a lion, and the fourth that of an eagle. . .*
> *--Ezekiel 10:14* [2]

> *At the very center, around the throne itself, stood*
> *four living creatures covered with eyes front and*
> *back. The first creature resembled a lion, the*
> *second an ox, the third had the face of man,*
> *while the fourth looked like an eagle in*
> *flight.* --Revelation 4:6-7 [3]

Christian art has also associated the four symbols with the gospels. Luke is Taurus, Mark is Leo, John is Scorpio and Matthew is Aquarius.

The signs of the equinoxes and solstices are called, in astrological language, the **cardinal** signs. Cardinal means that which is of prime importance, upon which other things hinge. **The cardinal signs symbolize the acting, creating, initiating quality of life.**

In Old Testament times, in the Age of Aries, the cardinal signs were Taurus, Leo, Scorpio and Aquarius. The life of Christ, the Lamb of God, marked the change of the ages, and Aries the Ram, with Cancer, Libra and Capricorn, became the new cardinal points. These four signs, as a group, are said in our age to express the qualities of action, and of initiative. Aries, the cardinal Ascendant, and leader of the "train," is the most direct expression of the action principle.

The cardinal signs are one of three families of zodiac signs. The other two groups are called **fixed** and **mutable**. Each of the three groups symbolizes a quality or mode of expression.

The fixed signs represent stability. Their quality is sustaining, durable and everlasting. Immediately following the cardinal signs, in counter-clockwise order, they are said to build upon, to structure and to sustain what the cardinal energy has initiated. Taurus, Leo, Scorpio and Aquarius are the fixed signs of this age. Long have these symbols been "fixed" in our collective consciousness, whether or not we consciously connect them with astrology. Even earlier than the living creatures of the Bible, they are found as parts of the sphinx in Egyptian art. Back nearly to the dawn of our recorded history bulls and cattle have been sacred symbols through much of the civilized world.

Immediately following the fixed signs are the mutable signs: in this age Gemini, Virgo, Sagittarius and Pisces. As the cardinal signs are initiating, the fixed sustaining, the mutable are disseminating. **Adaptable and flexible in their expression, the mutable signs "spread the word" and disseminate knowledge.**

Pisces is the constellation that rises just before the sun at vernal equinox. This is the Age of Pisces, and in this age, Pisces is a mutable sign. As the primary symbol of the changing order, Pisces must disseminate the truth and spread the word of the ideals of the new order. A later chapter will detail how Pisces and the Mutable Cross symbolically reflect the history and evolving consciousness of this age.

The action principle for this age, however, is cardinal, led by Aries, the "sacrificial lamb" of the old order. Actions are often based on past programming, and later chapters will also discuss some of the struggle and conflict involved in the attempt to understand and to teach the ideals of the new order, while acting upon unconscious motivations carried over from the old order.

To philosophize a bit on the esoteric meaning of numbers: A circle is our symbol for nothing (zero), but it can also be said to symbolize the eternal everything. It is life. It is **being.** It is nothing, but it contains the potential, the sum total, the wholeness of all that **is.**

The zodiac is a circle containing twelve symbols that represent twelve unique archetypal expressions of being. Separately they are a-part of what **is.** Together they are **whole** (the whole as the sum of its parts).

One could say then, that the basic nature of being

has three qualities of expression: eternal (lasting forever, permanent, without beginning or end); creative (that which acts, or causes); and ever-changing. The whole of being is of all three qualities. One is three, and three-in-one.

In the symbolic language of astrology the three qualities of being are expressed as: fixed (eternal), cardinal (creative) and mutable (ever-changing). It is said that the signs rising at the cardinal points, of equinox and solstice, most directly express cardinal quality; and the other signs follow in order. The signs are grouped:

cardinal	fixed	mutable
Aries	Taurus	Gemini
Cancer	Leo	Virgo
Libra	Scorpio	Sagittarius
Capricorn	Aquarius	Pisces

But **all** is eternal, creative and changing. Due to the precession of the equinoxes each of the twelve signs will take its place, in turn, as the cardinal Ascendant, and each, in turn, will express cardinality, fixity or mutability as its primary (but not only) quality.

It may be no coincidence that in Christian theology the nature of being (God) is expressed as a trinity: Father, Son and Holy Spirit. All three are co-equal: eternal, creative, proceeding. All, we are taught, are eternal and without origin. All comprise the creative force of the universe. All proceed (move onward) to change and evolve that which has been created, in a continuous spirit of wisdom, unity and love.[4]

God is Creator, and the primary personification of God for this age is the Son, Jesus Christ. Since the advent of the Lamb of God, Christianity has spread throughout the world, bringing the Word to billions of people.

It may be no coincidence that the cardinal creative principle of this age is Aries the Ram, while the Word is spread--the truths of this age and its new religion are disseminated--through the symbol of the Fishes. Think of it! The Age of Pisces. The "fishers of man." The "shoes of the Fisherman."

The Holy Spirit, proceeding from the Father and the Son, expresses itself in three forms or elements: fire, wind (air), and water. The Holy Spirit was given at Pentecost in "strong, driving wind" and "tongues of fire." In baptism by water one is born into new life in the Spirit.[5] The spirit descends into matter (earth) and the three elements are four: **fire, air, water** and **earth**.

The four elements of the ancients are the four basic substances or forms of being. They are expressed in astrology by the division of the signs into four groups. Each of the triune qualities contains one sign of each element group. Each substance, each form of being, is triune in nature; and each quality of being, when manifest in the world of matter, is composed of four basic substances. So the three plus one are four, and the four times three are twelve.

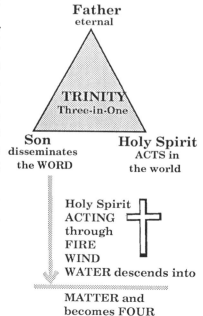

	cardinal	**fixed**	**mutable**
fire	Aries	Leo	Sagittarius
earth	Capricorn	Taurus	Virgo
air	Libra	Aquarius	Gemini
water	Cancer	Scorpio	Pisces

Form of being is associated not so much with actual substance, but rather with one's concept or experience of that substance. The temperaments associated with the four elements have long been a part of our idiom, whether understood in the context of astrological interpretation or not. For example, a fiery personality is understood to be enthusiastic, dramatic, joyous, demonstrative. The earthy temperament is "down-to-earth," with practical, common sense, stability. Airy people have their "heads in the clouds," occupied with abstract thinking and detached logic or rationalizations. Watery types are deep and murky, difficult to understand, motivated by feeling and emotion.

Now, one more method of grouping the signs is important in the understanding of basic astrological symbology: the principle of **duality**. Highly significant in human experience, duality is experienced by humanity in terms of life and death, light and dark, good and evil, positive and negative, masculine and feminine, and so on. Duality is symbolized in astrology in three ways.

One expression of duality is **polarity**. Alternate signs in sequence around the zodiac circle are said to be **positive** and **negative**. In astrological tradition the positive signs are called masculine, yang and extraverted. The negative signs are called feminine, yin and introverted. (These definitions have a "negative," meaning disagreeable, connotation for many contemporary astrologers--and for good reason. Negative became a synonym for "bad," just as the feminine was associated with evil in the thinking of our early symbol-makers, who were influenced by a highly patriarchal culture. I will deal with this influence at length in later chapters. For now, I am merely presenting traditional astrological definitions.) The signs associated with each polarity are as follows:

Positive	Negative
Aries	Taurus
Gemini	Cancer
Leo	Virgo
Libra	Scorpio
Sagittarius	Capricorn
Aquarius	Pisces

Secondly, each sign is said to have its complementary opposite, the sign that lies directly across the diameter of the zodiac circle. Each pair of opposition signs share with each other two basic qualities. They are both either cardinal, fixed or mutable. They are both either positive or negative. Even more importantly it must be understood that complementary opposites are really like two sides of one coin. Since each emphasizes character traits that tend to be weak and undeveloped in their opposition, conflict may be perceived. Actually they are like two halves of a whole. In order to achieve wholeness it is especially necessary to understand and integrate the opposition.

One of the themes of this book's analysis of the ages will be the interplay of opposition signs. The sign of the age is portrayed as the idea, or the collective concept, of deity. But the feet of humanity stand at the sign of opposition. If God is perceived as the epitome of the virtues of the sign of the age, then not-god (humanity), at its collective best and worst, epitomizes the sign of opposition. We mortals must strive for understanding of and integration with our God in order to become "holy" (whole).

As a brief example of the complementary opposites, the following section gives one of the issues common to each pair, and the contrasting manner in which each deals with that issue.

ARIES opposite LIBRA
IDENTITY

Aries asserts self, while Libra seeks self-identity through relating to others.

TAURUS opposite SCORPIO
MASTERY

Taurus finds security in mastery of the material world. Scorpio finds power through mastery of the inner self.

GEMINI opposite SAGITTARIUS
WISDOM

Gemini sees truth through reason and logic. Sagittarius sees truth through revelation and faith.

CANCER opposite CAPRICORN
COMMUNITY

Cancer protects and nurtures the home and family life. Capricorn advances and protects the professional and public life.

LEO opposite AQUARIUS
LEADERSHIP

Magnanimously and generously, Leo rules. Equalitarian Aquarius rebels against the rule of any individual.

VIRGO opposite PISCES
SERVICE

Virgo, the realist, is unselfishly dedicated to fulfill earthly human needs. Pisces, the visionary, is selflessly devoted to the needs of the spirit.

Finally, **each sign is a duality within itself,** in that its energies can be expressed constructively or destructively, materialistically or spiritually.

The **Aries impulse** to be always **first** is strong in

initiative and courageous leadership--or it is headstrong selfishness that demands its own way.

Taurus stubbornness gives the perseverance to achieve mastery--or obstinate resistance to necessary change.

The **Gemini duality** is versatile and adaptable, able to see new possibilities in a situation, from different points of view--or duality can also mean scattered, fickle irresponsibility.

The **Cancer maternal instinct** is nurturing and caring, warm and protective--or possessive, anxious and smothering.

The **Leo confidence** radiates warmth, strength and generosity--or is domineering, authoritarian and pompous.

The **Virgo** ability to **discriminate** is highly ethical and very efficient--or narrow-minded, petty and nit-picking.

Libra compromise keeps the peace with tact, diplomacy, moderation and balance--or anxiously vacillates in a constant search for approval.

Scorpio power to **control** can be turned inward for self-discipline and revitalizing strength--or outward, to manipulate others.

Sagittarius enthusiastically inspires others with idealism--or dogmatically insists what everyone must believe.

The **Capricorn** ability to **concentrate on reality** is responsible, practical and just--or opportunistic and unscrupulous.

The **Aquarius nonconformist** can be the humanitarian who strives for needed reform in society--or the radical who rebels against everything that restricts personal freedom.

Self-sacrificing Pisces serves with loving compassion and great empathy--or wallows in the self-pity of the suffering martyr.

The signs, as presented in this chapter, are only a small part of the complex language of astrology.

Each individual person can be described according to a unique composite of all signs as they characterize the planets and houses of the horoscope cast for exact date, time and place of birth. The horoscope interpretation is further clarified within the context of the individual's particular heredity and environment.

All individuals, however, are influenced by the collective world view of the time in which they live, even though they may be totally unconscious of that fact. A paradigm defined by a slow-moving precessional age spans many generations and links diverse peoples and cultures throughout the world. Most people are totally unaware of the synchronicity between the symbolism of the precessional ages and the collective unconscious. Yet religion, structured through the projection of that collective unconscious, bears striking correspondence with the astrological sign of each precessional age.

Genesis tells us that the stars are created to **serve as signs.** Perhaps they are evidence of a Divine Plan for the evolution of the collective consciousness and consequently, for the individual consciousness that is so **un**-consciously influenced by the collective.

The following chapters are given in the belief that a consideration of how the precessional ages through the signs of the zodiac have deeply influenced the source of our thinking, our history, our mythology and our scripture, will broaden our perspective on where we are and where we are going.

4

Genesis I:
An Allegory of the
Creation of the Universe

The author of the Book of Genesis and the next four books of the Bible, which are together called the **Pentateuch**, is traditionally said to be Moses. Modern biblical scholars have, for the most part, abandoned that view, and identify various sources and traditions.

The familiar first chapter of Genesis that tells of the six days of creation has been attributed to the Priestly source, which was written **later** than the other sources (between the 6th and 5th centuries B.C.). It depicts a cold, formal and transcendant deity, that contrasts greatly with the Chapter Two Yahwist version of a more personal God who walks and talks with Adam and Eve in the Garden of Eden. (The Yahwist version has been dated to about the 9th century B.C.) [1]

The Priestly and Yahwist sources vary in content as well as in style. For example, in the Priestly version, **people** are created (*"male and female he created them"*-- not female **from** male but **together** created) on the sixth day, **after** all the other creatures. In the Yahwist version **man** gets created first, then the Garden, then the animals and birds--and then only last, because the animals and birds were not deemed to be quite suitable companions for Adam, was **woman**, Eve, created from one of Adam's ribs.

It is the **second story of creation**, beginning with **Genesis Chapter II** and Adam and Eve, that has, as an underlying structure, the symbolism of the precessional ages in sequential order from Libra through Taurus. Part II of this book will cover that story in detail. First, however, it is important to consider **Genesis I.**

If we interpret Genesis literally, the third and fourth days are impossibly out of order. Earth could not have vegetation before the Sun was created. This could be explained in terms of primitive cosmology. Accordingly we might say that the authors of Genesis did not understand the true nature of the universe at all, and so they wrote allegorically according to the way it seemed to them that Creation might have been.

The **literal** theory, like it or not, carries the implication that there is **no** divine inspiration of Genesis. It is no more than a tale of speculation of how the world was made, written by primitive people who had only minimal factual information based upon their limited range of observation. This explanation might satisfy some scientists and a lot of atheists, but it will hardly please those whose religious doctrines include the idea that the Bible is of divine inspiration.

Let us take the position that Genesis *is* divinely inspired. Surely God would not cause the authors of Genesis to give us stories that could later be torn apart and disproved by science. That would make no sense at all.

If **truth** is really universal, then surely it must encompass our need for scientific accuracy, but also our need for a deity upon which to focus our yearnings for a sense of purpose beyond the split-second speck of matter to which pure science would reduce our lives. If it is our premise that God is Truth, and that the Bible is of divine inspiration, then the stories that it tells should reveal universal truth.   It seems quite obvious, then, that there must be much more to Genesis than historical chronology that is often inaccurate, or contradictory, or mere fairy tales.

If any story in the Bible falls into direct conflict with factual information that has been established through science, then we should still study that story for its symbolic content.   Correct interpretation of its symbolism should reveal information that is acceptable both materially (by science) and spiritually--in other words, **universal truth.**

Following is my allegory based upon Genesis I.   It is presented to demonstrate how the original version might be interpreted in a manner that is compatible with the discoveries of science.   It also introduces an underlying philosophy for this book which will be expanded and developed in successive chapters.

An Allegory

Day One
The Creation of the Elements of Matter

In the beginning, the Bible tells us, the earth was a formless void.

A mighty wind swept over the waters, and God said, "Let there be light." [2]

*B*efore the beginning there existed a Power.   The Power is Three-in-One.   The quality of **Spirit** is eternal, infinite and sustaining.   It always was and always will be.   In the quality of **Mind** is the principle of action, thought and creation; and in the quality of **Individuality** is the principle of expression and change.

Before the beginning the Power was at rest, until for reasons known only to Itself, It acted, drawing inward into a Center. In a sudden flash of light, blindingly brilliant, inconceivably hot, the Power expressed Its unique Individuality by exploding into the elements of the material universe. To this day It continues to express Itself with waves and vibrations of constant change, expanding outward in all directions from Its Center.[3]

At the moment of manifestation into matter, the Three-in-One became Three plus One: Four! **It was the beginning!**

DAY TWO
The Creation of Souls and the Principle of Opposites

God said, "Let there be a vault, to separate water from water."

*T*he Source, for reasons known only to Itself, desired companionship, and It projected out from Itself a multitude of souls that in the image of the Source were three-in-one: spirit, mind and individuality. In a separate dimension from the universe of matter, the souls were one with their Source, and as spirit they are always aware of that Oneness. Yet, as individuals they are given the right to their own minds. The souls went out from the Source, creating with their own minds, and experiencing the world of matter according to their own individuality. In the infinite wisdom of the Source, the truth was evident that a soul could only be a true companion who could freely choose to merge its own will with the Divine Will. Thus in the **Second Creation of the Source,** Heaven became separate from the universe *of matter, and with the birth of ego (free will), the **princi-ple of the opposites** began. At this time, the opposites were in perfect balance.*

DAY THREE
The Evolution of Life on Planet Earth

God said, 'Let the waters be gathered into place, so that dry land may appear. Let the earth bring forth vegetation.'

*I*t was the master plan of Mind that the souls should have infinite opportunities to experience matter in their sojourn back to the Source. A beautiful place of opportunity was created on a rather small bit of matter that we know as the planet Earth. Smoldering from the explosion of its origin, it was now caused to cool, as a blanket of gases was wrapped around it. The vapors formed rain, and the crevices and craters of Earth filled up with water. Slowly, over billions of the measures of time we now call years, the dry land began to produce growth, in infinitely changing variety. All of this came about in the **Third Creation of the Source.**

DAY FOUR
The Creation of the Divine Plan for Earth

God said, 'Let the lights in the sky serve as signs and symbols, to mark the days and years, and to shed enlightenment upon the earth.'

*ow it was a part of the master plan that there would be a means by which the souls who were to occupy Earth would be able to reach out and find **Universal Truth.** So Mind, the Creator, perfected the arrangement, causing the cosmos to appear in infinitely ordered patterns from the vantage point of Earth. Earth spun on its axis around a sun that would light its day and mark its seasons. The Earth, in turn, was orbited by a moon, which reflected variations of light from the sun, could shine at night, and provided a means to measure the cycles of time. Other planets also circled the sun, providing, each in its own cycle, symbols with which the creative minds of the souls could relate to each other and to the Source.*

*Around the distant stars, the Creator placed thought forms that would appeal to the spirit of the souls. Twelve of these thought forms, that we call constellations, can be seen in special relationship to Earth's path around the sun. These would serve as signs of each expression of the Individuality of the Source that each soul must experience in order to understand the Divine Will for its development upon Earth. All of this was the work of the **Fourth Creation of the Source.***

DAY FIVE
The Evolution of Animal Life on Earth

God said, "Let the waters team with countless living creatures, and let the birds fly about the earth." God blessed them and said, "Be fruitful and multiply."

n the depths of the waters, all manner of tiny creatures came into being. The creatures developed and changed and some became larger and some remained small. Over billions of Earth years some began to leave the waters to crawl upon the land and fly into the sky. Some adapted to life on Earth and survived to grow strong and hardy. Others could not adapt and so they perished and went back into the Earth and became a part of the matter that formed new species. The Earth nourished its creatures and with the blessing of the Source, they grew and multiplied and filled the Earth. From primal beginnings they evolved, climbing higher and higher into more complex and intelligent species. In the course of evolution the principle of opposites came to be expressed by the division of each species into two separate forms that were of the same species yet distinctly different in function. Through the union of these two, male and female, the bodies of new members of each species came into being. This was the time of the Fifth Creation of the Source.

DAY SIX
The Evolution of the Human Species and the Descent of the Souls

God said, 'Let the earth bring forth animal life of an even higher variety, and I will make man and woman after my own image and likeness, and I will give them dominion over the earth.'

*N*ow by this time Earth was filled with a great variety of creatures, on land and in the sea. It was a beautiful place, this planet, now ready to serve as an experience of matter for the souls. One species, the human, evolved to the highest level of intelligence of all the animals. Over many millions of years, the humans had painstakingly learned to use fire and make tools. Wily and resourceful, their superior intelligence had enabled them to survive and evolve still higher, even though many of their fellow creatures were much bigger

*or physically stronger. It was the human that was cho-
sen by the Creator to be the body/vehicle through which
souls could manifest into matter.*

*The first souls were sent to Earth. In order that
they might fully experience the principle of opposites it
would be necessary for some of them to occupy the bodies of the male of the species, while others occupied the
bodies of the females. Because of the physical structure
and the function of the bodies, the active-mind aspect of
the soul would be able to express itself more freely in
the male body, while the receptive-spirit aspect of soul
would be able to express itself more appropriately in the
female body. Each soul retained its triune nature, but it
expressed either the active (masculine) or receptive (feminine) principle in dominance over the other.*

*Each soul differed from every other soul in the
expression of its individuality. Into the bodies of the
first men descended the souls who chose to be active-
dominant, and into the bodies of the first women
descended the souls who chose to be receptive-domi-
nant. The Creator directed that all future souls to manifest into matter would enter through the bodies of the
children created by the unions of these first men and
women.*

I *t was now near the end of the **Sixth Creation
of the Source.** The Creator observed all of Its
work and found it good. The Creator reflected upon the
priciple of opposites and the*

**Six Creations became Twelve, as the
Three-in-One explosion into Four is Twelve.**

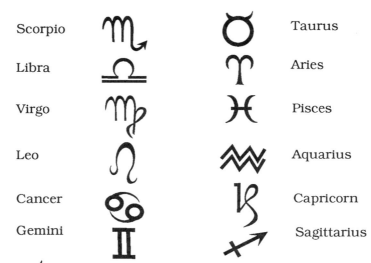

Scorpio	♏	♉	Taurus
Libra	♎	♈	Aries
Virgo	♍	♓	Pisces
Leo	♌	♒	Aquarius
Cancer	♋	♑	Capricorn
Gemini	♊	♐	Sagittarius

*T*welve parts to the Whole, or Twelve expressions of the One: this would be the cycle of experience for the souls in their earthly lifetimes. The Creator altered, ever so slightly, the movement of Earth on its axis, so that the point, from which its sun would be seen on the first day of each new cycle of seasons, would move slowly around the circle of constellations that would symbolize the Twelve expressions of the One. It was through the head of the Scorpion, symbolic of cre- ative transformation, birth and rebirth, light out of dark- ness, that the point of the spring equinox now passed.

The work of the Creator was complete. The Source returned to Three-in-One and rested, content. As a sym- bol of the time of rest, the Source blessed the number **Seven** and decreed it holy. Earth years passed and the vernal point moved on into the constellation of Libra the Balance, and thus began the first age of the first cycle of the Twelve-in-One, and the first Divine Lesson of the soul in matter.

The ages came and passed, as the precession of the equinoxes caused the spring point to pass before the *constellation that symbolized the ideal characteristics of the Source toward which all souls were to strive in that age. The autumn point, or opposition constellation, symbolized the primary ways in which the souls remained in bondage to matter.*

*   **Only through the expression of the characteristics of the opposition sign in accordance with Divine Will could the souls reach out for true understanding of the Divine Ideals of the Age.** The choice to serve ego, the self, rather than God, would cause a soul to remain out-of-balance and fall farther into the bondage of the material world.*

*   In the **Age of Libra**, the souls were given the opportunity to learn to relate to one another and to their environment in harmony, peace and balance. The bondage to **Aries** symbolized selfishness.*

*   In the **Age of Virgo,** the invention and use of practical tools of service for the benefit of all was the ideal. The bondage to **Pisces** gave birth to the fears and superstitions and suffering that came from selfishness.*

*   In the **Age of Leo,** the arts were born, and some souls learned to use the signs and symbols of the heavens, and of their own individual creativity, in the enlightened education and leadership of others. The bondage to **Aquarius** caused selfishness and fear to become rebelliousness and intolerance of groups other than one's own.*

*   In the **Age of Cancer**, the protective nurturing care of others was advanced; and the signs in the heavens were used to serve the growth of agriculture. In their bondage to **Capricorn**, some souls compounded the faults of previous ages by ambitiously climbing over the bodies of anyone whom they perceived to be in conflict with themselves.*

*   In the **Age of Gemini**, communities were born, and joined into nations. Communication, sociability and education were advanced through the development of*

writing.   In the bondage of **Sagittarius**, *idealism was perverted to the need to convince others of one's own ideas, and to scatter them into a shambles if they did not agree.*

In the **Age of Taurus**, *some souls were able to take hold and learn to control the material world and to structure great civilizations that provided a measure of stability for the growing masses.   In bondage to* **Scorpio**, *energy dissipated into sensuality; and the soul memory of a life beyond the Earth was corrupted into the idea that material possessions must be sent with the dead in order to provide for their comfort.*

As the spring point passed into the **Age of Aries, the Holy Age of Seven**, *the Source observed that the souls on Earth so misunderstood Divine Will that direct intervention was necessary.   It was then that the Word spoke as Spirit to the souls of certain individually chosen people who were highly evolved in the understanding of Truth, and the Word said, "**I am that I am**,"* [4] *clearly teaching the concept that* **One Power created the world,** *and that the signs in the heavens, which some humans mistakenly called their gods, were only a part of the creation of the One.*

The Lord thy God is one.
Thou shalt have no other
Gods before me. [5]

With this command, the Word began a statement of Divine Will in the form of ten laws, delivered with supreme clarity, that humanity might understand and choose to obey.

Although many souls taught by the Chosen People understood and obeyed, the vast majority either did not hear the Word at all, or worse, heard the Word, but misunderstood or disobeyed.   By the time that the Holy Age drew to a close, humanity, in bondage to **Libra,** *had* rationalized the **Law** into a thousand variations that perverted, altered and compromised it to suit the convenience of ego. As selfish ego had **t**ipped the Libran scales of justice badly out of balance, now also they corrupted the Arian concept of the One into an aggressive, jealous and unforgiving God who punished, and goaded them to punish, other souls for infractions of humanity's rationalizations of the Law.

It was then that God the Source, in the aspect of Individuality, manifested into human form--a male form, to symbolize the principle of His active intervention in the education of the souls. Born of a daughter of man, who was infused with the power of the Holy Spirit, He became the Son of God--

And the Word was made flesh
and dwelt among us . [6]

The spring point passed on into the constellation of Pisces.

In the **Age of Pisces,** the Son of God taught the souls the ideal of compassion and forgiveness, and He summarized the ten laws into two--and the two and ten were twelve, and the twelve was One, and the One was **Love**--and God so loved the souls of the world that He sacrificed His individuality on the cross of matter in order to teach them that the sacrifice of ego would bring them resurrection, and return them to Oneness with God the Source.

Many souls returned to the Source in this and in future epochs as, with a mystical act of faith in the Son, they surrendered their egos and acted entirely in accordance with Divine Will. Forgiven by Mind the Father, and through the grace of the Spirit Mother, they chose total accordance with the Individuality of the Christ, and returned to the Three-in-One.

But the majority of the souls, in bondage to **Virgo,**

became so caught up in the details of worship that they misinterpreted the teaching of the Christ and divided themselves into a multitude of separate sects, each claiming to have the only right version of the Word, and they continued the rationalization of the Law to the point of endless squabbles with other sects who believed a slightly different version.

Many other souls refused to accept the Son as the Individuality of the Source; while still others even refused to accept the concept that the Source existed at all, because they could not **prove** Its existence according to the detailed rules of their religion which they called **Science**.

It was near the dawn of the **Age of Aquarius.** By this time humanity had so advanced in Science that it had the power to bring upon itself a nearly total destruction. Still, led by the overblown **Leo**-bound egos of their rulers, sometimes with words and sometimes with aggressive action, each nation warred with the others, each claiming the supremacy of its own concepts, each so afraid of the differences from others that it could not see the Truth that united them all. Some souls dimly understood the Aquarian ideal of universality, but in their bondage to the ego concept of Leo dominion, they set themselves up as righteous judges of that which was best for the needs of their group as a whole, severe - ly suppressing the need for the creative expression of the individual.

But great advances were also achieved in the Age of Aquarius. Enlightened teachers taught the universa- lity of all religions, and the Oneness of Truth aligned even the most diverse factions of faith and scientific rea - son, for those souls who were willing to listen.

As the explosive growth of technology freed humanity from the bondage of the planet Earth and enabled it to explore the other planets in its solar sys- tem, the souls of the Earth could see that their home in *matter was much too small and vulnerable to be so divided. So they balanced their Leo egos with the Aquarian virtue of tolerance and stopped the wars before their planet was totally destroyed. The concept of Universal Love still evaded many, but the necessity for world community brought about a time of peace.*

*As the spring point passed on through Aquarius and into the **Age of Capricorn**, catastrophic earth changes brought about the realization that the ecological chain was badly out of balance. The attention of the world community was brought back from the outer limits of space to deal with its responsibility for Earth. Now it was evident that while the technological advances of the previous age had shattered the boundaries of the air, the Earth, upon which most humans still were bound and dependent, was in grave danger.*

*Now it was the time for souls to truly learn the lesson of individual responsibility for self and for others. Very few could hold themselves blameless for the ruination of the environment; and many souls finally came to maturity as they learned to conserve and restore. Others, bound to their **Cancer** insecurities and anxieties, abdicated their responsibility to parent-figure dictators who protected them, but with oppressive strings attached.*

*In the **Age of Sagittarius**, the lesson was Revelation. The circle of the Great Year was nearly complete, with all aspects of Creation now a part of the collective experience. The souls were now to focus on full assimilation of spiritual Truth. Those who were bound to **Gemini** adhered only to what they considered to be logical. Skeptical, or even cynical of faith, they blindly stood by whoever could present the most persuasively **reasonable** version of the "facts." Near the close of the age, the archetypal symbol of the dualism of all the opposites emerged. Antichrist seemed quite reason-ably to repeat all of the ancient legends of the Son. Many* souls, hopelessly bound to reason, and unable to make the leap to faith in Revelation, mistakenly thought that Antichrist was the long-promised Second Coming.

The Precession of the Equinoxes now reentered the constellation Scorpio, completing the circle; and the time of Judgment had come. Bondage to the material desires of Taurus (and of the materialistic aspects of all the signs) was now pitted in a final clash with the highest ideal of Scorpio: to rise above earthly sensation and be reborn into perfect union with the One.

God appeared to all of humanity in the form of His Individuality, the Son. With Him were all of the Souls who had become His true companions, in the human forms of the lifetime in which they had achieved their resurrection. The Souls on Earth who were ready to rise out of matter were welcomed Home. The souls, who of their own free choice, refused to surrender ego, remained bound to Earth. At the command of the Creator, the Earth erupted in a multitude of volcanic molten fires and destructions that altered its face for all time.

Many souls throughout the universe of matter still had need of the particular experiences that life on Earth could offer, and God looked upon the darkness of the abyss, and a mighty wind swept over the waters and cooled them, and God said, **"Let there be light!"** And there **was** light, and the cycle began again--

5

A Narrative on the Allegory

I was curious about what my skeptical daughter would think about my "rewrite" of Genesis I. She agreed to read it.

"Well?" I asked. "Do you understand what I'm trying to say?"

"Some of it, I guess. It's interesting the way you made the things that we know from science fit in with the Bible story without really making either one of them wrong. But there are a lot of things I don't quite get."

"Like what?"

"Well, first of all, what are these pictures at the beginning of each 'day'? They look like the zodiac symbols combined. But why?"

"There are twelve zodiac symbols, but only six days of creation. Yet the twelve are six **pairs** of complementary opposites.

"With my illustrations I show the pair that seems to me to best express the actions of Creation for that 'day'; and I also establish the sequence of the ages, in that the first symbols of each pair are the first six ages in the cycle. The second symbol of each pair then continue in order to complete the sequence of twelve."

"How do the symbols fit the days?"

"Key words for Scorpio and Taurus are regeneration and generation, or rebirth and birth. They seem most appropriate for Day One. Taurus brings to mind the seed that takes root and tenaciously begins to grow. Scorpio regeneration comes first because creation may well be just that. We don't know how the 'big bang' happened or exactly what came before, or if our 'big bang' was the **first** one.[1]

"Libra and Aries best fit the creation of the souls because Libra is the symbol most associated with rela-tionships--or the companionship described by the Source; and Aries represents the birth of individual ego with its free will to create and choose for itself.

"Virgo, the maiden of the constellations, is a per-sonification of Mother Earth herself. The waters of Pisces, the fishes, are her womb from which life emerges, and Day Three is the preparation of Earth to bear life.

"Leo/Aquarius is the next pair in sequence, and that is appropriate for the creation of the signs in the sky. Leo, in astrology, is said to be ruled by the Sun, our primary light and the ancient symbol for God. Aquarius is a symbol associated with the intellect and with Universal Truth.

"Cancer, another water sign, is the symbol most associated with nurturing and motherhood, and Capricorn is a sign of earth; so they go with the evolu-tion of animal life on Earth.

"Gemini, the twins, and Sagittarius, the half-man/half-horse, are both dualistic symbols. They fit nicely with the last day when the souls leave the 'spirit dimension' and enter matter into two forms of expres-sion: male and female."

"Well, O.K., I guess I kind of understand what you mean, but I really don't understand about your use of numbers like three-in-one becomes four and six and twelve and all that. What does that have to do with astrology, or religion, for that matter?"

"The three-in-one obviously refers to the trinity:

Father, Son and Holy Spirit in the Christian religion."

"Yes, I thought of that. But you don't use those words."

"The concept of the triune nature of God is not an exclusive idea with the Christians. It's much older than that, and has parallels in other religions, like the Brahma, Vishnu and Siva of Hinduism. There's probably a common thread that goes way back to before our recorded history, to when people first tried to imagine a reason for the mysteries of life that they couldn't understand. When you think of it, doesn't it seem only natural that they should eventually deify larger-than-life personifications of the family unit; father, mother and child?"

"Maybe, but why do you call the Trinity Mind, Spirit and Individuality?"

"I want to show that the concept of three aspects of one is universal and not specifically tied to Christianity. I thought those three words fit the allegory best, but there are others that have been used to express pretty much the same idea. Here in my notes I've collected some of the other possible groups of three."

MIND	SPIRIT	INDIVIDUALITY
Father	Holy Spirit	Son
father	mother	child
creator	preserver	destroyer
life	soul	form
life	quality	appearance
active	receptive	expressive
cardinal	fixed	mutable
initiative	sustaining	changeable
conscious	subconscious	superconscious (or Christ within self)
intelligence	substance	energy
wisdom	strength	beauty

Pointing to the last words on each list, I added, "I read once that there's a theory that the word 'God' originated from the initials of the Hebrew words for wisdom, strength and beauty."

"I notice," said Shannon, "that you have strength listed under spirit, along with **mother**, meaning **female.** I like that! But I thought the Holy Spirit was male, too."

"In the earliest centuries of Christianity, there were fierce arguments about whether the Holy Spirit was male or female. Of course, in that highly patriarchal period of history, only men were doing the arguing, so guess who won out![2] But male and female are polarities--opposites, and in God all opposites would have to be resolved into perfect harmony and balance. If God is either male or female, he or she would be out-of-balance and therefore **not perfect.** That would never do! God has to have all of the qualities of the masculine and the feminine in perfect harmony. If you can separate one aspect of God and attribute to it the characteristics of 'father,' then it only seems right that you should be able to call another aspect 'mother.' "

"Yes, right! Equal rights!"

"O.K.! I agree. And we can have fun with it. But I'm also very serious about the concept. It doen't make any sense at all to say that we, all humans, are created in the image of God and then to think of God as a man. It is not our physical body that is created in the image of God, it is our essence, our self or soul. And that soul is neither male nor female but both. Since we have **'fallen' out-of-balance** --and I think that is largely the meaning of the biblical 'fall'-- we are predominantly masculine or feminine."

"You have three words on the list that I've heard you use talking to astrologers, and I didn't know what they meant."

"Yes: **cardinal, fixed** and **mutable**. Now maybe

you'll understand them a bit. The circle of the zodiac
has twelve signs--you know that. They are divided into
three families called triplicities. The cardinal signs are
said to be active and to take the initiative. The fixed
signs are the builders, with the quality of sustaining
power; and the mutable signs are changeable and
adaptable. Throughout the whole Age of Pisces that
we've been in since the time of Jesus, we have thought
of Aries, Cancer, Libra and Capricorn as the cardinal
family. Aries is the Cardinal Ascendant of the zodiac
because at the beginning of the age the very first star of
Aries rose with the sun on the first day of spring, the
vernal equinox. But those signs weren't always cardinal. In the Age of Aries, Taurus was the Cardinal
Ascendant."

"You're losing me."

"All right, if you really want to understand that,
you can read my chapter on precession. But first, do
you get what I'm saying: that while in our out-of-balance imperfection, we may associate active, positive,
initiative with males, and receptive, passive qualities
with females, God is All-in-One in perfect harmony."

"Yes, I guess so. But lots of times girls are active
and take the initiative; and some boys are quiet and not
outgoing at all."

"Right! I have listed father, active, creator, cardinal with Mind; and mother, preserver, fixed with Spirit
only in keeping with current tradition. In the All-in-
One that is God, and in the image of God that is self,
mother could just as well be the creator, and **father**
the preserver. We think now, that Aries is the first sign
of the zodiac, the Cardinal Ascendant, and Aries is a
masculine sign, so cardinal is equated with qualities
that we think of as primarily masculine. But in the previous age, Taurus, a feminine sign, was the Cardinal
Ascendant, and the primary deities for most people
were goddesses. If you study through the myths and

legends of ancient Greece and Egypt, for example, you'll see that those goddesses were pretty dynamic!"

"How about Individuality?"

"In the physical body, we express the principle of opposites as either male or female. But as individuals we are unique people, expressing ourselves differently than anyone else. God is perfect, resolving all opposites, and can, at will, express uniqueness and individuality. As Individuality, God was expressed in the unique person of Jesus. Since Jesus was born out of a patriarchal society at the end of a masculine age, he was male. God's individuality was expressed in keeping with the appropriate symbolism for acceptance by the masses in that time."

"So when do we get a feminine age again?"

"I know it seems pretty slow, with women's lib still a controversial issue--but haven't you noticed that we're on the way? This is the Age of Pisces and Pisces is a feminine sign. In the culture from which Jesus emerged the status of woman was about as low as you can get, and patriarchal Judeo-Christian thinking in the early centuries of this age pushed it even lower-- spreading its influence throughout the world. Compared with that, we have come a long way. The signs of the zodiac alternate masculine and feminine, every other one around the circle. I think that there's a gradual shift in dominance at each change of the ages. Aries was the age of the patriarchs, and according to their teachings, men were always in control. But myths and legends of earlier times suggest a different idea. Pisces is a long age, and nowhere near over. In fact, the trend toward the elevation of the status of women, and the tone for the advent of a feminine age, was set in the early years of Christianity by the emphasis that was given to Mary the Mother of God. The ideals for the new age were taught in the very beginning of the age, but many of the mere mortals who helped to spread the word about those new ideals still, themselves, acted according to habitual patterns of thinking carried over from Aries and symbolized by the Aries Cardinal Ascendant. Changes in world view evolve slowly; old habits of thinking die hard. But they **do** change! I predict that when the Age of Aquarius finally comes, and Pisces becomes the Cardinal Ascendant, the battle for the equality of women will have been completely won, and in fact, society will be primarily matriarchal again. And it is more than likely that God will, once again, be called **She**!"

"Right on! When do you think that will be?"

"According to my theory, the Age of Pisces won't be over until about A.D. 2700. "

"Oh, bad news! I thought I'd live to see it."

"You may not live to see the end of the age, but you **are** living in a time where women are beginning to assume leadership positions in all fields; and you will certainly live to see much more movement in that direction, and to participate in it yourself. Remember, this **is** an age of a feminine symbol, but major ways in which the large masses of people think always take a very long time to change. There's always a struggle when a new order strives to supplant the old. You get a different perspective when you consider history over thousands of years instead of just a hundred or so. Then you find out that nothing is really new--there are just old ideas reworked or developed in a little different way. The pendulum swings so far in one direction and then it has to swing back."

"Can't we ever get a perfect balance?"

"That is the ideal toward which each individual soul must strive in order to return to God. But no, I don't think we can ever completely achieve it until our soul leaves the physical body and the material world forever and returns to union with the One. As I indicated in my interpretation of Day Two, as soon as the souls were created with free choice, the principle of opposites became a necessary fact in order for them to experience the world of matter. You just cannot perceive **good** unless you have some perception of **bad** to contrast it with; you can't see **light** unless you know what **darkness** is; you have no conception of **quiet** unless you know what it is to be **noisy.** I could demonstrate something about this with a lesson on composition from my old art teaching days--mixed in with a little metaphysics."

"How?"

"Here's a white piece of paper. What do you see on it?"

"Nothing, of course."

"But what could you draw on it?"

"Anything I want."

"Right! so in this **nothing** there is the potential for **everything** in the world. At this point we could say that this **nothing contains everything** and that nothing and everything are in a state of unity or balance. But within this unity your **anything** can only be seen if you **separate** it from the unity. So draw anything.

"Now this shape that you have drawn always existed as a potential, but now it can be seen because you have separated it from the everything that was within the nothing. In composition we call this a **positive shape.** At the same instant that you created this posi-  tive shape, a **negative shape** also came into being.

"The two are not alike; they are not in perfect unity or balance. From here on the problem in creating a pleasing composition for your picture is

chiefly involved with the attempt to achieve **balance** between the positive and the negative shapes. Of course, absolute perfection can never be achieved. What is pleasing to one viewer may not be to another. Maybe that's why a few artists have been audacious enough to hang huge canvases of white-on-white noth- ingness. Anyway, every single thing that you see around you can be called **positive** in that **it is creat- ed, it has manifested, it exists.** And in a state that is **not** directly manifested or created, **every positive car- ries within itself its negative or complementary opposite. You can't see or perceive one without the other.** So long as there is no manifestation, nothing and everything are in perfect harmony, and there is no perception of anything. There can be no perception at all unless perfect harmony is split in two. Something separates from the everything that is contained within nothing, and manifests. Something can then be per- ceived, but at the same time we can also perceive its complementary opposite that has not manifested--just like the positive and negative shapes."

"That's pretty hard to understand."

"O.K. I'll try again. You've heard of complemen- tary colors in art, I'm sure. Like the complement of red is--"

"Green!"

"Now stare hard at this bright red cap on my marking pen while you count to 30. Quick, now, look at this white paper."

"I can see the exact shape of the cap on the paper, and it is green! I can't put it into words, but I think I understand better, now, what you mean."

"Try to say it!"

"Well, the red cap obviously exists, but it seems like a green cap exists, too, in a way. But if I'm looking at the red, I can't see the green. But when I see the green, it's not red--does that sound crazy?"

"Not at all. You see, when something positive exists in a tangible, manifested state, its negative also exists, but is not tangible, not manifested. But when the negative appears, the positive disappears. But both exist. They **always** are together; **the difference between them is only in appearance.**"

"Are you suggesting that the only difference between positive and negative is in appearance; or like in the art sample, in the eye of the viewer?"

"You're getting sharp! Yes! **The problem is in association of positive with good and negative with bad.** Good and bad are a matter of individual perception. If you take all of the qualities of all twelve signs, all of the attributes of the masculine and feminine, any characteristic you can name, I could tell you how that characteristic could be used in two completely opposite ways; one that you would perceive as 'good' and the other as 'bad.' "

"Example! I've heard you say that one of the worst Sagittarius traits is 'open mouth, insert foot.' "

"Yes, Shannon, you Sagittarians are usually quite outspoken. Have I ever had the opportunity to learn that! Whether this trait is 'good' or 'bad' is a matter of whether the speaking out happens at the right time and in the right place. If the speaking out is a thoughtless, careless or deliberate put-down of someone else, you'd be better off to stay silent. But there are other times when to keep silent and not speak out would be wrong, like if your words might save another person from being hurt."

"But what about really bad things, like evil, or the devil?"

"I don't believe there **is** a devil, as such, any more than I perceive God as a white-bearded patriarch. God is All-in-One, perfect, resolving all opposites. God created everything, and I cannot conceive of a perfect God as the direct creator of evil, or Satan. All that God cre-

ated was good. All the souls at their original creation
were good, meaning that they were harmonious, in the
perfect unity that is the image of God. But God gave us
the privilege of choice, and the ability to think and create as we choose. **We** are the creators of that which
some perceive as evil, or Satan, whenever we choose to
be in conflict with Divine Order. God is Order; Satan
symbolizes that which is out of order."

"That's pretty heavy. I can see how I might really
be responsible for some of the bad things that happen
to me--like how I could avoid some of them if, as you
say, I learned when were the right times to speak out
and when I should shut up. But there are really evil
things in the world, things that I didn't create, but my
life is still affected by them."

"True. After all these thousands of years, humanity has managed to get God's creation pretty badly out
of balance. But every war, every act of crime, every
disharmonious action, large or small, can be traced
back to some soul's choice to place its own selfish ego
in conflict with the order and harmony of God's creation, or to misuse a human creation in a way that conflicts with the law of love. Remember how Jesus simpli-
fied all laws to that of love? If all of us loved our neigh-
bors as ourselves, we wouldn't need any other laws."

"That sounds **too** simple, or too ideal. We have to
take the world as it is, and it is a **mess.** What can **I** do
about that, especially if I come face to face with evil
that's coming from others?"

"At the bottom line, each of us is responsible for
the harmony and balance of our own soul. Sometimes
the only way to restore balance--peace--is to fight--war.
The ability to fight and the ability to keep the peace are
complementary opposite characteristics--chiefly
associated with Aries and Libra, by the way. Even
Jesus drove the money changers from the temple. But
the **intent** must be to restore **balance,** to bring unity

between the two factions who are fighting. It is out of balance to overemphasize Aries by fighting to complete-ly subdue or eliminate the other side; it is equally out of balance to overemphasize Libra by being so afraid to disturb the peace that you are a coward and allow your-self to be dominated."

"You talk like you don't think **anything** is com-pletely bad."

"That is exactly what I believe. There is only good in that which is one with itself, in harmony, in the image of the Creator; and then there is that which is out of balance, separated from harmony. **No soul is lost forever**. The soul is eternal, in the image of its creator God. A soul will continue around the circle, experiencing the same lessons that are symbolized by the twelve signs, over and over, until it finally accepts its unity with God. Notice that when I wrote the sym-bolism of the divine lesson that is presented in each age, each one of the twelve symbols is at one time the spiritual example and at the opposite time, the way in which humanity falls out of balance. The twelve signs are grouped into six pairs of opposites, but each sign is also an opposition within itself, in that its characteristic can be used in unity with God, or in disharmony.[3] So you could say that the twelve are twenty-four. But now add the two and the four together--"

"Six."

"And two into six brings us back to three, and the three is One."

"You still didn't explain the three and one is four."

"The number four has always been associated with the material world. The lower animals have four legs; the ancients thought that matter was made up of four elements. So when the Three-in-One creates the world of matter, it becomes four: Mind, Spirit, Individuality and Body. In astrology the concept of four is symbolized by grouping the twelve signs into four families called the quadruplicities, or the elements. The four elements are introduced in the very first verse of Genesis:

> *. . . the **earth** was without form. . . . a mighty **wind** swept over the **waters**, then God said, 'Let there be **light**.'* [4]

"The elements are given according to the zodiacal order of the age in which Genesis was written. **Earth** is for Taurus, the Cardinal Ascendant of that time. Wind is next, and wind means **air.** Next in zodiacal order after Taurus come Gemini, an air sign. And next in order is Cancer, a **water** sign. Finally, comes light, meaning **fire;** and next in zodiacal order is Leo, a fire sign.[5] So now you have the twelve signs grouped as six pairs, four elements, and three qualities."

"Do you also have a reason why seven is so special?"

"Seven is the sum of the trinity and the elements. Seven is used by the authors of the Bible as a holy number, representing the Sabbath. According to my allegory, and based on my theory of the order of the Great Ages, the seventh age is the holy age when God directly intervened in creation in order to help the souls discover Universal Truth.

"Now, it you multiply--explode--the three of the trinity and the four of the elements, you again have twelve. If you reduce twelve by adding the two and the one--there you are back at Three. And Three is One!"

"Couldn't all this just be a coincidence," she questioned.

"Call it that if you like," I retorted. "But it's a coincidence that suggests a magnificent Order!"

6

The Age of Libra

Members of my astrology workshop were arriving for our weekly meeting.

"How are you doing on that book?" I was asked.

"We talked before about how the Adam and Eve story fits the symbolism of Libra, and how the Noah story fits with Virgo. I decided to continue studying the rest of Genesis to see if the other ages were symbolically suggested. I was stumped at first because there's practically nothing between Noah and Abraham, and the historical Abraham is supposed to have lived at the dawn of the Age of Aries, at about 1800 B.C. That would leave a gaping hole between the legendary, and apparently real, massive flood of 13,600 B.C. and 1800 B.C., and would leave out four whole ages. But then as I continued to read about Abraham, I began to realize that the story contains definite transitions. If Abraham and his wife, Sarah, were used by the author of Genesis as allegory, or as symbolic devices, rather than as straight biographical history, then all of the "missing" ages are **there**, right in sequence, and easy to spot."

"Some say you can find a verse in the Bible to support anything you want to say, if you look hard enough."

"Yes, that is a truth that's been more than amply proved to me in my past confrontations with religious fundamentalists who wrench Bible verses ruthlessly out of context to 'prove' that God condemns all astrologers!"[1]

"Well, they'll have fits for sure if they ever read this book you're writing."

"Probably they wouldn't even read it. They'd get as far as the book cover and find out I am an astrologer, and condemn the book without a hearing. But that's their loss. I am convinced that zodiac symbolism is deliberately contained in many Bible stories, and that to ignore this is to ignore an important key in understanding what the stories mean."

"So what did you find in the rest of Genesis?"

"I've been working on an allegory that begins with Genesis, Chapter 2. I read it page by page and then paraphrase it to magnify the zodiacal and metaphysical symbolic content. If you're really interested, I'll read the stories to you and you can help me clarify the interpretation with your questions."

"O.K., shoot."

"Yes, we'd like to hear it."

"Good. Here are some of the Bibles I've been using. If you'd like, follow along so you can see what I'm taking each idea from."

The Story of the Creation of the Present Cycle

*I*n the ancient time, before the present Great Year, when the Lord God made the earth and the heavens. . .the stream of evolution welled up out of the *waters and the soil of the earth, and eventually formed a body that was suitable to serve as the vehicle for the souls who were of the Second Day of Creation. Millions of earth years passed, and uncounted Great Year cycles, while the human species completed its biological evolution. Now it was time for the evolution of consciousness to begin. As the vernal point passed by the head of the Scorpion and on to the Scales of Balance, the Lord God selected a male of the species Homo sapiens and blew into his nostrils the breath of Spirit, Mind and Individuality, and the man became a living soul.*

The Age of Libra

*I*t was in the east, in Eden, in a bountiful garden, that God sent the first soul to inhabit the body of a man. With the infusion of soul, man gained the potential to discover the meaning of life, and to create, as he chose, that which would serve his own ego, or that which would serve the will of God. In the middle of the garden were two trees that grew as a symbol in the mind of man of his great potential. They were called the Tree of Life, and the Tree of the Knowledge of Good and Evil.

The garden of Eden was fertile because it was watered each year by the flood from a river that divides into four branches, the Pishon, the Gihon, the Tigris, and the Euphrates. The whole of the land was known as Ur.

As the man cultivated and cared for the garden in Eden, the Lord God spoke to him from within the depths of his soul and the man knew that if he partook of the fruit of the Tree of Knowledge of Good and Evil, he would be doomed to die. The thought of death seemed uncomfortable, somehow, even though he knew not what it meant.

With his gift of conscious mind, man developed language and gave names to all of the creatures of the *ground and the sea and the air. But since none of the other creatures possessed a soul, none could be a suitable partner for the man.*

So the Lord God cast a deep sleep on the man, and while he was asleep, God caused one-half of the soul of the man to withdraw and enter the body of a female of the human species. God removed one rib of the man to symbolize the forming of the woman. The woman was not formed from the feet of man, to be beneath him, nor was she formed from the head of man, to be his master. She was formed from the side of man to symbolize her equality, as a child of and as a companion of God.

At this time, the man and the woman were innocent, having made no choices of their own wills. The Scales of good and evil, of light and darkness, of male and female--of all the opposites--were in perfect balance. The ideal of the soul was Libra the Balance.

Now the opposite to Libra is Aries, which in its materialistic expression places "I am," the ego, in conflict with the harmony of Balance. In the symbolic form of the cunning serpent, Aries spoke to the woman. "Did God really forbid you to eat of the trees in the garden?" the serpent asked. The woman's ego emerged and she thought to herself, "What does death mean?" The serpent [as her ego] spoke again. "No, I will never die! I lived before I came into this body, and I will live again after I leave it. What can I lose by gaining knowledge? The more I know, the more powerful I can become--perhaps even as powerful as the God who sent me here!"

The woman spoke her thoughts to the man and then she ate from the fruit of the Tree of Knowledge of Good and Evil, and she gave him the fruit and he ate it, too. Both the man and the woman chose, of their own free wills, to place their selfish egos above the divine example of harmony and balance.

With the loss of innocence, the man and the

woman knew that they were naked and vulnerable. They knew that even though they knew more than they had before, they still did not have all the answers. They knew that they had opposed the will of their Creator and provider. What did it mean to die? For the first time they knew fear.

When they felt the presence of God in the garden, they hid themselves. The Lord God called out to the man to come. The man said, "I heard you, but I was afraid because I was naked, so I hid myself." The Lord God said, "Why do you fear your nakedness? You would not know what fear is unless you had chosen to place your will ahead of Mine by eating of the forbidden fruit!" "It was all her fault!" cried the man. "She talked me into it!" And God asked the woman, "Why did you choose against Me?" "The serpent tricked me," answered the woman.

Then the Lord God said to the serpent:
"As Soul you are separate from all the animals and the wild creatures,

As ego you shall crawl on your belly, bound to the dirt of the material earth all the days of your life.

I will put enmity between you and the spirit of the woman and between your offspring and hers;

He who is to come will redeem you even though you will try to strike at this heel and reject and defy him."

To the woman God said:
"You are privileged as the female of your species to be the channel through which new souls will come to earth.

But as a reminder of your act of disobedience and of your vulnerability, I will cause this act of Creation, childbirth, to take place with pain.

Since you have initiated the act that has placed my
scale of harmony of the opposites out-of-
balance, I will cause that imbalance to be
reflected in the natures of you and of the
man.

You will reflect the dominance of receptive, intuitive
spirit, while the man will reflect the domi
nance of active, creative mind. The active
principle will be recessive in you, while
the receptive principle will be recessive in
him.

Through your individuality you will reflect the degree
of imbalance within your nature, and
throughout the ages your descendants will
strive to learn how to restore the balance.

So long as the opposites are out-of-balance, the man
shall be your master!"

To the man God said:

"So long as you choose the material world instead of
me, you will be bound by it.

Do not expect me to shield you from the consequence
of your egotistic choices. Whatever you do
will come back to you in kind. So long as
you work for material gain, you will sweat
and toil until you return from the ground
from which you came;

Your body emerged from the clay and the dust of the
earth. To dust it will return."

The man called his wife Eve, which meant 'living,'
because she would become the mother of all living.

The Lord clothed the man and his wife with gar-
ments of protection. Speaking to some close companion
souls who were above bondage to the earth, the Lord
said, "See, the human is like one of us in knowing what
is good and what is bad. To dwell in an earthly body is

to dwell in a state of separation from us. Lest the soul within the human choose to remain separate forever, I must prevent him from reaching out an earthly hand to take fruit from the Tree of Life."

So God banished Adam and Eve from the Garden of Eden. No longer could they dwell in that state in which every want and need was provided freely from God's abundance. Now they must work to provide for their needs, tilling the soil from which they came. Now, in order to survive, they must learn to read the signs in the sky, and they must learn the ways of all the plants and the animals and the cycles of the earth. Had they remained in unity with God, no toil would have been necessary--all was given. But now--no more. Long would be the ages until humanity's redemption.

In the east that meant the sunrise of the beginning of their cycles on earth, God settled Adam and Eve. And God stationed a cherubim [angel of knowledge], and the fiery revolving sword of the zodiac, to guard the way to the Tree of Life.[2]

"Comments?" I asked the class.

"Well, Libra symbolism is pretty obvious, for sure. Libra is the sign we associate with partnership and marriage, so what else but Adam and Eve. And Libra the Scales stands for harmony and balance. It fits."

"Yes," I said. "And note that Aries, in a way, still becomes the first age of man after all. As the opposition to the Libran ideal, Aries becomes the serpent that symbolized the choice of Eve and Adam to separate themselves from the perfect harmony of Divine Will. In typical human fashion, they then project the serpent out from themselves, disclaiming responsibility for their choice: 'The devil made me do it.' "

Another student spoke up. "But many books say that the serpent is symbolic of the lowest level of Scorpio. And you do have your allegory start with the rebirth in Scorpio. Maybe that could be an origin of the ancient symbol of the circle made of the serpent biting its own tail."

"Scorpio always gets the bum rap! " I exclaimed. "The only one with a serpent, indeed. Actually, every sign has a serpent side to its nature. It is the serpent when it is understood only at the materialistic level. This is the signifi- cance of the fiery revolv- ing double-edged sword. Each sign contains an opposition within itself in that its energies can operate materialistically or spiritually. During the cycle of the ages, each sign will be presented once as the ideal and once again as the oppo- site, or the way in which souls bind themselves to mat- ter. The only prominent biblical serpent is the one that tempted Eve. In a sense, the beginning of the souls' fall from innocence is symbolized by Aries. The serpent bit- ing its tail symbolizes the entire cycle of involution of Aries to Taurus via Pisces in which the soul who con- stantly operates on the materialistic level increases its separation from God."

"You said 'involution.' Why?"

"Involution means the state of being involved or entangled. It is retrograde development, or degenera- tion. Evolution means growth. Obviously, a soul who is constantly choosing the serpent opposition is on a path of involution.

"For now, though, let's go on to the second age, Virgo. The Virgin holds the wheat of the harvest in her arms, and at the dawn of the Age of Virgo, people were beginning to learn the rudiments of agriculture. Virgo symbolizes the acquiring of practical skills with which to serve humanity. The ideals of the sign are service, skill, industriousness, humility. The opposition is Pisces, which at its materialistic level is confused, fearful, deceptive and just loves to suffer.

"Symbolism for the transition from the Age of Libra to the Age of Virgo can be seen in the story of the sons of Adam and Eve, Cain and Abel. You'll see, in the Bible that Abel offered to sacrifice his best ram to God, and that God was pleased with him. The ram, of course, is the symbol of Aries, the materialistic opposition to the ideal of the outgoing age. So here, Abel offers to give up his selfish ego--Aries, and honor God--Libra."

The Age of Virgo

*A*s the first born, Cain had worked harder and longer than Abel to wrench his livelihood from the earth. Cain showed the Lord what he had produced, but was resentful when the Lord did not welcome him with the same favor as had been given to Abel.

The Lord said to Cain, "Why are you so crestfallen? It is good that you progress in skill and knowledge. This will improve your lot, and perhaps also the lot of others. Your pride in your accomplishment is its own reward. But ego is a demon lurking at your door; yet you can be his master."

But Cain misunderstood the meaning of the Word, and in his resentment, he killed his brother, Abel. When the Lord asked him where Abel was and Cain answered, "I do not know. Am I my brother's keeper?", he behaved according to the lowest deceptive manifestation of Pisces, and so bound himself to the material aspect, the serpent of the new age.

In his guilt and confusion, his new-found skills in agriculture failed him, and he became a restless wanderer, complaining all the while to God: "My punishment is too great to bear. **You** have taken away my property and caused me to wander homeless where anyone may kill me at sight."

"Not so," said the Lord. "If anyone kills Cain, Cain be avenged through seven ages before that soul can be

redeemed." And thus the Lord placed a mark on Cain,
to signify the number of the Age of Redemption.

Cain left the Lord's presence, continuing in his
cycle of involution.[1]

Cain and his wife, and the other descendants of
Adam and Eve, became the parents of many generations. In the 10th generation of the line of Adam was
born a man who was sent by God to teach the highest
example of Virgo. He was called by the name of Noah.

"The numbers there are intriguing," I was interrupted.

"Yes!" came another comment. "The use of seven,
there, really fits in with your lineup of the ages. The
seventh age from Virgo would be Pisces, which is the
Age of the Christ."

"Does the ten in the genealogy have a meaning?"

"Possibly," I said. "If Adam was 'one,' then Noah is
a **new** cycle, like an avatar of the new age."

"I have to say," laughed one whose chart had
Pisces rising, "Cain really does sound like a suffering
Pisces!"

"Let's get back to the story."

*N*ow as the generations had multiplied upon
Earth, certain highly evolved souls, the sons of
God, saw beauty within the souls of the daughters of
men and took them for their wives, and thereby provided the channels through which emerged the souls who
would become the heroes and heroines of many a legend and myth of the later days.[2]

"You know," I interrupted myself, "This could be a
place suggestive of extra-terrestrial intervention. Have
any of you ever read any of the books about that?"

"You mean like *Chariots of the Gods*?"

"Yes. And another good one is *The Sirius*

Mystery. It's really well researched, and makes a strong case for the idea that much of the advanced knowledge of the ancients was taught to them by visitors from the star system of Sirius."

Other class members commented: "It would seem impossibly conceited of us to think that in all the vast universe, ours is the **only** planet with intelligent life; or even the planet with the most **advanced** life."

"A God of the **whole** universe could work in ways that we can't even begin to comprehend. It's a lot to think about."

"Onward!" I returned to the story.

But too many people had misunderstood the Divine Will and indulged the selfish desires of ego. The Lord God said, "My souls shall not remain in these bodies forever; the body is only of matter. The maximum span of the soul in each body shall comprise one hundred and twenty years."

When it could be seen how wicked most souls had become, how nearly all of their freedom of choice was used in the service of their selfish egos, the Lord saw that a very harsh discipline was needed--an event that could wipe them away from the face of the earth so that their souls and others yet to come could have a fresh new beginning.

It was about this time that in the natural order of God's creation the glacial ice sheet had melted to the point that great flooding was imminent.

Among the men on the earth whose souls were very near in their evolution toward true companionship with the Lord God was Noah. He was a good man. He was practical, industrious, discerning, and blameless in that age because his will was completely in the service of the Divine Will. Noah and his good wife had three sons who, at this time, had each taken wives; and Noah and all of his family lived in close communion with God.

One day Noah heard the Spirit of the Lord speak to him from within the depths of his soul. He knew that great destruction would soon come, that the floods that were beginning in some areas would well up to cover all the land that he knew.

With his great mind, Noah was attuned to the Divine Mind, and he was instructed to build an ark so that he might save himself and his family and the creatures that would be necessary to repopulate Earth after the deluge.

So Noah, with the help of his family, built a large ark. They took great care in its construction, paying close attention to the details that God, through Spirit and Mind, gave to Noah.

When the ark was completed, they set out to select a male and a female of each living creature. These they housed in the various compartments of the ark; and then they gathered a supply of the kind of food each creature would need and stored that away in the ark also.

Of the animals and the birds that were "clean," meaning that they were favored as offerings to the Lord God, Noah selected seven pairs to be brought into the ark.

Now the Spirit again spoke to Noah and told him that only seven days remained until forty days of rain would cause the flood waters to rise and cover all the land.

So Noah gathered provisions for his family and they went into the ark.

The seventh day passed, and the floodgates of the sky were opened, and rain poured down upon the earth.

The rain continued for forty days, and the flood waters lifted the ark high above the earth until all the land was submerged, as far as Noah could see. All creatures who had been left upon the ground perished.

The waters maintained their crest for one hundred fifty days until God caused a wind to sweep over the earth, and the waters began to recede. On the seventeenth day of the seventh month from the beginning of the flood, the ark came to rest on the mountains of Ararat.

Noah discovered that life was returning to Earth by sending out a dove to fly across the waters. On the first trip the dove could find no place to light, but on the second trip it brought back an olive leaf, and on the third trip it did not come back at all.

Finally the earth was dry enough that Noah and his family and all the creatures that they had saved could come out of the ark. Then Noah built an altar to the Lord and, choosing from every clean animal and every clean bird, he offered sacrifices on the altar.

The Lord knew the sweetness of his soul's offering, and thought: "Never again will I allow Earth to be doomed because of man, since the desires of his ego oppose Me from the start.

"As long as the souls remain bound to matter,
seedtime and harvest,
cold and heat,
Summer and winter,
and day and night,
Opposition shall not cease."

Noah looked up at the sky and saw a beautiful rainbow. In the depths of his spirit, so closely attuned with God, Noah knew that God was giving him a sign of a covenant with all human beings that never again would the earth be so devastated by a flood.[3]

"Let's pause for a minute, here. Noah as a personification of ideal Virgo is so evident that it explains itself. But I did want to point out one thing. One's opposition sign is not always to be taken negatively. Noah, in his high expression of Virgo, was also able to draw upon the positive qualities of Pisces, in his highly attuned psychic sensitivity that opened him to the detailed instructions that were given to him.

"In Genesis 9:20, however, is the beginning of a short story about Noah that illustrates how the serpent can tempt even the highest soul."

*N*ow Noah was a man of the soil in that he was interested in the development of agriculture; but also in that he was still bound to his material body. No matter how closely a soul may be attuned to God, so long as it remains in the body, it is capable of being tempted by the serpent of materialistic desire, the ego.

Noah was tempted by the serpent of Pisces, and overindulged himself with the wine from his vineyard. As he lay drunk and naked, his son, Ham, father of Canaan, saw Noah's vulnerability. Ham could have chosen to help his father, but instead he gave in to the temptations of his own ego and exploited his father's weakness by telling his two brothers about it.

Shem and Japheth walked backwards with a robe and covered their father's nakedness. They did not look to gain anything for themselves in their act of selfless service.

When Noah woke up from his drunkenness, he said:

"Cursed be Canaan! The line of descent
of the soul of Ham will suffer bondage to
the desires of ego.

Blessed be the souls of Shem and Japheth. May
God expand them, while Canaan remains
a slave." [4]

"What can Noah's words mean?" A student interrupted. "Is that an allusion to reincarnation?"

"Yes, I think it is. Ham's actual son would not be damned because of his father's mistake. I don't think the author of Genesis had that low an opinion of God!

But this could be a way of saying that Ham's actions had placed him in bondage to return for another life in a lower condition, while Shem and Japheth would progress upward. It's a subtle reference, but the only explanation for it that makes any sense to me would be reincarnation. There are a lot of Bible verses that allude to reincarnation. Apparently they are a bit too subtle to have been spotted by those who did the scripture re-writes after the Ecumenical Congress of Constantinople in A.D.553 in which the Emperor Justinian forced the reincarnation doctrines to be declared an anathema."[5]

*T*he descendants of Noah and his children migrated out from the land of Ur, to populate all the lands of Earth. At first, these, the Indo-European people, all spoke the same language and shared similar physical characteristics.[6]

Although some souls progressed in the evolution of consciousness, the great majority chose the path of involution, drifting with the current that enslaved them more and more in the bondage of their materialistic desire. As slaves to ego they developed irrational fears that caused them to confuse the ideals of Virgo into fragmented notions of righteousness that found fault with everyone who was different from the self.

The transitory period as the spring point moved from the constellation of Virgo into that of Leo will be told through the legend of the Tower of Babel.

In the land of Shinar (ancient Sumeria) people settled who were especially skilled in their observations of the signs in the sky. They presumed to think that if they built a tower to improve their knowledge of the stars, they could become very famous and powerful and be like gods. They built a magnificent ziggurat; but their plans for dominion were thwarted by the wisdom of the Divine Plan, that at this time in history caused great *diversity in languages and cultures. The diversity came about because people spread out from their eastern origins, adapted to the climate and environment of new lands, and mingled with other humans who had evolved in other places.*

Later, people would use the Tower of Babel to symbolize how people came to speak in different tongues, and they would say that this was a direct punishment of the Lord for humanity's presumptuous effort to place pride above service to the Lord.[7]

"After the story of the Tower of Babel, Genesis lists the genealogy to the Patriarch, Abraham. If we try to tie all the stories of Abram/Abraham to the historical Abraham, Genesis loses clarity, because we would have to leap from times that clearly had to be prehistorical right up to the second millenium B.C., thus skipping over several entire ages.[8]

"Again, if we assume that Genesis is a bunch of collected legends and imaginings of men who were trying to explain their origin but weren't intellectually and scientifically advanced enough to know what really happened, then we can easily dismiss the gaps and puzzles.

"But if we choose to think that Genesis is of divine inspiration, then we must assume that it contains truth, if only we can decipher its symbolism.

"Probably there are many actual historical facts about the life of the historical Abraham woven through the Genesis story. But Abraham and Sarah and their children can also be taken as symbols.

"There may very well have been a patriarch named Abraham who actually lived during the period that we know as the Age of Aries. Some parts of Genesis may be based on actual historical events. But I also think that the authors of Genesis used Abraham and his family as literary devices to show the transitions between the ages. The sequence of the symbolism of the signs is just too striking to ignore. You'll see what I mean when I tell you the stories of the next ages. I should have them finished by the time of our class next week. I'll tell you about them then.

"The familiar story of Abraham begins with the Age of Leo. At the beginning of his story Abraham was called Abram and his wife was called Sarai. So--'to be continued' next week, with the Age of Leo."

8

The Age of Leo

*I*n the Age of Leo, great progress was made in all the arts. Stories and dramas were woven from the threads of legend and from the pictures that the creative imagination of the souls found in the sky. Deep soul memories of the thought forms that had been formed in the Fourth Day of Creation stirred their minds and spirits, and each in his or her own individuality expressed it in a different way. A few souls perceived the true significance of the signs and symbols in the heavens and knew that they were only channels for the Light. In their enlightenment, they strove to advance the lot of others, with no thought of personal dominion.

But most people misunderstood or perverted the signs according to their own desires. They misunderstood completely by thinking that the lights in the sky were gods or goddesses, instead of only signs and symbols of the One. Worse yet, some people were intelligent enough to figure out the meanings and predict the movements of the celestial signs, but they used their knowledge to manipulate and prey upon the fears and superstitions of the unenlightened masses.

Some say that it was in this age that the Great Pyramid and the Sphinx in Egypt were designed. The highly intelligent and enlightened souls who were the architects knew that it would be a very long time before humanity would be enlightened enough to use advanced knowledge wisely. So they kept their wisdom secret, passing it on only to others who, through passing rigorous tests of initiation, proved their spiritual worth.

They knew that the dark night of the soul, the low point of the Great Year, was coming and that humanity would so corrupt itself that even the advanced technology of these few would be lost. So they incorporated within the design of the pyramid detailed and precise measurements that could only be rediscovered when humanity, redeemed, began to advance out of darkness.

Abraham the Patriarch

*T*he Age of Virgo was drawing to an end as Terah, father of Abram, took his entire family, including Abram and his wife, Sarai, out of Ur. During the Virgoan era a great many members of the Ur race migrated to other lands, and became diversified into other cultures. After Terah's death in Haran, Abram was called by God to continue on to the land of Canaan, which was promised to be given to his descendants.

God said, "Your descendants [of the Ur race] will make a great world; all humanity shall find blessing through you."

Finding famine in Canaan (for it was not yet time for them in that land) Abram and Sarai moved on into Egypt. In those years, Egypt (land of Leo the Sun) was not a desert but was very fertile and advanced in its civilization.[1]

"Is it true that Egypt was not a desert then?" a student interrupted.

"Yes, it's true. I've read in several books that during the time of the Age of Leo a 'climatic optimum' was reached. The temperatures were much warmer in Europe, with the last traces of the glacier gone, and the Sahara was a grassland.[2] Some researchers insist that the Sphinx would have to have been built before the Sahara became a desert.[3] A recently published archeology book that I saw in the library started right out on page one by stating that the entire study of prehistoric times is in a state of crisis because new techniques such as radio carbon dating have rendered most existing textbooks inadequate or outright **wrong.** [4] It may yet be found that the Great Pyramid and the Sphinx date back to the Age of Leo."

Now Abram and Sarai had no child, for Sarai was barren. But Sarai was very beautiful. When they were about to enter the land of Egypt, Abram said to his wife, "You are so very beautiful that when the Egyptians see you, they will surely want your favors. If they know that I am your husband, they will kill me so that they can have you. Please say, instead, that you are my sister. In that way, things will go very well for me."

Just as Abram expected, the Egyptians praised Sarai's beauty. So Abram was able to prostitute his wife to the Pharaoh, and things went very well for him, indeed. From the Pharaoh, Abram received flocks and herds, male and female slaves, male and female asses, and camels.

The Lord, however, was most displeasd with Abram's and Sarai's behavior. Pharaoh and his household were struck with plagues until Sarai confessed the deception. Pharaoh summoned Abram and said, "How could you do this to me! Why didn't you tell me she was your wife? Take her and be gone!" [5]

"Now, here we need a bit of interpretation. The signs alternate around the circle, in masculine and feminine polarity. Virgo is a feminine sign, and Sarai represents the matriarchy and the outgoing influence of Virgo. Here, at the beginning of the Age of Leo, Virgo is the Ascendant, rising with the sun. As I said before in Chapter Three, the ancients considered the constellation rising with the sun at vernal equinox to be 'sacrificed' because the rays of the sun now entirely hid it from their view. Therefore, Sarai, symbolizing Virgo, is sacrificed to win favors for her husband. Another symbolic clue that the epoch has passed from a feminine- to a masculine-dominated order is that Sarai is barren.

"It is not consistent with the Divine Plan that Sarai should continue to be the dominant symbol here, providing for her husband. So God sees that things get rearranged the way they should be by getting Sarai thrown out of the Pharaoh's palace! Abram is typical of people who resist the new order and try to cling to the old ways. But this is Leo and he is to be the patriarch, and it's time for him to learn dominion."

A bram and his nephew, Lot, were both very wealthy. They had learned the arts that can give dominion during their stay in Egypt. Greatly had Abram benefited through the sacrifices of his wife. Abram and Lot and their entourage left Egypt and migrated toward the lands of Canaan and Jordan.

The herds and flocks of Abram and Lot were so vast that great difficulties arose during the journey. Quarrels broke out between the herdsmen of Abram and the herdsmen of Lot. It was quite obvious that no one encampment would provide the water and grazing area to support all the herds if they stayed together.

Abram said to Lot, "Let there be no strife between us, for we are kinsmen. The whole land is at our disposal. You may have first choice. Whichever area you choose, I shall go in the opposite direction."

Lot looked around and saw that the Jordan plain was as fertile as Egypt, as well watered as the Lord's own garden. So Lot chose the Jordan plain for his territory of dominion, and set out eastward. Abram remained in the land of Canaan. And so it was that Abram and Lot separated from each other.

Lot pitched his tents near Sodom. Now the people of Sodom were very wicked in the sins they committed against the Lord.

When Lot had gone, the Lord called Abram to walk about the length and breadth of the land of Canaan, and told him, "Look to the north, south, east, and west. All the land that you see I give to you and to your descendants forever. Your descendants are like the dust of the earth; if anyone could count the dust of the earth, your descendants too might be counted."

Now during these times, bitter wars were fought among the kings of the various territories. Abram remained at peace in his encampments until one day when a fugitive from a terrible defeat in battle came and brought him the news that his nephew Lot and all of his possessions had been seized by the victorious forces, along with all the food supplies of Sodom and Gomorrah.

Abram mustered the men of his household and went in pursuit. His party attacked at night and defeated the captors of Lot. He recovered all of the possessions of Sodom and Gomorrah, as well as those of Lot, and he brought back all of the women and the other captives.

When Abram returned to Sodom from his victory, the king of Sodom came out to greet him, and the king and the high priest of Salem, Melchizedek, performed a ceremony of blessing upon Abram. As was the custom, Abram gave the high priest a tithe of the spoils of victory.

The king of Sodom said to Abram, "Give me back my people, but you may keep all of the goods." But Abram replied, "I have sworn to God Most High that I would not take so much as a thread of anything that is yours, lest you should say, 'It was at my expense that

Abram is rich.' Nothing for me except what my servants have used up, and the share that is due the allies who joined me in battle." [6]

"Now do I need to identify the Leo symbolism in this, my 'zodiac-digest condensed' version of Genesis 13 and 14?"

"No," a student replied. "the whole theme is of kings and the struggle over dominion."

Another added, "The battling kings symbolize the lower nature of Leo, but Abram expresses the higher nature in that he is willing to lead and be victorious when it is necessary. But he helps without dominating, without taking spoils. He proves himself worthy of God's reward."

"Good," I said, "That's the way I see it, too. The next chapter tells of the covenant with Abram. It has some very interesting indicators of time that seem to fit right in with my theory of the cycle of the ages. Let's see if you can spot them."

*T**he Lord came to Abram in a vision and said, "Fear not! I am your protector, and I will give you great reward."*

Abram replied, "Oh, Lord, what good will any reward be if I have no child and must make one of my servants my heir?"

But the word of the Lord came to Abram, "No servant shall be your heir; your own child shall be your heir. Look up at the sky and the stars. Count them if you can. Just so shall your descendants be."

Although Abram had been quite unable to see a potential child in his stars, he, nevertheless, put his faith in the Lord. This added to his credit in the sight of the Lord, for surely it is the right attitude of a man toward his God, that his faith in the word of God stands above his attempts to interpret his own horoscope. [7]

The Lord said, "I am the Lord who brought you out of Ur of the Chaldeans to give you this land."

"Oh, Lord," asked Abram. "How am I to know that I shall possess it?"

So the Lord instructed Abram to bring him a three-year-old heifer, a three-year-old she goat, and a three-year-old ram, and also a dove and a pigeon. Abram brought all these. The three animals he cut in half and placed each half opposite the other. He did not cut up the birds. Birds of prey swooped down to eat the carcasses of the animals, but Abram stayed with them. After a time, the sun set, and as the deep, terrifying darkness fell around Abram, he went into a trance-like state.

Again the Lord spoke, "It is a certainty that your descendants will be enslaved in an alien land. They will be oppressed for four hundred years. But my day of judgment will come for the nation that will enslave them, and they will leave with great wealth. You, however, shall die in peace at a contented old age. The wickedness of the Amorites will not reach full measure until the fourth time-span. It is then that your descendants shall return here to the land which I have given you."

In the darkness, now, there appeared a smoking oven and a flaming torch, which passes between the split pieces of the animal carcasses. It was a sign of the covenant that the Lord had made with Abram.[8]

I looked up from my manuscript. "Get it?"

"Well, maybe," said one of the students. "I'm sure the numbers have meaning. This would be the third age, and three animals are cut up for sacrifice--and they are specifically three years old. But a heifer, a goat, and a ram suggest the wrong signs."

"O.K., I'll explain how I see that part. The chapter notes in the *New American Bible* say that a three-year-old animal was considered to be ritually mature.[9] That doesn't change the potential symbolic significance of three sacrifices here. I think it does mean that three ages are gone. The main reason I think so is because it is later specified that **four** time-spans will pass before the Exodus from Egypt--the Exodus clearly has to be the meaning of the prophecy about enslavement and deliverance. The use of the word 'time-span' is from the *New American* translation. In most Bibles, 'generation' is used; but that could still be taken symbolically as a period of time other than what the word literally implies. If it is taken to mean four **epochs,** then we are right on cue. The fourth epoch **after** the Age of Leo is the Age of Aries, in which the Exodus actually did take place."

"But what about the symbolism of the animals?" another student questioned.

"These were the common sacrificial animals all through the Bible. In some places, only one of them is specified, and there the symbolism seems to point to a specific age. You'll see this later. Here all three are used. I think it's the **number** that is the significant symbol in this case. I can't explain why the birds were brought but then not included in the sacrifice. Had they been, the number symbolism would be different; but then why are they there at all?"

"What about the last part of the vision, of the torch and the oven?"

"The ritual of cutting animals in half and then passing between them was an ancient practice to seal an agreement between people. One was to imagine that failure to keep the agreement might result in the same fate as befell the animals. In this vision we have the symbolism of the opposites. The animals are split in half, as each of the three ages has its opposite. The flaming torch must be the light of God; the smoke of the oven, the symbol of the sacrifice. God sealed the covenant with Abram in a vision of a ritual that Abram would understand because it was a common ritualistic practice of that time."

"If the prophecy refers to the enslavement in Egypt, why doesn't the Bible **say** Egypt? Who are the Amorites?"

"I wondered about that, too. In Chapter Ten, I found that the Amorites are among the descendants of Noah who came through Ham. The notes on the chapter, in the *New American* translation, place the decendants of Ham in northern Africa, which of course, could mean Egypt.

"Now before we go on to the story of Ishmael,there are some things I want to say about the astrological symbolism. This covenant of God with Abram in which Abram is promised the land for his descendants takes place in the Age of Leo. Leo is the beginning of the patriarchy. Libra is Balance; only in balance are male and female equal. It was only *after* the fall that Adam was given dominance over Eve. Virgo is a feminine sign; Leo is masculine. It is here in the Age of Leo the Lion that the covenant is made establishing Abram as the Patriarch. Later on it will be Judah, the Lion, who will emerge from the twelve sons of Israel to become the ancestor of the Redeemer. I say this now because there seems to be a pronounced shift back and forth between masculine and feminine symbolism at the transition between the ages.

"And one more thing--the Bible specifically says that Abram came from Ur of the **Chaldeans**. Who knows what that means?"

"Doesn't that have something to do with astrology?"

"Yes. The **word** 'Chaldeans' is synonymous with astrologers. Even the dictionary says so. Interesting note about the background and more-than-probable education of Abram, isn't it?"[10]

*S*arai felt that she had failed Abram because she had not been able to give him a child. So upset was she that she took her Egyptian maidservant, Hagar, and gave her to Abram for a concubine. "The Lord has kept me from bearing children," she lamented to her husband. "Lay with my maid, then; perhaps I can have a child through her."

Abram granted his wife's request, and Hagar, the maid, became pregnant. Feeling quite pleased with herself, and quite superior, Hagar looked at her mistress with disdain.

"How could you do this to me!" said Sarai to her husband. "I myself gave my maid to your embrace, but now that she is pregnant, she looks at me with smug superiority. May the Lord decide which of us is right!"

"She is your maid," Abram told Sarai. "Do whatever you want with her." Sarai was so mean to Hagar, that Hagar ran away.

The Lord found Hagar beside a spring in the wilderness. The Lord appeared in the form of a man, so as not to frighten her. "Where are you going?" he asked her, kindly.

"My mistress, Sarai, abused me, and I am running away."

But the Lord said, "Go back to your mistress and submit to her, and your descendants will be too numerous to count. You will bear a son, and call him Ishmael. He'll be a wild ass of a man, at war with everyone, and everyone at war with him. He shall camp in opposition to all of his kin."

Realizing, now, that the being who spoke to her was supernatural, Hagar exclaimed, "You are the God of Vision! Have I really seen you and still remain alive?" (In later days, the well at which Hagar encountered the Lord came to be called Beer-lahai-roi, which means "the well of living sight.")

And so it was that Hagar returned to the house of

Abram, and bore him a son. Abram named the son of Hagar Ishmael. By this time, Abram was eighty-six years old.[11]

"Sarai, the matriarchal symbol, is barren. She would like to remain dominant and in control, but this is not her time. As I've said before, whenever a new order comes in, there are always those of the old order who resist the change and stubbornly fight to keep the old ways alive. The line of descent is given to the patriarch now, whether Sarai likes it or not. The servant, Hagar, repeats the Sun-ruled symbolism of Leo in that she is Egyptian. But Hagar is **not** the wife; she is only a slave. Thus the child will be considered to belong only to Abram. Sarai, the wife, would be the legal mother. The patriarch dominates."

A listener asked, "Isn't Ishmael supposed to be the ancestor of Islam? I've read that somewhere. If so, light is shed on the prophecy about him."

"Yes," I said, "I've read that, too. Certainly fits the situation in the Middle East right down to the present, doesn't it? Ishmael, the father of the Islamic nations; and Isaac, the father of Israel; and the family feud still rages!"

Then I added, "One more side note before we go on to the Age of Cancer. Hagar is still a female, in spite of all this masculine symbolism. That she is a **slave** is another way of saying that the feminine principle is suppressed during this epoch. However, she still receives a vision, symbolizing that aspect of the spirit-intuitive that seems to be predominantly associated with the feminine principle."

9

The Age of Cancer

*T*he years passed and Abram reached the age of ninety-nine. Once again the Lord appeared to him, saying, "Between you and me shall be a covenant. You will become the father of a host of nations. Accordingly, your name shall no longer be Abram. You are **Abraham**, and Abraham is exceedingly fertile. Nations and kings will come through you. I will maintain my covenant with you and your descendants throughout all ages as an everlasting pact. I will be your God and the God of your descendants after you. The whole land of Canaan belongs to you and your descendants as a permanent possession. For your part, you must see that you and every male among you bear a mark of your agreement to live according to my Law. Throughout the ages, you and your descendants must keep the covenant with me. Circumcise the flesh of your foreskin. In this way my covenant shall be in your flesh as an everlasting pact. All males must do this, even your slaves. If any male is uncircumcised, he shall be cut off from his people; he has broken my covenant."

As Abraham knelt, the Lord continued. "No longer shall you call your wife Sarai. Her name is Sarah. Accordingly, I shall bless her; and I will give you a son by her. Her son shall I also bless. Many nations and rulers of nations shall issue from him."

Abraham smothered his laughter. "How can an

*old man of one hundred years father a child?   And
Sarah is ninety! How can she give birth?"*

*But then Abraham remembered that he was in the
presence of the Lord, and that he was helpless to deny
the new order.   He protested, "But what of Ishmael?
Won't you keep him in your favor?"*

*And God replied, "No matter what you think now,
Sarah will bear a son, and you shall name him Isaac.   It
is to Isaac that my covenant shall pass.   I will be his
God and the God of his descendants. As for Ishmael, do
not worry.   He is not lost.   He will be fertile and will
father twelve chieftains, and I will make of him a great
nation.   But it must be to the son of Sarah that my
covenant now passes."   With that, the Lord departed
from Abraham.*

*Abraham followed the instructions of God and
saw that every male in his household was circumcised.*[1]

"This chapter is loaded with symbolism!" a listener
exclaimed.   "Abram's age of ninety-nine is like the end
of a cycle; and the name changes certainly symbolize a
new order coming in."

"And," said another, "if the new order is truly to
change from the masculine Age of Leo to the feminine
Age of Cancer, then the covenant of circumcision takes
on a new and interesting significance, now, doesn't it!"[2]

"You've got it!" I laughed. "Its use in this particular
place in the narrative is like a symbolic castration, as
the patriarchy gives way to the matriarchy. The line of
descent now returns to Sarah!"

"You're going to get arguments over that statement."

"No doubt! But I don't mean to say that this is
the literal reason for circumcision. Surely that practice
was established for quite practical and secular reasons
of hygiene. And the best way in those days to see that
the masses did something that was in their best inter-

ests was to make a religious law out of it. I'm sure that
the Jewish laws against pork, which brought disease if
not properly cooked, must have a similar origin. I do
suggest that the author of Genesis used the ritual of
circumcision as a symbolic literary device to express the
change to a new order. I am even more convinced of
this as I have read on to find that other specific mentions of circumcision are also tied in with change of
orders--always from masculine to feminine, and **never**
mentioned in transition from a feminine to a masculine
age.

"Another point of interest is that even though we
think of Judaism and the Arian age as being very patriarchal and male dominated, orthodox Judaism still
insists that the line of descent comes through the mother only. In order to be Jewish, one must be born of a
Jewish mother. I read a piece about that in a newspaper once. It was about arguments among orthodox and
conservative factions over the rule. It said a number of
prominent Jewish families had been lost over it. For
example, the article said that Barry Goldwater convert-
ed to Christianity after he, as the child of a Jewish
father and gentile mother, was refused bar mitzvah on
the grounds that he was not a Jew because his mother
was not a Jew. It does make you wonder about the
ancient origins of this covenant."[3]

"Rabbi Dobin's book links the name change
directly to astrology," a student commented.

"Right! He uses Midrash interpretations of
Genesis to show that changing one's name also meant
getting a new chart for a symbolic new birth. When an
orthodox Jew is gravely ill, the nearest male relative
goes to the synagogue where a ceremony is performed
to add a new name to the Hebrew name of the sick person. This practice has its origin in the ancient Midrash
interpretation that where the 'planetary fate' of Abram
and Sarai denied fertility, the new destiny of the

moment of 'rebirth,' as Abraham and Sarah, promised many descendants. The Roman Catholic practice of taking a new name at confirmation probably originates with Genesis, too, whether anyone remembers it that way or not."[4]

A little later, the Three-in-One, personified by the Lord and two messengers, paid a visit to Abraham and Sarah. The Lord said, "I will return to you at about this time next year, and by then Sarah will have a son." Sarah laughed.[5]

"The Bible's chapter footnote on this verse says that 'laughed' or 'yishaq' is the Hebrew form of the name 'Isaac,' " I pointed out.[6]

*A*s the Three left Abraham's tent and moved on in *the direction of Sodom, Abraham walked along with them for a while. The Lord said that he had heard that the sins of Sodom and Gomorrah are very grave, and that he intended to go and see for himself.*

Abraham asked the Lord if the cities of Sodom and Gomorrah were to be destroyed; would the innocent be swept away with the guilty? He pressed again and again for an answer.

"If there are fifty innocent people, will you spare the city? Forty-five? Thirty? Only ten?"

The Lord assured Abraham, "For the sake of those ten, I will not destroy it."

Abraham returned home. The two angels of the Lord came to the house of Lot at the gate of Sodom in the evening. Lot perceived the angels only as two distinguished gentlemen, and he insisted that they spend the night in his house and join him for dinner. Later that evening, all the townsmen of Sodom gathered outside Lot's house and demanded that he bring the men out to them. Lot protested that the men had the shelter of his

*house, and therefore his protection. Instead he offered,
"I have two daughters who have never had intercourse
with men. You may do with them as you please, but
don't do anything to these men. They have the shelter
of my roof."*

*The angry townsmen sneered at Lot, and pressed
forward to break down the door. With that, the two
angels, with a blinding flash of light, dazed the towns-
people and pulled Lot back to safety. They told Lot to
take all of his family and leave the city, "The Lord has
sent us to destroy this place."*

*Suddenly, Lot realized that his guests were super-
natural. He hastened to warn his prospective sons-in-
law, who had contracted marriage with his daughters.
"Get up and leave! The Lord will destroy the city." His
sons-in-law thought he surely must be joking.*

*Dawn was breaking as the angels urged Lot on.
When Lot hesitated still, the angels seized the hands of
Lot and his wife and two daughters, and led them to
safety outside the city. "Flee for your lives," the angels
told them, "and don't look back, or you will be swept
away." The Lord told Lot that the small town of Zoar
would be spared, so he and his family could find safety
there.*

*Lot's wife looked back, and she was turned into a
pillar of salt.[7]*

"The destruction of Sodom and Gomorrah com-
pletes the transition from the Age of Leo to the Age of
Cancer. The symbols for the collective masses of the
outgoing age are Leo [now corrupted into dominion,
advanced secular culture, the overblown ego] and its
counterpoint, Aquarius [rebelliousness against authority, intolerance of groups and ideas other than one's
own]. These are represented by Sodom and Gomorrah.
The older order must fall to make way for the new.
Those who are willing to give up the old ways and trust

in the Lord are spared to go on. Lot is hesitant--and definitely misguided in his attempt to sacrifice his daughters to save the men. It is the masculine age [here symbolized by the implication of male homosexuality] that is to be sacrificed now. Lot's prospective sons-in-law refuse to give up the old order, so they perish. Lot and his virgin daughters make the transition, but Lot's wife can't resist one last temptation to disobey the Lord and look back. The pillar of salt symbolizes her fall back into materialism. Salt crystallizes in cubes; it is a solidified 'four,' and here means bondage to matter. One must go forward or die. There can be no ultimate denial of God's plan."

ot and his two daughters left Zoar and went to live in a cave in the hill country. The daughters bemoaned the fact that there were no men left, after the destruction, for them to marry. The older said to the younger, "Come, let us get our father so drunk on wine that he will lie with us and then we can have offspring." The two carried out the plan, and each became pregnant by her father, and gave birth to sons.[8]

A listener interrupted, "Here's a prime example of where a literal, rather than symbolic, reading of the Bible can get you in trouble. Incest is not condoned in society; in fact, is considered abhorrent and sick. Yet here is the family that has been chosen by God to be spared destruction, engaging in incest, with no mention of punishment or even of disapproval."

"Yes, it's a difficult section to interpret--unless you consider it as a symbolic literary device to show the shift to a feminine age-- the taking over of the line of descent by the matriarchy."

braham and his household now journeyed to the region of Negreb. During their stay in Gerar,

Abraham once again passed Sarah off as his sister to protect himself from the king, Abimelech. The king sent for Sarah and took her into his home. But before he could touch her, God appeared to him in a dream: "You will die because of the woman you have taken, for she has a husband. I know you took her in good faith; you thought she was Abraham's sister. This is why I keep you from sinning by telling you this before you touch her. Save yourself! Return her to her husband."

Abimelech and his court were horrified. Abraham was called to court. "What wrong have I done to you," said the king, "that you should bring such monstrous guilt on me and my kingdom?"

"Because I was afraid," answered Abraham, "that you would kill me on account of my wife."

So Abimelech restored Sarah to Abraham, and also gave him flocks and herds and slaves, saying to Sarah, "See, your honor is preserved with everyone."

And God restored health to the wife of Abimelech, and to his maidservants, for so long as Sarah was not restored to her rightful place, every womb in Abimelech's household was closed. Now they could all bear children again.[9]

"How encouraging," laughed one of the women, "that the king was so interested in a 90-year-old woman!"

"Proof again that you can't take these Bible stories too literally," chided the man next to her.

"Well, I'll take the role of the literal interpreter," retorted another of the women, "and say that Sarah must have been quite a sexy lady for her age!"

As the chuckles died down I offered my own interpretation: "This is a repeat of the motif of an earlier story that belongs to the Virgo/Leo transition; only then, Sarah, representing the outgoing matriarch, was prostituted, or sacrificed, and then sent out of Egypt.

Now, however, Sarah is at the near peak of her powers, and about to become a mother--the mother of the Age of Cancer. Abraham **uses** her for his own benefit--as one might expect of a time when Capricorn is the 'serpent'--but Sarah is protected by God and is not corrupted. In fact, the king made Abraham rich in his effort to vindicate Sarah and prove her honor had been preserved.

"With Sarah's pregnancy and the birth of Isaac, we are full-fledged into the Age of Cancer."

N̵ow Sarah became pregnant, and bore Abraham a son in his old age, at the exact time that the Lord had stated. Abraham gave the child the name of Isaac, and according to his covenant with God had him circumcised on the eighth day of his life. Sarah said, "God has given me cause to laugh, and all who hear of it will laugh with me. Who would have said that Sarah should bear children, and yet I have!" Isaac grew, and when he was weaned, Abraham gave a great feast.

As Sarah saw her son playing with the son of Hagar, the slave-woman, she demanded of Abraham, "Drive out that woman and her son. No son of a slave shall share Isaac's inheritance!"

Abraham was very upset at Sarah's demands, but God said to him, "Do not be distressed about Ishmael or about your slave-woman. Do as Sarah demands, for it is through Isaac that your descendants shall bear your name. But I will also make a great nation of Ishmael, for he, too, is your offspring."

And so it was that early in the morning, Abraham gave some food and water to Hagar, and then sent her and her son away. Hagar and the boy wandered aimlessly in the wilderness until their water ran out, and Hagar sat down in despair that the boy might die. The boy began to cry, and was heard by God. God's messenger spoke to Hagar from the heavens, "Don't be afraid, Hagar. Arise and lift up the boy, for he will become the father of a great nation." Then God opened Hagar's eyes, and she perceived before her a well of water, and she let the boy drink.

God was with the boy as he grew up. He and his mother lived in the wilderness, and he became an expert bowman. His mother found a wife for him in Egypt.[10]

A student interrupted: "I get that Sarah and Isaac represent the new order, and that's why Hagar and Ishmael must be sent away. But I'm not sure I understand the symbolism of Hagar's experience in the wilderness."

"I think it just means that no one is ever lost. Hagar and her son may be 'out' for now, but they will have another chance to be redeemed."

Meanwhile, Abimelech and the commander of his army came to Abraham and said, "God is with you. Swear by God that you will behave as loyally toward me in these lands as I have toward you."

Abraham agreed to swear, but questioned Abimelech about a well that his men had seized by force. Abimelech claimed never to have heard about the matter before. Abraham and Abimelech agreed to a pact. Abraham set apart seven ewes from his flock and said to Abimelech, "These you shall accept from me in acknowledgment that the well was dug by me."

Abimelech agreed and that is why the place was thereafter called Beer-sheba, which means in Hebrew, "the well of the seven." Abraham planted a tamarisk tree at Beer-sheba and invoked the name of the Lord. In this land he resided many years.[11]

"The symbolism here is not so clear, but it seems to be another story that belongs to the transitory period.　Cancer has to do with the establishment of home and security. The pact made in the settling of property rights is sealed with seven ewes (feminine symbols for a feminine age) and Beer-sheba was later said to be the place of seven wells. An oath with the number seven prominent may also refer, symbolically, to the seven planets that were known to the ancients, and to the sacredness of the number seven."

"About seven," a student asked, "do you suppose that the seven visible planets could be the origin of the idea that seven is a sacred number?"

"I think that is quite likely. The planets could also be the reason for the structure of seven days of creation."

*S*ome time later, God put Abraham to a test. God called out, "Abraham! Take your beloved son Isaac and offer him up on a holocaust on a mountain that I will point out to you."

Early next morning, Abraham set out with Isaac for the place that God had designated. He made Isaac carry the wood for the holocaust, while he himself carried the fire and the knife. Isaac asked his father, "Father, here are the fire and the wood, but where are the sheep for the sacrifice?"

"God himself will provide the sheep for the holocaust," Abraham answered his son. The two continued up the mountain.

When they came to the place where God had told Abraham to go, he built an altar and arranged the wood on it. Then he tied up Isaac and put him on top of the wood on the altar. Just as he reached out for the knife to slaughter his son, God called out from heaven, "Abraham! Do not lay a hand on the boy. I know now that you are totally devoted to me, since you did not withhold from me your own beloved son."

Abraham saw a ram that was caught in a thicket.

He took the ram and offered it as a sacrifice in place of his son. And then Abraham named the place Yahweh-yireh, which means "the Lord will see."

Again God spoke, "Because you did not withhold from me your own beloved son, I will bless you mightily and make your descendants as countless as the stars and the sand of the seashore. Your descendants will overcome their enemies, and all the nations on earth will find blessings through them. All this will I do for you because you obeyed my command." [12]

"This is a familiar story, and, of course, a central teaching of it is the lesson of faith. God had already promised Abraham that through **Isaac** he would father a new nation. Would God break a sacred covenant? Of course not! In his unquestioning faith in the word of God, Abraham obeyed past any logical expectation, thus proving his love for God exceeded all. But in the light of our theme of Genesis, as the story of the ages and of the Divine Plan, what do you think this passage means?"

"Well, obviously it foretells the sacrifice of Jesus."

"And I'll bet that the use of a **ram** here is deliberate."

"Yes," I answered. "It would be at the end of the Age of Aries the Ram that the Redeemer is born. At the close of the epoch, the Ram would become the Lamb, and the Lamb is sacrificed to bring in the new age. Jesus would place unquestioning faith and obedience to the word of God even above his own life; and **God would so love the world that he would sacrifice his beloved son."**

*A*t the age of 127, Sarah died in the land of Canaan, and Abraham performed the customary mourning rites for her. Then he addressed the people of Canaan, "Although I am a resident alien, will you sell *me a piece of property for a burial ground for my dead wife?"*

The Hittites answered, "You are an elect of God. Choose the best of our burial sites."

In the negotiations that folowed, a man named Ephron offered to give Abraham the property that Abraham had especially wanted. But Abraham insisted upon paying for the land. The price of 400 pieces of silver was agreed upon. Thus Ephron's field was conveyed to Abraham by purchase in the presence of all the Hittites who sat on Ephron's town council; and after the transaction, Abraham buried Sarah in a cave in the field, which was now his property.[13]

"Cancer symbolism?" I asked.

"Abraham has bought property. No longer is he an alien and a migrant. He now has a permanent home."

"Four could be a symbol that this is the fourth age."

"And silver is associated with Cancer, too."

"And also," I added, "the fact that Sarah has died is our first clue that the Age of Cancer is drawing to a close. If you take a quick look at the Bible, you'll see in the 24th chapter of Genesis how the transition begins, and by the 25th chapter, the symbolism of where we go next will be obvious."

The Age of Gemini

*B*y now Abraham was a ripe old age, and he had been greatly blessed by the Lord.   One day he instructed his senior servant, "Put forth your hand under my thigh, and swear by the God of heaven and earth that you will not procure a wife for my son from among any of the daughters of Canaan, but you will go into my own land and select a wife from among my kindred."

"But what if the woman is unwilling to come back with me?" asked the servant.   "Shall I then take your son back to the land from which you migrated?"

"No, never take him there for any reason," said Abraham.   "God, who took me from the land of my kin, promised me by sacred oath that I should have **this** land for my descendants. He will send his messenger before you so that you will obtain a wife for my son. If then the woman is unwilling to follow you, you are released from this oath, but never take my son there!" The servant swore the oath as instructed, placing his hand under Abraham's thigh.

The servant, bearing many fine gifts, left for the land of Abraham's kindred.   He brought his camels to the well outside the city in the early evening, at about the time when the women go out to draw water.

He prayed to the Lord to help him find the right girl by this sign: "If I ask a girl to give me a drink, and she offers water to me and to my camels, too, I shall know *that she is the one that you have selected for the wife of Isaac."*

Scarcely had he finished his prayer when Rebekah, a beautiful young virgin, who was related to Abraham through his brother, came down to the well and filled her jug. The servant addressed her, "Please give me a sip of water."

"Take a drink, sir," offered Rebekah, "and I shall draw water for your camels, too." The servant watched as she watered the camels, and then he took out a gold ring and fastened it upon her nose. Then he placed two heavy gold bracelets on her wrists, asking her, "Whose daughter are you? Is there room in your father's house for us to spend the night?"

She answered, "I am the daughter of Bethuel, son of Milcah, who is wife of Nahor; and there is plenty of room in our house."

"Praise the Lord!" exclaimed the servant. "He has led me straight to the family of my master's brother."

Rebekah ran off to tell her family about the visitor. When her brother, Laban, saw the golden ring and bracelets, he rushed out to welcome the man at the well. So the servant went into Rebekah's home, where his feet were bathed, his camels were cared for, and a table was set for him. But he said, "I will not eat until I have told you my tale."

So the servant explained in detail his mission and his oath to find a wife for the son of Abraham. He told of his prayer at the well, and of Rebekah's fulfillment of it. Rebekah's family, believing that his was truly the will of the Lord, consented for Rebekah to marry Isaac. The servant then gave many costly gifts to Rebekah and to her family.

Early next morning, the servant asked to leave to return to Abraham, but Rebekah's brother and mother replied, "Let her stay with us for just ten more days." But the servant said that he did not want to be detained. Rebekah was then asked what she wanted to do, and she consented to go with the servant without delay. So Rebekah and her nurse and her maids left with the servant of Abraham and with the blessings of her family.

One evening as Isaac was out in the field, he saw camels approaching. Rebekah, from her camel, saw Isaac in the field, and asked the servant, "Who is that man?" The servant replied, "That is my master!" And Rebekah covered herself with her veil.

And so it was that Isaac took Rebekah into his tent and married her. In his love for her, he found solace after the death of his mother, Sarah.[1]

"A nice and proper little romance, isn't it? Can you see the transition in symbolism?" I asked.

"The ring in her nose is certainly a return to an age of masculine dominance!" one of the women ruefully commented. "And I suppose Abraham's insistence that the wife come from his homeland and kin points to a switchback of the line of descent from Sarah the matriarch to Abraham the patriarch."

"What's the oath of the hand under the thigh?"

"The Bible footnotes say that there was a Hebrew concept that children issue from the father's thigh. He who took such an oath was thought to bring a curse of sterility upon himself if he did not fulfill his sworn promise.[2] This oath, used in this particular context, seems to be yet another reference to the line of descent returning to the patriarchy. Even the use of gold could be a symbol, for gold is associated with Leo and Sun, the beginning age of the patriarchy; while silver is most often associated with Moon, which is feminine."

"So Cancer is about to wane. I wonder about the similarity of the word Cancer with Canaan--it seems that most all the references to Canaan so far have pointed toward this epoch."

"Yes, I wondered about that, too."

At the age of one hundred and seventy-five, Abraham breathed his last, and was buried next to his wife, Sarah.[3]

"He was a lot older than that, according to your version.   He lived all the way through the Ages of Leo and Cancer, and that would make him more than 4,000 years old when he died."

"Older than Methuselah!"

"For sure!" said Tom, my class expert on trivia. "I read in an almanac once that if you added up the age of Methuselah, you find that he was 369 years old when Noah was born. If the flood started when Noah was 600 years old, then Methuselah--who lived to be 969 years old--died in the year of the flood. This brings up the question, did Noah leave his grandfather out in the rain?"[4] Everybody laughed.

"Yet another reason why we shouldn't take the Bible too literally," I said.   "You know, there is a very authoritative precedent for saying the Abraham stories are allegorical.   In Galatians, Chapter Four, Paul has just told the story of Abraham and his two sons, one by the slave-girl and one by the free-born wife.   Verse 24 begins: *'All this is allegory.'* Paul, of course, has a different interpretation of the allegory than I do. He compares Hagar to the covenant at Mount Sinai and to the Jerusalem of Paul's day.   But Sarah relates to the Jerusalem on high, and in Paul's words, *'it is she who is our mother.'*[5] Actually, when I think of it, that's not so far off from my theory, because I consider Sarah to be the symbol of the female principle, or the symbol, in her age, of the Divine Mother."

"How do you explain the age of 175 which the Bible says was Abraham's age at death?"

"Well, it seems rather farfetched to believe that the

real historical Abraham could have lived to be that old. Possibly it has to do with a different method of calculating time that was handed down, or it could be that the numbers have a symbolic significance."

Another student suggested an answer. "According to numerology 1+7+5=13 and 1+3=4. Four is the number of Saturn or the material world. One correlation might be that the allegorical Abraham lived in part of four different ages: Virgo, Leo, Cancer and Gemini."

"We have to keep in mind," I said, "that the allegorical Abraham is as different from the historical Abraham as our present- day 'Uncle Sam' differs from the real 'Uncle' Samuel Wilson, after whom he was modeled."[6]

A braham's son, Ishmael, had twelve sons before he died. The Ishmaelites settled in the vicinity of the Egyptian borders, each of them pitching his camp in opposition to all of his kindred.

The blessings of God were with Isaac.

When Rebekah, the wife of Isaac, became pregnant, the children in her womb jostled each other so much that she went to consult the Lord, who said to her:

"Two nations are in your womb, quarreling while
still within you;

But one shall surpass the other, and the older
shall serve the younger."

There were twins in her womb! And when the time of their delivery came, the first to emerge was reddish, and his whole body was like a hairy mantle. They named him Esau, which means "hairy." Esau's brother came out, gripping Esau's heel. The second born twin was named Jacob.

As the twins grew up, Esau became a skillful hunter, and was a man who lived in the open. Jacob, however, was a simple man, who preferred to keep to his tents. Isaac preferred Esau; but Rebekah preferred

Jacob.

One day, while Jacob was cooking a stew, Esau came in from the open, famished, and saying, "Let me gulp down some of that red stuff. I'm starving!" But Jacob said, "First give me your birthright in exchange for it." "Look, I'm dying of hunger." said Esau. "What good will the birthright do me?" "Then swear to me," insisted Jacob. So Esau gave Jacob his birthright in trade for bread and lentil stew. He ate, then went on his way. Esau cared little for his birthright.[7]

"Twins! Right on schedule."

"Right! Age of Gemini--the first mention of twins in Genesis. And as you shall see, twin symbolism runs all through this next section. But first, let's clarify the symbolism that is loaded into this short story of the birth of the twins.

"Gemini is the sign of duality--the symbol in which the principle of the opposites is most pro-nounced. In Esau and Jacob, the masculine/feminine polarity can easily be seen; and also the complementary opposite signs of the age.

"First there's the symbolism of the heel. In the mythology of the ancients, the heel is the symbol of contact between spirit and matter. The man who stands upright, and has a soul, makes contact with the earth at his foot. The vulnerability of the heel is told in stories other than those in the Bible. The most familiar is probably that of Achilles, who lost his immortality because of an injury to his heel. To this day 'Achilles heel' is a common symbol for one's weakest point. The very first biblical reference is in Genesis 3:15 where God says that the serpent will strike at the heel of man.

"Gemini is the sign of the age, so Esau, as first born, represents the spiritual concept of the Age of Gemini. Jacob, grasping Esau's heel, represents Sagittarius, opposition sign of the age and symbol of the material bondage of the souls.

"Gemini is a masculine sign. So Esau, as first born, symbolizes the masculine polarity, and the shift from the old, feminine, matriarchal Age of Cancer to the new, masculine, patriarchal Age of Gemini. But Gemini is the symbol through which, more than any other, we must fight the battle of the opposites.

"All humans are dual; we are spirit and matter, we can choose obedience or rejection of Divine Will. And though we may express dominant characteristics of either masculine or feminine, each soul carries within itself the recessive characteristics of the opposite sex. The body may be male or female, but the soul, in the image of God, is androgynous. In God, male and female are perfectly balanced. So long as a soul remains bound to the material world, it is out of balance.

"The description of the characters of Esau and Jacob make it pretty obvious that Esau is masculine and Jacob, although a male, expresses a dominance of character traits that are commonly thought of as feminine. So the twins represent not only the shift of the ages, but also of the duality of human nature.

"The inner battle of the soul begins with a 'first score' for the enticements of the material world, when Esau sells his birthright to Jacob for a good meal. At this point, his hunger satisfied, Esau thinks little of his spiritual 'birthright.' Already the twins fulfill the prediction of the Lord to Rebekah. The older twin now serves the younger, in that the spiritual nature of man binds itself to the lures of material satisfaction."

*W*hen there was famine in the land, Isaac moved his camp to Gerar, the territory of Abimelech. The Lord instructed him not to go into Egypt but to stay in this land.

The covenant of the Lord with Abraham now passed on to Isaac, and again the promise was repeat-

ed that the descendants of Abraham would be as numerous as the stars and this land belonged to them.

When the men of Gerar asked questions about Rebekah, Isaac said, "She is my sister." Rebekah was very beautiful, and Isaac feared that if he called her his wife, he would be killed so that they could have her. But one day Abimelech happened to gaze out his window and saw Isaac fondling his wife. He called for Isaac and said, "Surely she must be your wife. How could you have called her your sister?"

Isaac answered that he feared for his life. "But how could you do this to us!" exclaimed Abimelech. "What if one of my men were to lay with your wife? It would have brought great guilt upon us!" And Abimelech gave all of his men a stern warning that anyone who molested either Isaac or Rebekah would be put to death.

Isaac, with the blessings of the Lord, became very rich in this region. His crops were bountiful; his herds multiplied. Abimelech's people, the Philistines, became very envious. Abimelech asked Isaac to move his camp away because his herds were crowding the area. So Isaac established a permanent camp at the Wadi Gerar, where he reopened the wells that his father's servants had dug long ago when Abraham was alive. (The Philistines had stopped them up after Abraham's death.)

But now, as the servants of Isaac dug and reached spring water, the shepherds of the region quarreled with them, saying, "The water belongs to us!" They quarreled over the first well, which was named Esek (challenge), and over the second well, which was named Sitnah (opposition). But over the third well they did not quarrel. It was called Rehoboth, and it was said, "The Lord has now given us plenty of room to flourish in this land."

Later, at the site called Beer-Sheba, the Lord appeared to Isaac and repeated his blessings to stay *with Isaac and multiply his descendants for the sake of his father, Abraham. Isaac built an altar there to invoke the Lord and pitched his tent there as his servants began to dig the well.*

Abimelech came to Isaac, accompanied by his councilor and his general. "Why have you come?" asked Isaac. "You hate me and drove me away from you." They answered, "We are convinced that the Lord is with you, so we propose a pact between our two sides that henceforth we shall act kindly toward each other." They feasted together that night, and early the next morning they exchanged oaths. Abimelech and his men departed in peace.

That same day, Isaac's servants reported, "We have reached water!" Isaac called the well Shibah, and that is still the name of the city Beer-sheba to this day.[8]

"Here, Isaac, like his father before him, passes his wife off as his sister to protect himself. This truly seems to be a literary device to symbolize transition, because this is just where it shows up in the text. In this case, moving into Gemini the Twins, the masculine and feminine principles are at first equalized. The king decrees that neither Isaac nor Rebekah shall be molested. Rebekah, symbolizing the matriarch and the outgoing female principle, is **not** prostituted and does **not** leave. She stays right with Isaac the patriarch in the new Age of Gemini."

"What about the wells? In a way it's another repetition of an earlier theme, but it is quite a bit different here."

"This story, like the one just before, about Rebekah and Isaac being 'equalized,' seems to be a literary device of transition. The first two wells cause quarrels: 'challenge' and 'opposition.'[9] These are negative possibilities of the Twins. But in the beginning of an age, the ideal must be presented positively. So Isaac rises above the 'opposition' by creating a third well and all realize that there is no need to argue--there is plenty for all. Two, the 'opposition,' is resolved into harmony by three, the Trinity. The opposing sides form a new pact of peace. Later, more wells are dug and the sacred 'seven' is invoked again by the choice of Shibah, which means seven, as the new name for Beer-sheba."

Now meanwhile, when he was forty years old, Esau married Judith and Basemath, two women of the Canaanites. This was a source of embitterment to Isaac and Rebekah.[10]

"The twin symbolism continues on with two wives for Esau. Isaac, repeating his father's directive for the new order, does not want wives for his sons from Canaan, Cancer, the old order."

*W*hen Isaac became so old that his eyesight was failing, he called Esau to him, saying, "You see I am so old I might die at any time. Go out and hunt some game and then prepare an appetizing dish for me to eat, so that I may give you my special blessing before I die."

Now Rebekah eavesdropped during the conversation, so when Esau left to go hunting, she told Jacob what she had heard and instructed him to quickly bring her two choice kids from the flock so that she could pre-pare them for Isaac. "You will bring it to your father," she said. "Then it will be you who receives his bless-ing."

"But Esau is hairy," worried Jacob, "and I am smooth-skinned. If Father feels me, I'll bring curses upon myself, rather than a blessing!"

"Just do as I say." ordered Rebekah. "Let any curse upon you, my son, fall upon me instead. Go get the kids!"

Later, Rebekah dressed Jacob in Esau's best cloth-ing, and she covered his hands and the hairless part of his neck with the skins of the kids. She handed him the appetizing dish she had prepared and sent him to his father.

Jacob told Isaac that he was Esau, his firstborn. Isaac, suspicious on account of Jacob's voice, asked him to move closer so that he could touch him. When he felt the hairiness of the hands and smelled the fragrance of Esau's clothes, Isaac was fooled.

And so it was that Isaac gave to Jacob the bless-ing of the firstborn:

"The blessings of God be upon you. Let people and nations pay you homage.

> *Be master of your brothers, may your mother's*
> > *sons bow down to you.*
> *Curses on those who curse you, and blessings*
> > *on those who bless you."*

Just as Jacob left his father, Esau returned from the hunt. When he appeared to his father, bringing his appetizing dish, Isaac was seized with uncontrollable trembling. "Who was it then that I blessed? Now he must remain blessed!"

Esau sobbed bitterly, "Bless me, too!"

Isaac explained the deception of Jacob, but insist-ed that even though achieved through a ruse, the bless-ing could not be taken back. He could not break his word.

Esau bore a great grudge against Jacob and plot-ted that after his father died, he would kill Jacob. When Rebekah heard of that plan, she told Jacob and sent him away to stay with her brother. "Stay there until Esau's anger subsides," she said. "Then I will send for you to come back. Must I lose you both this day?"[11]

"Battle of the opposites: score 'two' for material-ism," I commented. "And this story also, of course, symbolizes the struggle between the masculine and the feminine. Every age contains a lengthy struggle between the old and the new orders. Here, the old matriarchal age is not ready to relinquish control. Rebekah wants the blessing of the firstborn to go to her favorite son, Jacob, thus retaining the feminine line; so she decides to trick Isaac into giving his blessing and the birthright to Jacob."

"There's much more than that," interrupted a listener. "I've read more than one interpretation of this story. Since Jacob is in fact the carrier of the line, later to found the twelve tribes, he is usually reasoned to be the 'good,' or the more spiritual twin; while Esau is eternally the sinner because he thoughtlessly sold his birthright in the first place."

"But," said another, "I've read other interpretations that acknowledge that Jacob behaved despicably, but rationalize that God sometimes uses weak, sinful men to achieve an ultimate purpose that we cannot hope to understand and therefore should not question."[12]

"Well, any way you look at it," said a third, "if we take Esau and Jacob as literal and historical characters, we must accept that Jacob, the major patriarchal figure, later to be known as Israel, is a deceptive, nasty trickster who twice cons his rather stupid dupe of a brother out of his rightful inheritance."

"O.K., then," I said. "Doesn't it make better sense to take the story of Esau and Jacob as a symbolic parable to illustrate the duality--Gemini--of human nature? The way I see it, the twins are symbolically **one** person. Esau, the spiritual side of one's nature, has been lured and tricked by the deceptive enticements of the material world and has fallen prey to the lower side of his nature, Jacob. Thus spiritually corrupted, he plots to kill Jacob. But one cannot kill a part of oneself, nor can one blame one's weaknesses on another person.

"Rebekah, for her part, seems now to realize the damage she has caused through her feminine--old order--tricks, so she sends Jacob away, thus accepting the new order.

"The next three chapters of Genesis are devoted to Jacob, and Esau is barely mentioned. It is not until Chapter 32, **after** Jacob has decided to beg the forgiveness of his brother, Esau,[13] thus symbolically reaching out for the spiritual side of his own nature, that he meets God face to face. Jacob's reconciliation with the spiritual is symbolized as God **changes his name to Israel**--born again! He has *'contended with divine and human beings and has prevailed.'* [14]

"The opposition, Sagittarius, in the form of Jacob/Israel, has been spiritualized and balanced with Gemini--Esau; and Gemini has been balanced within itself, in the reconciliation of the two sides of the nature of Israel. Israel has now earned the right to carry on his father's name, so it is that through his descendants the Age of Gemini will pass on into the Age of Taurus."

"It works," they agreed. "But you skipped a lot of material."

"Ah, yes--the three chapters. Actually, I think I'll go even further and summarize chapters 26 through 36 with one commentary, rather than tell each story in detail.

"The Gemini symbolism continues to be carried through these chapters in some pretty obvious ways. Previous to this time of Gemini, the Bible only mentions one wife for each man. But Esau and Jacob each marry two wives. Jacob's two wives, Leah and Rachel, each have a maidservant who becomes a concubine to Jacob.

"Gemini symbolism is carried out in the competition between Leah and Rachel. Rachel is Gemini, the first choice; while Leah is Sagittarius, the opposition sign who for a while supplants Rachel as the first wife. Each woman has her 'alter-ego' in the person of her

maidservant. The 'good' of each will ultimately prevail.
The order to the ages passes appropriately, in that
Rachel's first son, Joseph, will bring in the Age of
Taurus. But Leah gives birth to Judah, through whose
line will come the Redeemer; and it is her sign of
Sagittarius that will bring the Revelation.

"Rather than paraphrase each story in detail, I
have prepared an essay on the twelve tribes of Israel
that come from the sons of Jacob whose births are
described in chapters 29, 30 and 35 of Genesis."

11

The Twelve Tribes of Israel

To study the twelve sons of Jacob, who founded the twelve tribes of Israel, presents an intriguing puzzle. Many authors have considered the twelve tribes to represent zodiacal symbols,[1] but they differ on which one is which. The Bible lists the twelve many times but frequently changes the order in which they are listed. Even the death-bed blessing of their father differs in order from the actual order of their birth.

The only interpretive key that every author seems to agree upon is that Judah represents the lion, or Leo. To try to alter that would be to ignore too many obvious references to him such as "lion" and "kingship."

Reuben is usually given as Taurus because the story of the birth of the twelve tribes is related to either the historical period that encompasses the Age of Taurus or to the beginning of the Age of Aries, when Taurus became the Cardinal Ascendant. Since Reuben is the firstborn, he, of course, must represent the first sign of the zodiac. This would seem logical, because if you then go in the forward motion of the zodiac, the second son, Simeon, is Gemini; the third, Levi, is Cancer; and the fourth, Judah, is Leo--right on target!

The only trouble is that aside from Judah, the whole affair gets very muddy. You really have to beg the issue to get the biblical references to Simeon and Levi to sound anything like the characteristics of

Gemini and Cancer; and Reuben does not sound much like a Taurus, either, when in his father's death-bed blessing Reuben is called "unstable as water."[2] (Maybe that could be true of some Taureans on especially bad days, when they act like the worst of their Scorpio opposites, but it hardly suggests a proper symbol for God's plan for a new age.)

Then, just before Israel's death, he, in effect, removes the exclusive right of Reuben and Simeon to be numbers one and two in birthright, by claiming the sons of Joseph as his own and making them equal to Reuben and Simeon (Gen. 48:5-7).[3] The death-bed blessing of Israel to Reuben and Simeon-Levi, mentioned as a pair, could be taken as further evidence of the removal of their birthright: To Reuben was said, *"You shall no longer excel."* Of Simeon and Levi was said, *"I will scatter and disperse them."* Joseph is blessed as the *"prince among his brothers."* [4]

The first reference after Genesis to the twelve sons of Israel is in Chapter 1 of Exodus. They are given as those who migrated with Israel into Egypt and are listed in the following order: Reuben, Simeon, Levi, Judah, Issacher, Zebulun, Benjamin, Dan, Naphtali, Gad and Asher. Joseph is not included since he was already in Egypt.[5]

This order is **not** the actual birth order of Jacob's sons.[6] But it **is** the correct birth order if we honor the mother line, as we might expect would be done in the matriarchal Age of Taurus. Here the legal wives of Jacob clearly predominate over the offspring of their maidservants, who were only concubines. The four sons of the maidservants are placed at the end of the line. All of the sons of the first wife, Leah, are in order at the beginning. They are followed by the son of Rachel, Benjamin. He is really the youngest of the twelve, but he moves up in order apparently because of Rachel's status as a legal wife.

The death blessing of Moses, in Deuteronomy 33,

is in a slightly different order, inserting Rachel's children before the last two who were born of Leah, but all of the concubine's children are still at the end of the list.[7] Other listings in other books of the Bible, particularly ones that clearly belong in the Age of Aries, begin with Judah in the lead.[8] Now Judah is not Aries, he is Leo--so why is he chosen as the father of the new line of descent through David to Jesus?

Aries is a patriarchal age, of this there is no doubt! But by now, the Israelites have a long history. My theory is that they saw the birth of the patriarch to have been in the Age of Leo, that this idea is **symbolized** by the story of Abram. Those who think that the Israelite leaders who made up these stories **really** thought that the world was created just a couple of thousand years before their time, should think it all through again. Keep in mind that **very advanced astronomy** was known to the Egyptian priests with whom Moses obviously must have studied, since he was reared as a prince of Egypt.

In my opinion, there is no lasting and arbitrary assignment of one sign for each tribe. No individual or group expresses one sign only. We are all a composite and variable. I think that the zodiacal designation of each tribe varies. The differing arrangements are a symbolic device that was deliberately used by Moses, and by others under his influence, who contributed to the authorship of the Pentateuch.

Just as the secrets of the pyramid were reserved for only initiates, I think that Moses kept most of his knowledge secret, knowing that it could be misunderstood and misused. But he preserved it hermetically, in the symbolism of these first books of the Bible that he either wrote or caused to be written through his influence.

It is highly probable that the twelve tribes of Israel are zodiacal symbols. Let us look at that in the light of

my theory that one of the things that Genesis symbolically preserves for us is the knowledge of the Great Ages
of the precession of the equinoxes.

In Genesis 29 and 30, the actual order of the
births of the sons of Jacob is given, along with references to the meaning of each name. The meanings
given do not fit well at all if Reuben is Taurus and the
zodiac proceeds in counterclockwise order. But they do
make sense in clockwise, or precessional order, with
Reuben as Scorpio. Since this is a story of creation,
perhaps the order of birth is the order of Creation.

Reuben is the firstborn of the first wife, Leah, who
was at first unloved and barren. But when God saw
that she was unloved, he made her fruitful. Reuben's
name can be interpreted as: *"he saw my misery; he
will love me."* In the last Age of Scorpio, the world was
to a large extent cold and miserable under the glacier.
We could paraphrase to say, "God sees the misery of the
world, and he will restore it."   Reuben represents
Scorpio.

Leah named her second son Simeon, which
means *"he heard."* In the Age of Libra, God has "heard"
and has restored, and a new cycle of Balance has
begun. In Libra, the principle of the opposites begins in
balance, so here neither the patriarchy nor the matriarchy dominates. Simeon represents Libra.

Of her third son, Levi, Leah says, *"Now my husband will become attached to me."* Levi represents the
Age of Virgo, when the mother-wife-matriarchal line
was established.

With the birth of Judah, Leah says, *"I will give
grateful praise to the Lord,"* and after that she stops
having children. By "coincidence" it happens that
Judah still comes out as Leo the Lion, even in precessional order! The Age of Leo is the first patriarchal age,
and the "mother" is now barren.

Rachel, who was Jacob's first love, but only his

second wife, due to the deception of her father, has so far been barren. Now she cries, *"Give me children or I shall die!"* Jacob admonishes her that he cannot take the place of God who has denied her. Rachel then offers her maidservant to Jacob as his concubine, so that through her slave, at least, she can have offspring.

Rachel's maidservant gives birth to Dan, a name given to him by Rachel to mean, *"He has vindicated me."* Thus the age changes to Cancer, the sign most closely associated with maternal qualities, and the mother-matriarch line returns, vindicated and fruitful.

Naphtali, the second son of Rachel's slavewoman, represents the Age of Gemini. The meaning of his name can be paraphrased, *"I engaged in a fateful struggle with my sister and I prevailed."* Gemini symbolizes the struggle of the opposites, or the twins of spirit and matter within self.

The still barren Leah, not to be outdone, gives her own slavewoman to Jacob, and the maid gives birth to Gad, whose name means to Leah, *"What good luck!"* Gad would represent the hope for the future, and the end of the now present struggle (Gemini) in the coming Age of Taurus.

Of the second son of her slavewoman, Asher, Leah says, *"What good fortune!"* or "they call me fortunate." In the Age of Aries, the nation of Israel is established in full flower as the chosen people of God.

Now one day, Reuben finds some mandrakes (an herb that the ancients thought promoted conception) and brings them to his mother, Leah. Rachel wants the mandrakes and the sisters quarrel bitterly over them. Then Rachel offers to trade the mandrakes for a night with Jacob. The result of Leah's purchased night with Jacob is Issachar, whose name means, *"I have paid for you,"* or *"my reward."* Issachar represents the Age of Pisces, which is the fulfillment of the matriarchal cycle (opposition sign to Virgo), and is the age of the reward--

the elevation of the Virgin through whom has come the Redeemer.

The next son is Zebulun, also born of Leah. This is Aquarius, the fulfillment of the patriarchal cycle that began with Leo. Leah says, *"My husband will offer me presents, now that I have borne him six sons."*

Finally, the Lord smiles on Rachel and she is fruitful, giving birth to Joseph, who in this line-up represents the Age of Capricorn. Says Rachel: *"He has removed my disgrace,"* or to paraphrase, "he has elevated my status" [a top goal of Capricorn]. She also says, *"May He add one more son"* [one more age].

Rachel, here representing the Divine Mother, dies in childbirth with Benjamin, who represents the final age and the close of this cycle, before the world faces the judgment, destruction and rebirth in the next Age of Scorpio. It is Benjamin who represents the Age of Sagittarius.

Rachel calls her last son Ben-oni, which can be translated either *"son of my vigor"* or *"son of affliction."* (Presumably the contrast of translation can refer to which way each soul can go at the end of the cycle.) Israel, however, renames this last son Benjamin, which means *"son of the right hand,"* or the *"father's help and support."* In this way, it is foretold that the Christ, who would bring in the Jupiter-ruled Age of Pisces, will return in the Jupiter-ruled sign of the Revelation, the Age of Sagittarius![9]

While the precessional line-up makes sense in reference to the naming of the sons, it does not fit at all with the character of the sons or tribes as expressed in the death-bed blessings of Israel and, later, of Moses. In these, and in several other listings in the Bible's early books, the sons or tribes are given in what apparently was the law of the mother line; the sons of Leah are at the head of the list, followed by the sons of Rachel, and at the end of the list, the sons of the slavewomen.[10]

In some of the several references to the tribes that could be associated with the Age of Taurus, the sons of the slavewomen are mixed up in age order, but generally they follow the pattern I have suggested, according to the supremacy of the wives. In the actual blessing to all of his sons at this death-bed (in Genesis 49), Israel mentions Joseph and Benjamin last; but he has already, when alone with Joseph (in chapter 48), elevated the house of Joseph to equality with Reuben.

Israel, representing Gemini, is dying, along with his Great Age. The Age of Taurus is dawning. If we call Reuben Taurus, as most analysts do, and follow forward zodiacal order, but place the wives' sons before the slaves, as is done in Exodus, Numbers and Deuteronomy, we would get the following order: Reuben as Taurus, Simeon as Gemini, Levi as Cancer, Judah as Leo, Issachar as Virgo, Zebulun as Libra, Joseph as Scorpio, Benjamin as Sagittarius, Dan as Capricorn, Naphtali as Aquarius, Gad as Pisces and Asher as Aries.

If we were to leave Joseph second to the last, in chronological age order, he would be Pisces. I have read more than one good supporting analysis of Joseph as Pisces, based on his psychic ability to have and to interpret prophetic dreams, but I just do not agree. Joseph is no Pisces. Capricorn, I could believe, as he rises to be vizier of Egypt, and ruthlessly uses the famine of the people to collect all of the flocks and the lands of everyone in the country in order to secure his status with his boss, the Pharaoh. Genesis 47 describes Joseph's acquisitions after the settlement in Goshen and anyone knowledgeable in the characteristics of the signs could recognize Capricorn or Taurus; but Pisces--never! Scorpio, I could also believe, as Joseph is left for dead by his brothers, but "rises again" to a whole new life, and then gets even with his brothers, even while providing for them. (Scorpio is a water/intuitive sign, too, so that accounts for the dreams.) But Joseph as Pisces just does not work. The "matriarchal order" makes more sense.

In the case of some of the sons, the death-bed blessings of Moses in Deuteronomy 33 support the same sign characteristics as in the death-bed blessings of Israel. Moses follows the "matriarchal order," but does not in all cases use the same tribe to represent the same constellation as does Israel. But Moses' death was in a different age, and the symbolism is therefore of a different teaching than that of the time of Israel's death.

Now, remember, the house of Joseph has been made **equal** to Reuben, so we could say that Reuben (Taurus) and Joseph (Scorpio) are interchangeable. On his death-bed, Israel tells Reuben that he is "unruly as water" and "shall no longer excel (lead)," because he has defiled his father's bed by sleeping with one of Israel's concubines. So Taurus, having given in to the temptation to behave in a typical manner of his serpent-opposition sign of Scorpio, is consequently kicked out of his place as first in line. In his blessing of Joseph, Israel makes it quite clear that Joseph is to replace Reuben as the prince (first) among his brothers. So the house of Joseph makes the advance from the material to the spiritual expression of the new age. Joseph is no longer Scorpio--he is Taurus.

All that Moses has to say to the tribe of Reuben is, *"May Reuben live and not die out, but let his men be few."* The finest and best of everything is given to Joseph:

> *"These shall come upon the head of Joseph*
> *and upon the brow of the prince among his*
> *brothers,*
> *The **majestic bull**, his father's first born,*
> *whose horns are those of the wild ox*
> *With which to gore the nations,*

> *even those at the ends of the earth."*
> *(These are the myriads of Ephraim and these*
> *are the thousands of Manasseh.)*
> *--Deut. 33:17* [11]

Reuben is admonished by his father and symbolically dismissed for the present. Joseph moves to his rightful place as the spiritual representative of the Age of Taurus, vizier of Egypt, the primary civilization of the new age.

In the twelve tribes, Joseph will be represented as Taurus by his son, Ephraim. Joseph died in Egypt. So, his sons carried on his birthright in the Exodus.

In the Genesis blessing of Israel, Simeon and Levi are together, and the same things are said about both. This has led some analysts to say that they are together Gemini, the Twins. They then solve the problem of a missing sign by putting in Dinah, the only daughter of Israel;[12] or by saying that the twelve were only complete when Joseph's two sons replaced him.[13] Others have valiantly tried to justify the violence, fury and willfulness with which Israel characterizes Simeon and Levi as the intellectual aggressiveness of Gemini and the emotional aggressiveness of Cancer.[14]

I think that Israel's scathing criticism of Simeon and Levi refers to the wickednesses and excesses he had perceived in the two ages just passed, Gemini and Cancer. He curses them and says they will be scattered and dispersed.

Joseph's other son, Manasseh, replaces Simeon in the order, representing Gemini. Later in the Bible, there are several references to the tribe of Manasseh as being split into two half-tribes, thus carrying out the Gemini symbology.[15]

To keep the entire house of Joseph together (as nearly all passages do) Benjamin would have to be moved up in the order and replace Levi as Cancer. The characteristics that would result of this position seem to fit, as Moses says of Benjamin, *"Benjamin is the beloved of the Lord, who shelters him all the day, while he abides securely at his breast."* [16] Israel is not so generous: *"Benjamin is a ravenous wolf; mornings he devours the prey, and evenings he distributes the spoils."* [17] At a much more material level of expression, this, too, could describe the Cancer protective and maternal instincts.

Reuben and Simeon are now displaced as Taurus and Gemini. Where do they go? The clue is in Israel's words, and in his choice to bless Joseph and Benjamin last in the final forward zodiacal positions of Pisces and Aries, even though he has previously stated the leadership of the house of Joseph. Reuben is called *"unruly as water,"* indicating a water sign, and is the son of his father's *"sorrow."* This would be a lower expression of Pisces. Joseph, whose son will be given Reuben's place, is blessed second to the last in order, the position of Pisces.[18]

In the blessing of Joseph, Israel alludes to the Mighty One who will prevail in the Age of Pisces. So here, very briefly, we do get a connotation of Joseph, blameless in his father's eyes, as Pisces. But it is not yet time for the Redemption. Reuben represents Pisces, unredeemed, in place of Joseph, who has been selected to bring in the Age of Taurus.[19]

Benjamin is given a violent characterization, which could be taken as the final sign of Aries, and his blessing is last in order. Simeon replaces Benjamin at the end of the line, representing the lower nature of Aries. The second son of Joseph, as said before, becomes Gemini; and Benjamin, moved up in line to join the house of Joseph, becomes the third sign, Cancer. No place remains for Levi.

If Levi, in the blessing of Israel, was meant to be the other half of Gemini, then surely he is representative of the half who spiritually redeems himself, because Levi is the tribal origin of Moses, and is **removed** from the line-up of the tribes to become the priestly class.[20]

But if Levi, originally **third** in line, was meant to be Cancer, the symbolism would still work. It is of the higher nature of Cancer to make one's own needs subservient to the nurturing care of others. In the blessing of Moses, the Levites are clearly designated as the priests.

Next comes Judah, who seems to remain Leo the Lion, no matter how we line up the twelve! Israel says, *"The scepter shall never depart from Judah,"* and Moses intimates the Judaic line for the Messiah with these words:

"The Lord hears the cry of Judah:
   you will bring him to his people.
His own hands defend his cause
   and you will be help against his foes." [21]

According to Genesis 30, Issachar was born just before Zebulun. Both Israel and Moses bless the two of them together. Both Israel and Moses mention the name of the younger son, Zebulun, before the elder, Issachar. I cannot explain why the order is reversed, but I can associate the characteristics with the signs as follows:

Zebulun, in the words of Israel, will dwell by the sea and ships; and Moses contrasts Zebulun, in his *"pursuits"* with Issachar living a very settled life--he accepts the burden of being a serf in order to be settled and enjoy the pleasant country.

If Zebulun is to represent the next constellation after Judah, which is Virgo, then his characterization as a trader primarily on the sea alludes to the age of the flood, and later, the massive migration of the Ur race.

Issachar, as Libra, wants to be at peace at all costs, even to the compromising point of placing himself in servitude to another.

The next constellation in line is Scorpio, and the next son blessed by Israel is Dan.   Dan is to achieve justice, as Scorpio is the symbol of Judgment.   As the serpent or horned viper (symbol of the lowest manifestation of Scorpio) Dan will lurk by the roadside to bite the horse's heel so that the rider tumbles backward. The horse is clue to the fact that Scorpio is adjacent to Sagittarius, symbolized by a man-horse centaur.   The heel is symbolic of mortality or matter, since the foot is the part of the body where humanity makes contact with earth. [ref. page 112]

Moses' blessings change the order of the sons of the slavewomen, and Dan does not seem to represent Scorpio there.   The story of the blessings of Moses are at a much later time and no doubt have a different symbolic secret to unlock.

Israel next names Gad, who *"shall be raided by raiders but he shall raid at their heels."* [22] That will be for the Centaur, Sagittarius.   The Centaur is an image of a man trying to raise himself out of his lower nature (half-horse) to reach for the spiritual.   At the same time that Sagittarius must struggle to save itself, it is also noted for its attempts to bring revelation to others.

Asher represents Capricorn, symbolic of the goat who climbs to the top of the mountain and gains status and material security.   *"Asher's produce is rich, and he shall furnish dainties for kings."*[23]

Naphtali would represent Aquarius.   Of him Israel says, *"Naphtali is a hind let loose which brings forth lovely fawns."*   The meaning of this is pretty foggy, but here goes: Aquarius is known for the breaking of boundaries and fighting to be free.   Perhaps this foretells that in the Age of Aquarius, boundaries will be broken and bring forth peace (the fawn).[24]

That brings us down to the final two: Pisces, then Aries.   I have already explained how that works symbolically for Joseph/Reuben and Benjamin/Simeon.

In summary, it is my theory that the naming of the twelve sons of Jacob in Genesis 29:31-35, 30:1-24, and 35:18 contain, in symbolic form, the order of the precessional epochs, a clue to the characteristics of each, and a prophetic clue as to the timing of the birth and the second coming of the Christ. In this first biblical list of the twelve, the sign representation is as follows:

Scorpio--Reuben
Libra--Simeon
Virgo--Levi
Leo--Judah
Cancer--Dan
Gemini--Naphtali
Taurus--Gad
Aries--Asher
Pisces--Issachar
Aquarius--Zebulun
Capricorn--Joseph
Sagittarius--Benjamin

The death-bed blessing of Israel contains, in symbolic form, the forward zodiacal order of the Age of Taurus, clues to the characteristics of each sign, criticism of the wickedness of the ages just past, designation of Joseph as the primary symbol of the Age of Taurus, and the prophecy that Judah will ultimately receive the birthright. Judah will always be the king (Leo) and the line of descent (to the Messiah) will pass through him. The order of the signs is now as follows:

Taurus--House of Joseph (Ephraim)
Gemini--House of Joseph (Manasseh)
Cancer--Benjamin (Joseph's only full brother)
Leo--Judah
Virgo--Zebulun
Libra--Issachar

Scorpio--Dan
Sagittarius--Gad
Capricorn--Asher
Aquarius--Naphtali
Pisces--Reuben
Aries--Simeon

Although the major parable of the transition into the Age of Taurus is the story of the death-bed blessings of Israel, the transition was first indicated in the tale of the rape of Dinah. Dinah, only daughter of Jacob, was seized and raped by the chief of the region in which they lived. He was willing to marry Dinah, but her father and brothers would not hear of her marriage to an **uncircumcised** male. (Here, for the first time since the **last** transition to a feminine age, circumcision is mentioned.) So all of the men of the tribe agreed to become circumcised, thus symbolizing the return of the matriarchy and the onset of the feminine Age of Taurus.[23]

That brothers Simeon and Levi pushed the vindication of Dinah too far, by murdering and robbing her suitors, is indicative of the turmoil and tragedy that accompanies the struggle of a new order to supplant the old. This, then, led up to the punishment of Simeon and Levi for their excesses, when Israel gave his death-bed blessings.

12

The Age of Taurus

*T*oward the end of the Age of Gemini, Joseph, the favorite of Israel's sons, had a dream. He told it to his brothers: "We were all binding sheaves in the field, when my sheaf suddenly stood upright, and your sheaves formed a ring around it and bowed down to it." Since Joseph was not the firstborn, and therefore had no right to supremacy, his brothers naturally resented the implications of the dream.

Then Joseph had another dream, and again told it to his brothers, "This time the Sun and the Moon and eleven stars **all** bowed down to me." He also told the dream to his father, who said, "Can it really be that your mother and I and all of your brothers will come to bow before you?"

While Israel pondered whether or not Joseph's dream might be prophetic, the brothers plotted against Joseph. They said to each other, "Let's kill him. We can say that a wild beast devoured him."

But Reuben, the firstborn, stopped them, saying, "We must not kill him. Just throw him into a cistern." (Reuben hoped to rescue Joseph later.) So the brothers stripped Joseph of the beautiful coat that his father had given to him and threw him into a cistern.

A bit later, a caravan came by, and the brothers decided to sell Joseph to the traders for twenty pieces of silver. Now Reuben was gone at the time, so twenty *coins would represent two for each remaining brother,* **two** *being symbolic of the dual Gemini nature of each one.*

The brothers smeared Joseph's coat with blood so that Israel would think that Joseph had been killed by a wild animal.   While Israel mourned the loss of his favorite son, the traders sold Joseph to the chief steward of the Pharaoh of Egypt.[1]

Now Joseph fared well in Egypt right from the start.   Blessed by God, he was successful in all that he did.   Displaying a typically Taurean sense of responsibility and practicality, Joseph was entrusted with the household and all the possessions of his master.

When Joseph was tempted by the serpent-sensuality of the Taurus opposition sign, Scorpio, in the form of his master's seductive wife, he resisted, remaining loyal to his master's trust.   But misunderstood because of the false accusations of the seductress, Joseph was thrown into jail.   Because Joseph's behavior was in accordance with Divine Will, God remained with him, and Joseph was soon placed in charge of the entire jail.

Two servants of Pharaoh, who were also in jail, became very disturbed by dreams.   Joseph, with the help of God, correctly interpreted their dreams.   Later, when Pharaoh had a dream that none of his sages could interpret, a servant, who was now out of jail, remembered Joseph and told the Pharaoh about him.

Summoned by Pharaoh, Joseph interpreted the dream of prophecy of seven years of abundance to be followed by seven years of famine.   (Pharaoh had dreamed of seven lean cows devouring seven fatted cows.)   Joseph advised Pharaoh to collect a huge reserve of food in preparation.

Greatly impressed by Joseph, Pharaoh placed him in command of all the land and people of Egypt, and charged him to make the necessary preparations for their welfare.

The seven years of abundance passed, and were followed by the seven years of famine. In the famine, all of the world came to Joseph to obtain rations of the grain that he had caused to be held in reserve.

Among those who traveled to Egypt for rations were ten of Joseph's brothers. As they bowed before the grand vizier of Egypt, they never thought for a moment that he might be their brother, Joseph, for they thought him to be dead or, at best, a slave. But Joseph recognized them, and succumbed to the Scorpio temptation to get even. The brothers had told him that they had two more brothers, one who had been lost, and the other who was at home with their father. Joseph threatened them with death if they did not produce the brother who remained at home, in order to prove they were honest men and not spies.

The brothers talked among themselves of their anguish, saying that this was their punishment for their mistreatment of Joseph. Reuben exclaimed, "I told you so!" All this was said in front of Joseph, whom the brothers thought did not understand their language, since he had spoken to them through an interpreter. Joseph, moved by their words, turned away from them to weep, but regaining control, he held Simeon hostage, and sent the others off to fetch Benjamin at their home.

Unknown to his brothers, Joseph ordered that the money they had paid for their grain provisions be placed in the sacks with the grain. At their first night encampment, the brothers discovered the money, and they trembled with fright because they could not understand. "Why had God done this to us?" they worried.

At home, they told their father all that had happened. But Jacob refused to let Benjamin go to Egypt. Finally, the family had used up all the grain, and was starving again, and Jacob was forced to agree to the Egyptian vizier's demands. He sent his sons off to Egypt, with gifts for the vizier, and extra money, too, just in case the return of the previous payment had been a mistake.

When Joseph saw his brothers return with Benjamin, he ordered a feast prepared and invited them all to join him. Apprehensive that it was a trap, the brothers confessed to Joseph's steward that they had found the money in their bags on the last trip. The steward told them, "Surely God must have returned it, because I have received all the money that was due from you." With that the steward led Simeon out to them, brought them all into Joseph's house, and gave them water with which to wash their feet. When Joseph came in, all of them bowed before him and gave them their gifts.

The brothers were quite amazed to find themselves seated at the table exactly according to their ages, from oldest to youngest. After a merry feast, Joseph carried out his plan to teach them one final lesson. He ordered his steward to fill their bags with provisions, include the money as before, and to place also in Benjamin's bag a silver goblet from the table. After the brothers had set off on their trip home, he sent the steward to overtake and arrest them for theft. The brothers protested that none of them would do such a thing as steal the master's goblet, and if any of them was found to have it, they would all become his slaves. The steward replied, "Only the one who is found to have the goblet shall become a slave; the rest can go free." When the goblet was found in Benjamin's bag, all of the brothers returned to face Joseph. He lectured them sternly, saying, "How could you do such a thing? Why do you repay good with evil?"

Judah stepped forward to plead with Joseph that he had promised to return Benjamin to their father safely, and offered himself into slavery instead. Deeply moved, Joseph at last revealed, "I am Joseph, your brother!"

Joseph reassured his dumbfounded brothers that they should no longer reproach themselves for the wrong they did to him, for it was the will of God that he should be sent into Egypt in order that lives might be saved during the famine. God had only used the brothers to carry out the Divine Plan. After the brothers all kissed each other in joyful reunion, Joseph sent them to bring back the whole family, with the promise of Pharaoh that they would be given land and all that they needed for a good living.

The spirit of Jacob was lifted when he heard the good news, and Israel said, "My son Joseph is alive! I must see him before I die!"[2]

[All through Joseph's absence, the biblical authors refer to his father as Jacob, even though God has already renamed him Israel. Only in this passage, Genesis 45:28, does he become Israel again. Apparently the name Israel represents the triumph of the spiritual over the material, and only when Jacob operates at the highest level of faith and obedience to God is he called Israel.]

And so it was that Israel and all of his descendants migrated into Egypt and settled in the land of Goshen.

It was with the blessing given to his sons before his death that Israel symbolically completed the change from the Age of Gemini to the Age of Taurus.

Long after the death of Israel, the Pharoah and the Hebrew population continued to profit from the wisdom and the practical administrative ability of Joseph. He lived to see his son's children to the third generation. At the age of 110 he died and was buried in Egypt.

A few of my Tuesday evening class members had arrived early and were reading my version of the Joseph story.

"And so ends the Book of Genesis," I said,   "with the beginning of the Age of Taurus." I was encouraged by their interest and comments:

"You're right! It's easy to see Joseph as a Taurus. With his ability to organize and build and save, it all fits."

"Even the Pharaoh's dream brings in the specific Taurus symbolism of the cows."

"But now what?" I was asked. "Genesis is over, but you've only covered six ages in detail."

"The next book of the Bible, Exodus, takes us quickly into the Age of Aries," I said, "whose primary teacher was Moses."

"Are you planning to continue on through the Bible stories to get us up to the present?"

"Not in the same chapter-by-chapter format," I replied. "My thesis for this work is that Genesis is a story that reveals in symbolic form both the actual physical sequence of the creation of our world, **and** a divine plan for the evolution of the souls who would inhabit that world. From a study of the precessional ages of the past we can learn something about our collective origin, reflect on where we are now, and project the likely course of our future development.

"Genesis is the story of the creation and evolution in the **past.** It chronicles the ages of the past up to the Age of Aries, when the Old Testament was written. Most of the rest of the stories in the Old Testament concern the Age of Aries, except, of course, the prophecies for the future.

"A great deal of astrological symbolism is used throughout the Old Testament--much more than most people would imagine. Either they do not know how to look for it, or they are determined that it can**not** be there because they are prejudiced against it! I could not even attempt to detail it all in one book. I do want to discuss the major biblical figure of the Age of Aries, Moses; and, of course, Jesus and the New Testament with the symbolism of the present Age of Pisces. But first, I have just a few more thoughts about the Age of Taurus.

"We do know that Egypt was one of the most highly advanced civilizations in the Age of Taurus. One need to look no further than the pyramids and massive monuments to see how efficiently the Egyptians managed the material and acquisitive attributes of the sign. Taurus is a feminine sign, and the primary deity was the goddess Isis. Another major deity was the bull-god, Apis. That the Egyptians were also firmly involved with the materialistic attributes of the opposition sign, Scorpio, is evidenced by the preoccupation with death and the elaborate preparations for burial and the extensive possessions that were buried with the dead. The Scorpion death-rebirth symbolism of the phoenix-rising-from-the-ashes was prominent. Images of the Egyptian scorpion goddess, Selket, were placed in tombs to welcome the dead with open arms. An insignia of the initiate to the temple was the coiled headband with a serpent standing upright, symbolizing the spiritualization of matter.

"The cult of the bull existed in many parts of the world during the Taurean Age. Its sacredness in the civilizations of Minoa on Crete, and in India, are among the most familiar. Now that we are into a time of recorded history, many examples can be given. But since my thesis is Bible symbolism, I shall concentrate on Egypt as the setting for the Bible stories of this time.

"As is true with all ages, Taurus opened with the presentation of a spiritual example of the higher qualities of the sign, as personified by one or more legendary characters--in the biblical case, Joseph. But during the course of each age, it seems that the majority of people are lured by the material desires of their egos. They express the opposition sign at its lowest level and finally manage to corrupt the primary symbol of the age, too, so that it is expressed in qualities of its lower nature, rather than according to the God-like spiritual qualities that were exemplified by the legends of the inception of the age.

"By the end of the Age of Taurus, the Egyptian culture was decadent and declining more. Taurus and Scorpio were being expressed at their most materialistic level by the rulers and the masses. Only a few understood the true meanings of the ancient truths that were preserved in the architecture of the Great Pyramid. Most people worshiped the idols and images that represented the various qualities of God without realizing that they were only symbols of the One who had created them all."[3]

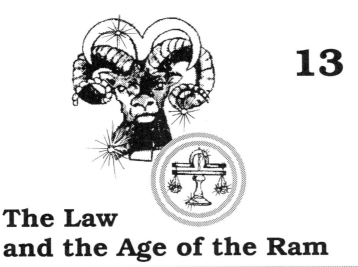

13

The Law
and the Age of the Ram

In the great civilization of Egypt, the high priests in their pyramid observatories saw that the vernal point had passed into the constellation of Aries. Accordingly, the bull-god, Apis, was replaced as the principal deity by Amon, the ram-god.[1] In other parts of the world as well, the old order passed to the new. Ram deities appeared; and the Aryans invaded India, bringing their God of Fire.[2]

In the time that we now call the 14th century B.C., the Pharaoh, Amenhotep IV, in his higher understanding, tried valiantly to force worship of the One God. Aton, symbolized by the sun-disk, represented the single, universal God, source of all life. Amenhotep IV changed his name to Akhenaton, which meant "service-to-the-Aton." After the death of Akhenaton, the majority of people fell back into the old ways, returning to polytheism and the worship of Amon and other animal deities.[3]

Little is said in the Bible of how the descendants of Israel got from the position of honor they enjoyed under Joseph to the maltreated slaves they were at the time of the birth of Moses. Exodus 1:18 mentions that a new king, who knew nothing of Joseph, came to power. This was presumably well after Joseph's death. The new Pharaoh perceived the Israelites as increasingly numerous, powerful, and therefore dangerous. Accordingly. he forced them into slavery.

Most people are familiar with the story of the Exodus, if not from the Bible itself, then through the popular movies that have been made of it. But no one has been able to pinpoint exactly when it took place. Some put it at around the 14th century B.C., while others believe it fits better in the 12th century during the reign of Ramses II. This Pharaoh's great penchant for monument building presupposes the backbreaking labor of many slaves.[4]

In the hearts of some of the greatly oppressed Israelite slaves, the memory of the God of Abraham remained alive. It was to such a slave family, to a husband and wife of the priestly tribe of Levi, that Moses was born.

From Midrash interpretations of Exodus, we learn that Pharaoh's astrologers warned him that the birth of a savior for the Israelite slaves was imminent. A son would soon be born to a Hebrew family who could be expected to grow up and lead Israel out of slavery. But Pharaoh's grand plans were dependent upon many more years of slave labor. An uprising he did not need. So Pharaoh ordered the Hebrew midwives to kill all newborn males. Of course, the midwives made up any and all excuses to avoid carrying out that order!

"The savior of Israel will be smitten by water," predicted the astrologers. So Pharaoh ordered his soldiers to seize all newborn Hebrew males and throw them into the Nile.

Now the Egyptians were very fatalistic about their astrology, but they held a philosophy of free will. The mother of Moses perceived that her newborn son was an unusual child, and she was determined to outsmart the Egyptian astrologers. She hid her child for three months until the planetary aspects would indicate that the Hebrew savior had been thrown into the river, and then she set her son afloat on the Nile in an ark made of bulrushes. The baby's sister followed the ark to see where the river would take it.

And so it was that even as Pharaoh's astrologers reassured their master that the Hebrew savior was surely drowned in the river, Moses floated safely to the palace of Pharaoh and was found and adopted by Pharaoh's daughter. The Hebrew slave child grew up in the court of Pharaoh as a Prince of Egypt.[5]

As a prince, Moses would have received the finest education possible. He would have been instructed by the High Priest and initiated into the temple. Most likely, he was strongly influenced by what he learned about the history of Akhenaton and the worship of Aton, the one universal God.

Exodus does not tell us at what age Moses found out that he was a Hebrew. It does tell us that--

After Moses grew to manhood, he visited his kinsmen and observed their forced labor. When he witnessed an Egyptian striking one of his kinsmen, he killed the Egyptian and hid him in the sand. Pharaoh found out and sought to kill Moses, but Moses fled to the land of Midian, across the desert.

During the many years that Moses spent in Midian, he married the daughter of a shepherd, had a son, and worked for his father-in-law, tending the flocks. Meanwhile, the king of Egypt died and was succeeded by another who was even more determined to hold the Israelites in cruel slavery.

One day, as Moses tended the flocks, he saw a bush that was on fire, yet was not consumed. As he moved closer to get a better look at this most remarkable sight, a voice called out to him from the bush saying, "Moses, come no nearer before you remove your sandals. This place is holy ground. I am the God of your fathers, the God of Abraham, of Isaac, and of Jacob. I have witnessed the affliction of my people in Egypt. Come, now! I will send you to Pharaoh to lead my people, the Israelites, out of Egypt!"

*When Moses asked the God in the burning bush to say his name so that he could tell the Israelites who had sent him, the voice replied, "**I Am Who Am. You shall tell them I Am sent me to you.**"*

*And so it was that in this epoch of the fire sign, Aries, the One God is introduced in a vision of fire, with the legend that is still associated with Aries to this very day: **I Am**! God had chosen the people of Israel to teach the masses that God is **One**.*

Moses returned to Egypt, and with the help of his Hebrew brother, Aaron, confronted Pharaoh with the demand to "Let my people go!"

As always, a great stuggle took place between those who try to hang on to the the old order, and the new order which must inevitably come. Moses performed a series of signs to convince Pharaoh, but at first Pharaoh's wise men were able to match the signs with their magic arts. But Moses had the inevitability of the Divine Plan in his favor; God was on his side. Soon, he sent plagues upon the Egyptians that Pharaoh's magicians could neither match nor explain. As the Egyptians were made increasingly miserable with pestilence, boils, hail and locusts, many implored the Pharaoh to let the

Israelites go, but Pharaoh remained obstinate. At first, the Israelites, too, doubted Moses; but as one plague after another hit the Egyptians but spared Israel, the Israelites were filled with hope that they would indeed be saved.

The final plague was to kill every firstborn person and animal of Egypt. God, through Moses, instructed the Israelites to slaughter lambs and to mark every door of every Hebrew family with the blood of the lambs. All homes with doors so marked would be passed over by the killing plague. The Israelites were to stay inside all of that fearful night; and while they waited for the Passover, they were to eat of the roasted lamb, of unleavened bread, and of bitter herbs. This ritual they were to observe each year thereafter, in celebration of their deliverance.

At midnight that night, all of the firstborn of Egypt died, from the firstborn of the Pharaoh to the firstborn of his prisoners in the dungeons. So Pharaoh arose in the night and summoned Moses and Aaron to him and told them to take all of the Israelites and leave Egypt immediately.

As Moses and the massive exodus of Israel pro-ceeded out of Egypt, God led the way, appearing to them as a column of fire, enveloped in smoke by day and glowing brightly by night.

After the Israelites had gone, Pharaoh regretted his decision to release them from captivity, and sent his chariots and warriors after them. Pharaoh's army caught up with Israel, camped by the Red Sea.

It was then that God instructed Moses to lift up his staff over the sea, and the sea split into two walls of water, allowing all of Israel to pass to the other side along a dry corridor of sea bed. As the chariots pursued, the sea walls crashed down upon them, hurling them into the midst of the sea.

All of Israel sang with joy, and the women danced

with tambourines in celebration of their salvation.[6]

In the third month after their departure from Egypt, the Israelites came to the desert of Sinai, and the mountain spewed forth smoke and fire, and trembled, as God spoke in sounds of thunder.[7]

Moses went up onto the mountain and there God spoke to him, giving him rules to govern the behavior of all Israel. Moses came down and related all of the ordinances of God to the people and then he erected at the foot of the mountain an altar and twelve stone pillars for the twelve tribes of Israel. Bulls were sacrificed. Half of the blood of the bulls was splashed onto the altar and the other half Moses sprinkled upon the people, saying, "The is the blood of the covenant which the Lord has made with you in accordance with his words of law."[8]

Again Moses went up onto the mountain, for God had promised to give him stone tablets inscribed with ten primary commandments for the instruction of the people. After Moses went up, a cloud covered the mountain for six days. On the seventh day, the Lord called to Moses from the midst of the cloud as, below, the Israelites saw a consuming fire appear on the mountaintop. Moses remained upon the mountain for forty days and forty nights. There he received detailed instructions for the organization of the sanctuary and for the consecration of priests.[9]

For the ordination of the priests, a bull was to be slaughtered and its blood poured out at the base of the altar. Its inner organs were to be burned on the altar, but the flesh and hide and offal were to be burned outside of the camp, since this would be a sin offering for atonement. Next a ram was to be sacrificed and its blood splashed on all sides of the altar and then the entire ram was to be burned on the altar since it is "a sweet-smelling oblation to the Lord." Another ram was then to be slaughtered so that Aaron and his sons, who were to become the priests, could be anointed with its blood. Some of the blood was to be mixed with holy oil to anoint the priestly vestments. The flesh of the ram was to be eaten by the priests.

"Throughout your age," instructed the Lord, "two lambs must be offered upon the altar each day, one in the morning and the other at twilight, as a sweet smelling oblation to the Lord."[10]

When all of the instructions to Moses were completed, the fiery finger of God inscribed the Ten Commandments upon two tablets of stone.[11]

Meanwhile, the Israelites had become impatient and fearful in their long wait for Moses to come down from the mountain. They turned back to the old ways and fashioned a calf out of molten gold. They sacrificed to the calf, crying, "This is your god, O Israel, who brought you out of Egypt."

And the fiery God, who had no name save "**I Am**" smoldered upon the mountain, threatening to consume them in a blaze of destruction. Moses implored that Israel might be spared, and God relented.

Moses came down from the mountain, bearing the stone tablets in his arms. When he saw the golden calf and heard the sounds of revelry, his wrath flared up and he threw the tablets down and broke them on the base of the mountain. He caused the calf to be fused in the fire, ground into powder, and sprinkled on the water that flowed down in a stream from Mount Sinai. This he made the Israelites drink.

"Whoever is for the Lord, let him come to me," he cried. All of the Levites rallied to Moses, and he ordered them to slay those among the Israelites who were especially sinful. Moses then offered himself as atonement for the sins of Israel, but the Lord answered, "Only him who has sinned against me will I strike out of my book. Lead the people where I have told you. When it is time for the people to be punished, I will punish them."[12]

Moses once again spent forty days and forty

nights up on the mountain, fasting as he cut two new stone tablets and inscribed upon them the Ten Commandments of the covenant. When he came down, his face was so radiant that the people were afraid to come near him until he called them to him. So he veiled his face.

The entire community assembled to build the sanctuary according to the Lord's instructions to Moses.

Moses continued his intimate relationship with God. When Moses went into the sanctuary, he would unveil his face and a column of smoke would guard the entrance while Moses talked with God. When Moses came out, the Israelites would see his radiant face, so he would again put on the veil until the next time he went in to converse with God. When the Lord was in the sanctuary, a great cloud of smoke settled over it. By night, fire could be seen in the cloud. Only when the cloud lifted could the Israelites break camp and continue on their journey.[13]

For forty long years, the Israelites wandered in the desert. Even after all of the wonders God had performed for them, still when they hungered or thirsted, they grumbled with impatience. But Moses implored God on their behalf, and food appeared as manna from heaven, and water flowed out of rocks. Still, the people rebelled whenever they felt in the least way threatened.[14]

One day, after long years of journey, the community came to Kadesh, and water was sorely needed. Once more they complained to Moses, "Why did you lead us out of Egypt to bring us to this wretched place where there is no water?" Moses and Aaron fell prostrate to appeal to the Lord, who appeared to them and said, "Take your staff, assemble the community, and order the rock to bring forth water."

Moses addressed the community, "Listen to me, you rebels! Are we to bring forth water for you out of *this rock to still your grumbling?" And Moses struck the rock twice with his staff and water gushed out in abundance.*

But the Lord was angered with Moses for his outburst of temper that suggested a lack of faith in the mercy of God toward his rebellious lot of people. Twice he had struck the rock; once would have been quite enough.

The Lord proclaimed to Moses, "Because you were not faithful to me in showing my sanctity before all Israel, you shall not cross the Jordan to lead this community into the land I will give them."

And so it was that in his old age, and in a much different way than the astrologers of Pharaoh had dreamed of so long ago, the savior of the Israelites was indeed "smitten by water." Moses continued to lead the people, revered as their greatest prophet, who knew the Lord face-to-face. But he was to die without crossing the Jordon River and without seeing the Promised Land.[15]

I had just finished reading my version of the Moses story to a good friend. I had asked for her comments on my work as one who was well-schooled in scripture but not at all in astrology.

"It hits most of the main points of that movie *The Ten Commandments* but a few things are quite different. Although you've skipped over a lot that's in the Bible, most of the things you have covered are lifted quite accurately--except for the direct references to astrology."

"Yes, those are from Rabbi Joel Dobin's book *To Rule Both Day and Night*. They are rabbinical interpretations of scripture from the Midrash. My reason for the choice of the particular stories that I took directly from the Bible was, of course, because they highlight the most obvious symbolism of the new Age of the

Ram."

"Well, I'm not up on astrology. I remember rams being mentioned here and there, but you'll have to spell it out for me."

"O.K., to start at the beginning, the first time Moses is confronted by God is in the form of a burning bush--fire--and the words '**I Am**." This obvious Aries symbolism is everywhere evident from ancient history to the present. Look at this calendar: Aries, the first fire sign; its motto, 'I Am'--though seldom is it directly associated with the story of Moses.

"The next reference is, of course, that the blood of a **lamb** is the sign of protection for the chosen people during the first Passover."

"And the lamb is still part of the Seder, and lamb is a traditional spring dish for Christians as well. But it is never mentioned as having anything to do with Aries."

"As with so many traditions that get handed down over hundreds of years, how many people give much thought to origins? Why is lamb specifically designated here in scripture as the symbol of Passover? Why not a calf, a kid goat, or a pigeon? Is it only coincidence that here, in this period of history when it is a fact that the vernal point was moving out of the constellation Bull into the Ram, the author of Exodus chose this particular symbol? Here's an aside that has nothing to do with the Moses story, but will further illustrate my point of how origins get lost and misconstrued. Why is it traditional to serve hot cross buns at Easter?"

"Why, it's because the cross represents the cross of Christ."

"Yes, that's what most people think now. But the tradition goes way back before the Christian era. In ancient Babylonia, little round buns were served at spring equinox marked with the cross of the Bull's own sign--Age of Taurus, a sign of earth--and the ancient glyph for earth, still used today, is a circle with a cross inside."[16]

"That is interesting. And I guess we can't lose sight of the fact that the times of the celebrations of Passover and Easter are set in connection with the spring equinox, rather than as actual historical anniversaries of events. We build and develop on the ancient festivals of spring as rebirth, renewal, and resurrection with the new meaningfulness of our religious faith."

"Very true! Now back to the allegorical or symbolic content of the text: We find Israel being led out of Egypt and the old ways into a whole new era, led by God in the form of a column of fire! And they are led to Mount Sinai where God's presence was symbolized by volcanic fire. At the foot of the mountain, twelve pillars are erected for the twelve tribes that symbolize the twelve constellations. **Bulls** are sacrificed, as it is the era when the constellation of the Bull is sacrificed to the rays of the sun. And Moses went up on the mountain to receive laws of the new covenant and of the new era. Note the details of the ritual for the consecration of the new priesthood. Is it only coincidence that the **bull** is to be burned outside of the camp as a sin offering; while the **ram** is to be burned upon the altar as a 'sweet-smelling' offering, and is to be eaten by the priests after its blood has been used to anoint them?"

"When you put it that way, it does seem as though it might have been deliberate literary symbolism of the change of precessional ages."

"Even the tablets of the Ten Commandments fit within zodiacal symbolism. The opposition to Aries is Libra, the constellation Balance. Libra is the Law. It seems that it is through the archetypal characteristics of the opposition symbol of each era that humanity either succeeds or fails in reaching for an understanding of the ideals of its deity."

"You'll have to explain that."

"Well, let's take Aries/Libra as an example. The Old Testament was written in the Age of Aries, and God is portrayed in its writing as essentially an Arian archetype. Aries is the 'me first' sign, and the primary ideal presented by Arian symbolism and by the Aries position in the cycle of the Divine Plan is that God is **One**--omnipotent and transcending all others. The very energy of the life force personified, our Aries deity is fiery and assertive in leading his people to pioneer new lands. He takes active initiative in a most straightforward manner, demanding that his people follow his lead without question. Unlike the old concepts of deity who, according to the Taurus archetype, were often personified as goddesses or the Divine Earth Mother from which all life came forth, the Aries deity was unquestionably a positive-masculine force, like the Ram with head and horns bent down to thrust forward. He led his people to freedom from bondage and protected them, but as each of the twelve zodiacal archetypes has the potential of evil contained within its good, so our Aries deity of the Old Testament is seen to be a jealous and vengeful God who is not in the least above wrathful, violent punishment of those who are slow to recognize his 'me first and only' position, or who disobey his laws.

"Now, the zodiac constellation opposite to Aries the Ram is Libra, the Scales of Balance. As long as anyone can remember, the scales of balance have symbolized justice and the law. Libra comes from Latin and means 'scales.' Add two more letters to it and we have library, our word for a collection of books. The Latin word for book is *libri* or *liber*. *Liber* also means 'free,' root of our word liberty. The similarities, here, imply to me that 'justice' is related to proper 'balance,' that balance is related to 'books' and the knowledge that can be gleaned from them, and that 'balance' and 'books' are related to 'freedom.'

"Now Aries loves freedom--**is** freedom--a law unto itself--me first and only! The collective ideal, the personification of God in Old Testament times is unmistakably an Aries. But if we project our deity 'out there,' then where are we? The other end of the line projected out to Aries is Libra. **So if the collective God is Aries, the collective 'not-God,' or human society on Earth, is Libra.**

"It is my theory that the collective consciousness tends to act out primarily the archetypal characteristics of the opposition symbol to the current age. It is through the virtues of that sign that we collectively create the best of our civilizations; and it is through the faults of that sign that we collectively create our failures and our downfall.

"In truth it can be said that the first law of nature is balance. Nothing is ever lost, and every cause has its effect. Neither the ideal that is projected nor we who are doing the projecting can ultimately prevail over the other. The scales must balance. When we are 'out-of-balance,' we corrupt not only ourselves, but also our ideal. And then our ideal manifests in a manner that contributes to our downfall.

"Now I have set the first age of man in the Great Year cycle as the Age of Libra. The ideal and the deity is Balance--the law and order of nature and the cosmos. Adam and Eve are Aries, possessed of individual egos and freedom of choice. Not realizing their essential unity with the Divine Order, they projected the law 'out there' and then chafed under the restrictions that they imagined this projection placed upon their freedom. The Tree of Knowledge of Good and Evil is a tree of separateness. The eating of the apple is the choice to be separate, to work against law and order rather than within it. Had they truly achieved knowledge, they would have known that they were free only insofar as they worked within the law.   It was **ignorance**, not knowledge, that caused them to fall.   'Original sin' is the concept of humanity as separate from God.

"By the Age of Aries, humanity had come halfway around the circle as Mother Nature still strives to restore the balance that was lost.   Now the archetype of our original 'fall' was projected as the ideal: **'I Am,'** the Divine Self, was all-powerful and definitely 'out there.' The deity was the Lawgiver, and all humanity must obey to win His favor.   And the world acted out the characteristics of Libra.

"Some of the most admired characteristics of Libra were acted out by the major civilizations of the period. Think of the harmony and proportion that was the art of classical Greece, not to mention the libraries of the highest classical knowledge.   Aesthetic perfection degenerated somewhat as the glory of Greece gave way to the eminence of Rome--but Rome at its best was noted for its Senate and the Law.

"Of course, few would not admire the simplicity and 'rightness' of the Ten Commandments of Moses as the prophet of the Lawgiver.   But Libra, remember, was in this time, the 'not-God,' the collective archetype of humanity.   And Libra has faults as well as virtues.   For one thing, as the age wore on, the spirit of the law became lost in form.   This is one of the problems that, at the end of the age, Jesus sought to correct as he pointed out instances where the Pharisees' compulsion for correctness and protocol and ritual in the form of various laws became a betrayal of the greater Law of Love.

"Aries is said to be 'ruled' by Mars, the god of war. But really, Aries is the individual--the hero--who fights for his right to reign supreme.   It is Libra that is the symbol of the militant collective.   Collective fighting is war.   And so the collective need to adhere to a set con-vention--a code of law--became corrupted into a justification of imposing the particular code of one's group onto all others. The Age of Aries became a period in history that was marked by constant brutal wars of conquest. The God of Aries was corrupted into an angry and vengeful figure, and his people obeyed the law often not with any sense of love, or even of reason, but only because they feared violent retribution."

"So it seems that humanity failed quite miserably in understanding its projected ideal," said my friend.

"For the most part you could say that. Yet civilization always continues its upward spiral, too. Most would believe it a gain that monotheism was firmly established, even if it is still not really understood. Civilization owes much to the principles of law and order that grew out of this age. Even the wars of conquest contributed to such things as the standardization of systems of measurement that greatly aided progress."

"O.K., that was quite an explanation, and plenty of food for thought. But let's return to the Moses story. I'm interested in the rest of the symbols. I suppose the golden calf, then, must be a throwback to the old order of Taurus."

"Right. A calf is a little bull, as if most of the 'steam' is out of the Taurean archetype now. But still, in their fear of the unknown and the new, the people revert back to the old ways and the old God. Moses caused the golden calf to be fused in the fire, ground up, and sprinkled into the water (spirit) that flowed down from the God on Mount Sinai, and the water was drunk by the people. The old god was assimilated into the new. All gods are One, and according to the Hebrews, no idol is necessary or desired to confuse that issue."

"I see where the symbolism of fire is mentioned again," she commented. "so we need not detail the rest. It's quite evident that if the story is followed for symbolism rather than just as a chronology of historical events, it takes on all kinds of meaning. Whether or not these stories of the forty years of wandering are literally true or not, they certainly seem to symbolize a personal stuggle for faith and trust in God. Now that you have explained what Aries means, I am amused that whenever Moses is admonished by God, it seems to be when he has acted with a typically Arian fault."

"Yes! And when he is intimately attuned with God, his face is radiant!"

"Forty seems to be a frequently used number to symbolize a time of trial. Is there a special meaning for that?"

"Forty is an augmented four, and four is the number of earth, the cross of matter. In our life on Earth, we are all bound by the limitations of time and space. Four represents the suffering that comes with that limitation. There are many examples of forty used to represent a period of suffering, penance and testing as a preparation for reward--like the novice must prove worthiness to become an initiate, or one must do penance before being redeemed. Think of the forty days of rain in Noah's story, the forty days of Jesus' temptation in the desert, and the forty days of Lent before Easter. I'll be covering the symbolism of numbers more completely in a later chapter."

"All of this has been quite interesting. I still have questions, and I'm not sure I agree with some of your interpretations. It's certainly far from a fundamentalist point of view. But I do think I'll go home and reread Genesis and Exodus in my own Bible, with these ideas of yours in mind."

"Good! That's one of the main things I hope this book will motivate people to do."

14

The Virgin, the Son and the Age of the Fishes

*I*t was near the end of the Age of Aries. The great Roman Empire, once enlightened in its concepts of law and justice, had become decadent. Debauchery reigned in the court of Caesar. Who even bothered to think of, much less care about, the greatly oppressed people of the conquered provinces?

Among the conquered and oppressed were the Lord's chosen people in Israel. Once triumphant in their exodus from Egypt, they had sealed a sacred covenant with God at Mount Sinai, agreeing to obey the Ten Commandments, and to receive the Promised Land.

But as the years went by, fewer and fewer of the chosen people understood the simple clarity of God's ten laws. In order to suit the convenience of their weaknesses and their selfish desires for power, the leaders altered and perverted and rationalized the ten laws into a thousand variations. Unwilling to accept responsibility for the problems that they brought upon themselves, they blamed God, saying that their Lord was wrathful and unforgiving, and punished every sinful soul.

Now defeated, oppressed, and in shame, the people longed for the fulfillment of the ancient prophecies that promised a redeemer--a Messiah--to deliver them from evil.

It was in this troubled time that god sent the angel Gabriel to visit a young woman of Israel named Mary, who lived in the little town of Nazareth. Mary was engaged to be married to Joseph. He was of the House of David, the lineage that had been prophesied for the Messiah.

"Hail, Mary," Gabriel greeted the young woman, as she sat alone in her room. "The Lord is with you. Blessed are you among women."

Mary was frightened by this strange visitor, but his presence radiated a kindly love, and she was calm as he went on to say, "Do not fear, Mary. God loves you and has chosen you for a special favor. You are to bear a son and give him the name of Jesus. He is to inherit the throne of David and will rule over the house of Israel forever. His reign will be without end."

Greatly troubled by these words, Mary asked the angel, "How can this be possible, since I am a virgin?"

And Gabriel answered, "The Holy Spirit shall be within you and the power of the Most High will over-shadow you. The holy child to be born will be called the Son of God."

Observing Mary's still questioning expression, the angel went on. "Elizabeth, your kinswoman, has also conceived a son, even though she is past the age of childbearing and has always been sterile. Nothing is impossible with God!"

So Mary accepted the will of God for her destiny, and said, "Behold the handmaiden of the Lord. Let it be done unto me according to your words."

With great haste, Mary decided to visit her cousin, Elizabeth, for she needed to speak with someone about her vision; and who else but Elizabeth, who shared in the angel's prophecy. She set out on the long journey.

Running up the path to Elizabeth's house, Mary called out, "Elizabeth!"

As soon as she heard Mary's greeting, Elizabeth

called out with great joy, "Blessed are you among women, and blessed is the fruit of your womb. But who am I that the mother of my Lord should come to me? The very moment that I heard your voice, the baby in my own womb leapt for joy. Blessed is she who believed that the words of the Lord will be fulfilled!"

Mary's heart sang with happiness, "My soul does magnify the Lord, and my spirit has rejoiced in God, my savior, for he has looked with favor on his handmaiden in her lowliness. All ages to come shall call me blessed. God who is mighty has done great things for me; holy is his name!"

Mary remained with Elizabeth for about three months, to assist until the delivery of her son, who was named John. He was destined to be called the baptizer, the prophet of the Messiah, who would be born of Mary.

When Mary returned home, she told her betrothed, Joseph, of the visitation of the angel, and of her pregnancy. Joseph was deeply disturbed. He loved Mary, but her story seemed so impossible. Could he trust her that much? Could he accept a child that was not his? He wanted to break the engagement, yet if he did so, she would be stoned. The Law dealt very harshly in such matters. What could he do? He fell into a troubled sleep. As he slept, he dreamed. And an angel appeared in his dream and said to him, "Joseph, son of David, do not fear to take Mary as your wife. The child she is to bear is conceived through the Holy Spirit. The babe will be a son and you are to call him Jesus. He will save his people from sin. Remember the words of the prophet, Isaiah: 'The virgin shall be with child and give birth to a son, and they shall call him Emmanuel, a name which means God is with us.' "

When Joseph awoke, he did as his dream had directed him to do. He took Mary as his wife, and protected her, respecting her virginity.

Now, in the time of Mary's pregnancy, a decree

went out from Caesar Augustus, ordering a census of his entire empire. All were obliged to register in their own town. Since Joseph was of the House of David, he had to return to Bethlehem. It was an arduous journey to expect of a woman who was by now heavy with child. But Joseph and Mary had been told of the special destiny of her baby, and they knew that the ancient prophecies also decreed that Mary must accompany Joseph to Bethlehem, for it was there that the Messiah must be born. So they set off on the long walk together, Mary often riding upon the small donkey that carried their provisions.

Just as they arrived in Bethlehem, Mary's labor began. No proper lodging could be found. There was not even time to locate the kinsmen of Joseph. Seeing Mary's condition, an innkeeper offered to let them stay in the warm cave where his animals were kept. And so it was that Mary gave birth to her firstborn son, and laid him in a manger, because there was no room for them in the inn.

In a nearby field, shepherds were keeping night watch over their flocks. Suddenly the night sky exploded into brilliant lights and the shepherds all experienced the same vision of angels singing joyfully. The shepherds shook with fear, but an angel said to them, "You have nothing to fear! I bring you good news to be shared with all the people. On this day, in David's city a savior has been born to you--the Messiah! Let this be a sign for you; in a manger you will find the baby, wrapped in swaddling clothes." And a multitude of angels sang, "Glory to God in heaven and peace to his people on Earth."

The shepherds went in haste to Bethlehem and found Joseph, Mary and the baby, still lying in the manger. They saw and they believed, and later they spread the good news to whomever of their friends would listen.

*E*ight days later, Mary and Joseph brought their firstborn son to the temple in Jerusalem to be circumcised and consecrated to the Lord according to the laws of Moses. They gave the child the name that had been told to Mary by the angel--Jesus.

At that time, an old and pious man named Simeon lived in Jerusalem. Through his sense of the Holy Spirit, Simeon knew that he would not experience death until he had seen the one who was to be the long-awaited Messiah. Inspired by the Spirit, Simeon came to the temple in time to see Mary and Joseph and Jesus there. Taking Jesus in his arms, Simeon said:

> "Now, Lord, you have fulfilled your word;
> and your servant may depart in peace,
> For my eyes have witnessed your redeemer;
> A light for the Gentiles,
> and the glory of your people, Israel."

The child's mother and father marveled at those words. Simeon blessed them and then said to Mary:

> "This child is destined to be the fall
> and the rise of many in Israel.
> His sign will be opposed.
> Yes, and a sword shall pierce even
> your own heart--that the thoughts of many
> hearts may be revealed."

Also at prayer in the temple was a prophetess named Anna, in the fullness of her eighty-four years. She, too, recognized Jesus as the promised Messiah. Giving thanks to God, she talked to all who would listen about the deliverance of Jerusalem.

*M*eanwhile, to the east, in the land of the Chaldeans, three learned men consulted with each other in great excitement.

"See here!" said one. "I know it is now!"

"Yes," replied another. "For months, now, Jupiter

and Saturn have conjoined in Pisces, the sign of the new age. Now Mercury and Venus are also conjoined. The vernal equinox nears and the constellation of the Ram is lost in the sunrise. The Fishes now rise before the sun. The new age is at hand."

"And Mars," said the third, "now opposes from the constellation of the Virgin, as the signature of his mortal birth."

"And on this very night," exclaimed the first, "Luna is also with the Fishes. The great king of the Hebrews that Gjamasp predicted is born. I am sure of it!"

"Yes! Three hundred years ago, he predicted that a new king of the Hebrews would be born when the Great Mutation occurred in the sign of Pisces. This new king could be the avatar of the Age of Pisces."

"The avatar will no doubt be born of a royal line. And we know the time of his birth! Do you suppose we could actually find him?"

"Let us go to the capital city, Jerusalem, and share firsthand in this most important event."

After a period of preparation, and careful notation from their star charts, the three astrologers set out by camel for the long journey to Jerusalem. Each night after the sun set, as they approached Judea, they could see the Great Conjunction rise in the sky, twinkling before them like stars, assuring them of their path.[1]

Upon their arrival in Jerusalem, the astrologers inquired in the court of King Herod about the child. King Herod was visibly agitated at their inquiries. He summoned his priest and scribes to ask where the Messiah was to be born. "In Bethlehem," they informed him, "for the prophet Micah has written, 'But you Bethlehem . . . from you shall come forth for me one who is to be ruler in Israel.' "

Herod called the astrologers aside and questioned them as to the exact time of the nativity. Then he instructed them, "Go on into Bethlehem and find the child. When you have done so, report to me so that I, too, can go and pay homage to him."

By now it was nearly a year since the birth of the child. As they camped that evening on the way to Bethlehem, the astrologers again consulted the sky. Mars was now rapidly approaching conjunction with Saturn, a sign of impending danger. "No wonder Herod seemed so disturbed," they said to each other. "He is threatened by the child we seek. We must hurry."

Immediately they broke camp and drove their camels hard across the last few miles to Bethlehem, all the while keeping in sight the guiding lights in the sky above them. The next day, in the tiny town of Bethlehem, they had no trouble locating the house of the family that had a son with the birth date they were seeking. Kneeling before Mary and her child, in this winter of the year that would later be called 6 B.C., they presented the gifts of gold, frankincense and myrrh, that in later times would be called the very first Christmas gifts.

To Joseph they gave the warning that the child might be in danger. And then they left for their own country by a route that would take them safely out of the reach of Herod.

In a dream that very night, an angel appeared to Joseph. "Get up right now," the angel said. "Flee with the child and his mother into Egypt, and stay there until you receive a further sign. Herod is searching for the child to destroy him."

So Joseph awoke, and in the concealing darkness, made haste with his family in the direction of Egypt. In this way, the prophecy of Hosea was fulfilled: "Out of Egypt I have called my son."

When Herod found out that the astrologers had deceived him and escaped, he furiously ordered the massacre of all male infants, two years and under, in the town and the area of Bethlehem. Since the calcula-

*tions of the astrologers would have the child about one
year old now, Herod thought in this way he could be
sure to eliminate this upstart ruler.*

*Two years later, Herod died, and the angel again
appeared in Joseph's dream and told him that it was
safe for the family to return to Israel. So the family
moved back to Mary's home town of Nazareth. And the
child grew in size and strength, filled with wisdom, and
the grace of God was upon him.[2]*

I had asked my class to discuss the story of the
transition into the present Age of Pisces.

"It's the old familiar story for sure; as faithfully
told as the script for a Christmas pageant--" began one.

"Except," interrupted another, "for the consider-
ably beefed-up role you gave to the three astrologers!
We'll forgive you for that, of course, though I know of
some who wouldn't."

"Yes," said a third. "So anxious are some to disas-
sociate religion with any connection to astrology that
they make the astrologers into kings, or call them wise
men and insist that the term 'wise men' does not necessarily mean astrologers. Anyone who made any honest
attempt to look at the history of the period would know
that a man who was ignorant of astrology would never
be called 'wise.' "

"It's difficult to understand," I said, "how anyone
could interpret the Nativity according to St. Matthew
and disclaim the involvement of astrology. The Star of
Bethlehem had to be a sign that could be interpreted
and followed only by those who were trained to read the
messages in the sky. If the 'star' were a great, big, obvious out-of-the-ordinary phenomenon that moved across
the sky and then hung right over the stable, why, the
whole population would have turned out to gawk and
question. And **that** most definitely does not fit in with
Matthew's theme!"

"What do you mean by Matthew's 'theme'?" I was asked.

I replied with a question: "How many of you have read and compared all four gospels?"

"I have," said one, "and they really don't agree with each other on many points. Take the nativity, for example. Mark and John don't mention it at all. Matthew tells about the astrologers, Herod's massacre, and the flight to Egypt; but doesn't mention a thing about shepherds or a manger or a presentation in the temple. In fact, Matthew has the astrologers visit the Holy Family in a house. Luke, on the other hand, tells us of the angel's appearance to the shepherds, and of the manger, and of the circumcision; but doesn't say a word about astrologers or a threat from Herod that caused a flight to Egypt. The two versions are very different from each other. The typical Christmas pageant, like your story, combines both gospels.

"I didn't realize that," said another. "I guess I've heard most of my Bible stories from the movies rather than from reading the original source. It seems so strange that the versions should be so different. What is the true history?"

"No one really knows," I answered. "The earliest gospel was not written until at least 70 years after the time that Jesus is thought to have died. It is highly unlikely that any actual eyewitness of the events of the life of Jesus had anything to do with the authorship of the four gospels. In fact, if we had to go by the history that was recorded during the time that Jesus was supposed to have lived, we would be hard put to prove that he ever existed at all. It is truly amazing--and also pretty credible evidence of his uniqueness--that this one man should so impact world history; when during the time of his actual life and death he was apparently considered by the authorities and scholars to be only the vanquished leader of a minor insurrection, too insignificant to write about."

"So what do we have, then, in the gospels?"

"We have some stories handed down by word of mouth that may or may not be actual history. Probably most of them are at least **based** on actual events. The **essence** of the teachings of Jesus comes through in agreement in the four gospels--although the historical content differs, and in some cases even seems to be contradictory."

"Well," commented one, "when I read the newspapers and see how differently even some current events can sound depending upon who's telling them, it's little wonder that the events of the life of Jesus could get remembered in different ways after 70 years or more had gone by."

"It's not so simple as faulty memory, or even just a matter of editorializing," I explained. "I believe that all of the gospels are true--just as I believe that Genesis is true. But I think that none of them were ever intended to be history textbooks. Some events of history are no doubt included, but the intent is to **teach,** and a large amount of symbolism--and literary license, if you will--is used according to particular points that the author wanted to make. Or, in some cases, there were points that the author wished to conceal from superficial reading. Take our two stories of the nativity for example. Matthew wanted to make the point that the Messiah was for **all** people, not just Hebrews. There's no mention of a humble background for Jesus here. If this were the **only** gospel account, we might even assume the family of Jesus to be aristocrats. They have taken a house in Bethlehem, are gifted with great riches, and are able to flee to Egypt when they are threatened by Herod. Their son is called a king, and Herod takes that possibility seriously, which implies that the family of Jesus might have a legitimate claim to a royal line of descent. But none of Joseph's or Mary's people are said even to be aware of the birth. Only strangers--astrologers, presumably Gentile--who have come from a great distance recognize Jesus as the Messiah. Even Herod, the only Jew mentioned in this nativity version, does not become aware that the birth is imminent until he is tipped off by the astrologers' queries. If you read the rest of Matthew, with the theme of 'Messiah of **all** people' in mind, you'll see that the theme is repeated in many other ways.

"Now on the other hand, Luke's theme is 'Messiah of the poor.' He goes to great lengths to emphasize the humility of Jesus and his family and of those who recognize that the Messiah has come. None of the rich and powerful are said to even be aware of the birth. Only the lowly shepherds receive the vision that leads them to the humble manger to find the baby. This theme, too, is often repeated throughout the Gospel of Luke."

"Now I understand what you mean by 'theme.' "

"It's a real mistake to try to reduce the Bible to a history textbook and then quibble over the historical accuracy of its stories. That just misses the main point. We must not forget that 'gospel' means 'good news.' When the early church fathers began to realize that Christ just might not come again any day soon, as they expected, they decided that they needed a written, permanent version of the teachings of their religion. The main all-over theme of the gospels was the **good news** that Christ had risen. This was the main point to be made. Then there are secondary points taught through such devices as the themes of Matthew and Luke that I've already identified. Jesus himself taught mostly in parables--stories that intrigued the listener and contained a truth. The lesson was often implied rather than directly stated. Those who were ready to receive the teaching understood. Sometimes different people understood the teachings on different levels; and some heard, but failed to understand anything beyond the superficial, interesting little tale that was being told. To be sure, the Bible contains history, but much of it is more allegory or parable than literal, factual history. That doesn't make it one bit less valid--in fact it implies more depth than we can ever completely discover.[3]

"An important thing to keep in mind in attempting to understand scripture, or any ancient writings for that matter, is that it has been a prevailing attitude of those who considered themselves to be among the most enlightened and educated throughout all the ages to assume that the masses would not be able to understand the 'higher mysteries'! It has been assumed that higher knowledge in the hands of people who were not prepared spiritually and intellectually to comprehend its proper use in the service of God might be misused in a way that could be dangerously harmful. Such knowledge could only be entrusted to one who had been 'initiated.' The early church leaders and the authors of the gospels were not at all immune from this attitude. I have wondered sometimes, in reading the gospels, if this is the attitude that still prevails among those authorities who now 'interpret' scripture; or is it just that some of the knowledge that was symbolically and hermetically contained within certain stories has been so completely lost and forgotten that even top-notch biblical scholars don't understand it anymore. I've come across some passages that are obviously loaded with symbols that are either ignored in the footnotes or are interpreted only superficially. Now do the translators and interpreters know what they mean, or don't they?"

"Give us an example of one."

"In John 11 is the story of the raising of Lazarus. After Jesus has received word that Lazarus is sick, still he delays going to him for two more days. Finally he tells his disciples that they are going to see Lazarus. The disciples protest that there is danger in that area of

Judea from Jews who recently tried to stone him. Jesus answers in verses 9 and 10.

> *Are there not twelve hours of daylight?*
> *If a man goes walking by day he does not stumble*
>   *because he sees the world bathed in light.*
> *But if he goes walking at night he will stumble*
>   *since there is no light in him.*[4]

The only footnote for this passage explains 'no light in him' in these words: 'the ancient Palestinians apparently did not grasp clearly the entry of light **through** the eye, but seem to have thought of it as being **in** the eye.'[5] Now, does that make clear why Jesus would reply as he did to the threat of stoning if he returned to Judea?"

"No, it doesn't even make sense. What do you think it means?"

"It seems that it should have been obvious that the word 'light' as it is used here, does not mean literal daylight or literally being able to see, but rather refers to spiritual light. Not so obvious is the use of 'twelve,' a number that I think relates, at least indirectly, to zodiac symbolism throughout many books of the Bible. I would interpret the passage, then, as follows:

> Are there not twelve expressions of spiritual light?
> If a man walks a spiritual path, he will not be
>   harmed--his whole world is bathed in light
>   and he is protected by God.
> But if he walks the path of darkness (expressing
>   the twelve in a materialistic manner that
>   denies the light), then he will bring harm
>   upon himself because there is no spiritual
>   light in him.

In this manner, Jesus is saying that since he walks in the light of the spirit, he has no need to fear any harm."

In the discussion that followed, the consensus of opinion was that it is more likely that the translator of that passage missed the deeper meaning than that he deliberately avoided it.

"The use of symbolism in the gospels certainly suggests that at least some early Christian writers and quite possibly Jesus, himself, were knowledgeable in astrology and in the ancient mystery religions. Yet contemporary church authorities ignore this quite completely in their explanations--or often lack of explanation--of the obviously symbolic passages. Why is this so? A brief historical sketch of the western culture where Christianity found its center will help explain.[6]

"Nothing makes a group more united than outside persecution, so we can rightly assume a great spiritual closeness among the early Christians who hid in the catacombs and identified each other with the secret sign of the fish. They believed that Christ's promised Second Coming, and their own enraptured deliverance from this Earth, was due at any moment, and that was all that really mattered to them.

"But as the dangers of Roman persecution decreased, the disagreements among the faithful increased, and accusations of heresy abounded. Various factions wrangled over differing ideas of doctrine, each small community [church] supporting its opinion with this or that passage from the letters of St. Paul, and each labeling any dissenting person or church 'heretical.' The corrupted Aries attitudes of Old Testament time were far from overcome, despite the teachings of Jesus to the contrary. The symbol of the old age had become the 'rising sign,' the Cardinal Ascendant, of the new age. Jesus' teachings would be spread by men acting in the manner of Aries. Initiative in the new age was motivated by habit patterns carried over from old Arian concepts. Old patterns of thinking, like old ages, die very slowly. Heretics and unbelievers were to be stamped out, violently if necessary.

"The Second Coming didn't come and the original

apostles died out. New generations began to realize that Christians might have to live in the world for a long time, so some kind of authority to settle all the wrangling was obviously necessary. The theory was accepted that the apostles had appointed bishops to succeed them, and that only those in direct line of succession from the apostles could ordain new priests. As the bishops began to meet to regulate the affairs of the church, the wrangling over doctrine proceeded with greater order. One of the methods through which they sought to unite the many rather independent and loosely related churches was to begin to collect and select a group of definite Christian writings to form a New Testament. Soon, sometime in the 2nd century, the term 'Catholic' came into general use. The word means 'universal,' meaning 'all,' but in the actual fact of the matter, a better definition would be 'exclusive' or 'orthodox.' The strongest faction within the churches grew up in the capital city of Rome, and the Bishop of Rome was proclaimed to be the direct successor of St. Peter and therefore the head of the church.

"With the recognition of Christianity by the Emperor Constantine in 313, persecution ceased, and the bishops found themselves to be quite powerful. Now disputes with the prevailing hierarchy could be put down with the help of the state.

"One doctrinal dispute, for example, at the Church Council at Nicaea in 325, centered around a priest named Arius, whose name bears an amusing similarity to the zodiac sign of Aries. I was amused by the name and by the dispute--which was called, no kidding, the Arian controversy--because the ideas of Arius hark back to the absolute monotheism that characterized the ideal of the old Arian Age. Arius argued that since the father (God) must have existed before the son (Christ), the son could not be eternal and the father's equal. The majority of the bishops thought that this could not be so because if Christ was not fully God, the salvation of the believers in him was not assured. Arius was declared a heretic and Emperor Constantine obligingly had him exiled. The Nicene Creed--for this new religion of the Age of Pisces--was adopted, stating that Christ is of 'one substance with the Father.' In another amusing bit of synchronicity, 'Nicene' rhymes:

> The Arian Age went out
> Though Arius had some doubt
> That the Creed Nicene
> Of the New Age Piscine
> Said the truth of what God was about."

"Shame on you! That's a terrible poem."

"Yes, I agree, but I couldn't resist it.

"At the risk of oversimplification of a complicated subject, much of the controversy with which the early church hierarchy dealt was with a variety of sects that could be loosely grouped under the term 'Gnostic.'

"Gnosticism, derived from the Greek *gnosis*, to know, was a broad synthesis of ideas that included the ancient mystery religions and astrology, along with elements of Judaism, Greek philosophy, and old Iranian, Syrian and Egyptian religions. In general, the Gnostics held that salvation is accomplished not by the power of God nor by human faith alone, but by spiritual growth through esoteric knowledge. The Christ-redeemer had a central place but it was to communicate or reveal to men the saving knowledge, rather than to actually *be* their salvation.[7]

"Gnostic ideas and symbolism undoubtedly influenced some of the books that wound up in the New Testament, but Gnostic thinking was increasingly suppressed as the church institution took hold. The official doctrine that prevailed was that Christ's sacrifice on the cross completely redeemed humanity and that salvation is a gift from God through faith in Christ that is conferred on the recipient regardless of any merit.

"Both astrology as related to Gnostic philosophies, and astrology as the forerunner of the science of astronomy were plunged into the Dark Ages, along with practically every other brand of rational inquiry, by about the 5th century. The attitude of the early church hierarchy seemed to be that knowledge (gnosis) as the path toward truth (God) was unnecessary, if not outright evil; and that faith alone could bring salvation--and that is all that mattered. The proper attention of humanity should be on ascetic preparation for a reward in the hereafter. After all, they thought, why should one waste time on such material matters as science, when Christ was due to return at any moment and whisk the faithful off to Heaven and heap great tribulations on everyone else?

"But then, one wonders if perhaps at least a few influential members of the hierarchy were not immune to the attitude that an emphasis on faith alone, and a suppression of free inquiry, gave them much better control over the masses. The spectacular book-burning of the great Library of Alexandria in the 5th century so thoroughly contributed to such suppression that by 1633 the Christian world was still ignorant of the knowledge about the cosmos that had been known to the classical Greeks. Galileo was condemned before the Catholic Inquisition for the 'heresy' of insisting that Earth was not the center of the universe, but instead was only one of a group of planets orbiting the Sun. One of the books known to have been burned at Alexandria contained just that very concept for which Galileo was persecuted. It was written by Aristarchus at least 200 years before the birth of Christ.[8]

"In order to understand the decline of astrology along with other systems of knowledge in the early centuries of the Age of Pisces, largely due to suppression by the church, it is important to consider two points:

1. A wide gulf exists in the understanding of any system of knowledge between those who have been carefully educated in the system, and further, have acquired the insight that transmutes their knowledge into wisdom; and those whose knowledge and understanding are limited to the level of popular practice.

2. Although higher knowledge, or wisdom, was considered by the ancients to come as a direct revelation from God, those who believed themselves to possess such knowledge tended to keep it secret and pass it on to new 'initiates' only after a careful period of preparation.

"This idea of 'initiation' was not limited to the so-called mystery religions. Christianity, too, was secretive in the early years. Sure, the vision was to spread the good news to everyone, but the reality was that everyone might include someone who pretended to be a faithful new convert, but would blab and get you thrown to the lions. New converts were brought in cautiously and carefully schooled in the Christian mysteries before being initiated, confirmed, and allowed to join the community at the Eucharistic table.

"When Christianity became the official religion of the Roman Empire, great masses of people were instant converts. Careful preparation was no longer necessary for protection, and the numbers were overwhelming. The new Christians brought with them a background of worship of a wide variety of gods and goddesses, of rituals and of superstitions. The leaders of the young Christian church had a job on their hands of mammoth proportions.

"Here, let us pause to define superstition. Superstition is 'a belief that is not based on reason or knowledge, in or of the ominous significance of a particular thing.' It can be further defined as 'the irrational fear of what is unknown or mysterious, especially in connection with religion' and 'any blindly accepted belief or notion.'9

"Now surely a great many new converts to Christianity received a genuine gift of faith, and also assimilated some accurate knowledge to support their faith. But honesty must necessitate the admission that a great many others merely traded an old set of superstitions for a new set of superstitions.

"They may have given up burning incense before the statue of their favorite goddess and the like; but their new religion often went no deeper than a new set of practices that were performed in the hope of good fortune or of avoiding misfortune. One might believe, for example, that sprinkling holy water on one's bed at night would ward off evil spirits--or even more irrationally, that bad fortune would befall on Friday the13th because Christ was crucified on Friday and there were 13 present at the Last Supper at which he was betrayed.[10]

"Now astrological knowledge has always covered a very wide range of understanding, too. At the highest levels it has probably been thousands of years since the stars and planets and the Sun and Moon were thought to **be** gods rather than creations of the one God. Astrologers in the centuries of transition between the ages of Aries and Pisces chiefly concerned themselves with improving their ability to measure and predict the positions of the signs in the sky so that they could better interpret those signs in terms of practical matters of human life. Great thinkers wove astrology into their metaphysical philosophies.

"But even at the lowest popular level, many still persisted in thinking of the planets as gods and goddesses to be feared and placated. Even if they no longer believed that the planets were deities, still their understanding of astrology was at the level of superstition--of omens and portents. Because astrologers were often able to predict events, popular understanding tended toward fatalism.

"It is probably safe to assume that any higher astrological knowledge among early Christian leaders was possessed by those who could be included under the term 'Gnostic.' And as has already been said, the Gnostic faction lost out in the struggle for control of the church hierarchy. So the higher metaphysical interpretation of astrology was suppressed with Gnosticism, and even the attempts to measure and map the cosmos for purely practical purposes were suppressed with the general disapproval of the church toward all of the sciences.

"With 'high' astrology forced into obscurity, what persisted? Why, popular astrology, of course. The superstitious level of astrology got blended right in with the superstitious level of Christianity, and the church authorities had to contend with rooting out the 'old' superstitions and finding acceptable Christian substitutes with which to placate the people. Christian feast days, for example, were deliberately set for dates that were on or very near the ancient popular festivals that originated with astrology. In the 4th century, Jesus' birthday was set for December 25 for winter solstice, which was considered by the ancients to be the birth of the Sun. The church called Christ the 'sun of justice' (Malachi 3:20), and 'light of the world,' in a symbolic sense, but his day of worship was still called **Sun**day.[11]

"In Old Testament times, the rabbis had been trained in astrology but also in the idea of free will and of 'Divine Election.' The chosen people of Israel, when exercising their free will to be obedient to God's laws, were above planetary influence. Frequently, the rabbis found it necessary to speak out against the low-level superstitious and fatalistic understanding of astrology that persisted within the uneducated masses of people. But on a higher level, they accepted and practiced astrology themselves. This is why astrological symbolism is so prevalent in Old Testament writing.   The carry-over from this rabbinical knowledge helps account for the astrological symbolism in some of the early Christian writings.[12]

"Now the priests of this new Christian religion contended with the same old reality that had plagued the rabbis.   The largely illiterate masses tended to reduce religion and philosophy to the level of superstition.   These priests, however, were no longer schooled in astrology, and so they ceased to understand it other than as a superstitious practice of the masses that had to be discouraged.

"Astrology had always been a spiritual science.   In truth, it could be called a mother of both religion and science.   In the most ancient of times, humans looked up to the skies and observed the patterns and repeated cycles of the bright lights that they saw.   As the beginnings of science, they recorded and marked out the cycles, and learned from this work that they could improve their lives by predicting the best planting and hunting seasons.   Since their very lives seemed so dependent upon what went on in the sky, especially the activity of the fiery sun, and the comings and goings of the elusive moon, it was only natural that they should deify them, and link their attempts to predict the cycles to the idea of understanding the whims and wills of the gods and goddesses.   In the ancient roots of every religion, astrology can be found.

"In ancient ages and even onto the beginning of this present age, science and religion were not separate. Learned people were not super-specialists as they tend to be today. The priest was the philosopher and the scientist.   Long after the philosophers-scientists-priests figured out that the stars and planets were only matter, creations of a Creator, the highest purpose of astrology was **still** to search for a meaningful relationship between humanity and the cosmos, and to argue for the cause of that cosmic order--God!

"But now, in the Dark Ages of the Age of Pisces, astrology faded into obscurity mainly because it was a **science**--a system of knowledge; and as such was deemed unnecessary to the total emphasis on **faith** that was the ideal of the new order.

"And so it was that, for probably the first time in all of history, astrology became separated from religion. The most scientifically minded continued their observations and calculations, but no longer linked what they were doing to religion. If their knowledge of 'high' astrology was philosophically oriented, they kept it to themselves or communicated it only to other 'initiates.'

"The urge of the mind and spirit **to know,** however, is far from easily squelched. Over the centuries, astrology gradually crept back into favor and by the time of the Renaissance, every court had its official astrologer, including the papal court. [13] Theologians, such as St. Thomas Aquinas, had accepted astrology with the qualification that it had always been a tenet of higher astrological wisdom: While men under the influence of their passions may stand under the influence of the heavenly bodies, man as incarnate spirit is above these determinations and is free. 'The wise man rules his stars.'[14]

"Some 16th century popes to favor astrology were Julius III, who used it to set his coronation date; Paul III, who used it to determine the proper hour for every consistory; and Leo X, who founded a chair of astrology at Sapienze. In this time, all respectable universities included astrology.[15]

"The Renaissance period was a golden age for astrology in western culture. At this time, astronomers were still practicing astrologers; and giants in the field, such as Tycho Brahe and Johannes Kepler made huge advances in the science that vastly improved chart calculations. Kepler is considered to be the father of modern astronomy.

"The invention of the printing press helped to popularize astrology among the people as many astrological almanacs were circulated. Unfortunately, however, when astrology sifted down to the lower level of the masses, it tended, as always, to be misunderstood in a superstitious manner, and to be accompanied by even more misunderstood low-level dabblings in magic and the occult. Because of this, there were condemnations by Popes Sixtus V and Urban VIII, concerned mainly with the suppression of 'pop' astrology combined with the occult.

"The power of the church was definitely waning in this period. When one pole of opposition is overemphasized, and the other pole is severely suppressed, the stage is set for a violent eruption. A pendulum can swing only so far in one direction and then it must swing back.

"The problems of this Age of Pisces can be illustrated in astrological symbolism, with the poles of the cross of matter that is also the major Christian symbol. At the top of our cross is our visionary ideal of Pisces--a compassionate, loving, forgiving concept of God that encompasses all people everywhere with love and faith in life eternal. At the opposite end of that pole, at the bottom, we are anchored in the down-to-earth reality of Virgo. We are at the moment still very much mortal, bound to material affairs, and must be concerned with what is useful, practical, and realistically within our grasp. It is from our reality of Virgo that we must reach out for our ideal vision in Pisces.

"Just as Jesus on the cross had two insurgents, one to the left and one to the right, we humans, symbolically impaled on our cross of matter, have two symbols in square--conflict--with our central pole. With these we must contend as well, as we attempt to balance our **vision** with our **reality.**

"One of the insurgents is said to have expressed faith in Jesus and was promised paradise. When *'one of the twelve, Thomas (the name means Twin),'* insisted on reasonable proof of Jesus' resurrection, and was allowed to probe the wounds, Jesus said:

> *You became a believer because you saw me.*
> *Blessed are they who have not seen and have*
> *believed.*   John 20:24-29 [16]

"The pendulum began its swing at the point of Sagittarius, faith in **Revelation.** At the opposite end of that pole is the 'twin'--Gemini, symbolizing **Reason.** [17]

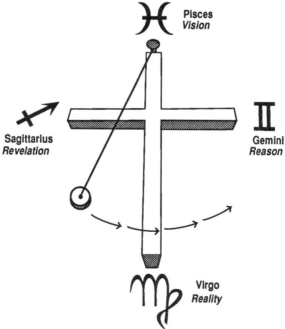

"The early church leaders--who, as **all** mortals in this age, are symbolized by the opposition sign of **Virgo**-were concerned with how to put the mystical Pisces vision of Jesus into a framework of practical reality. They began with a typically Sagittarian dogmatic insistence on blind faith in a collected group of principles that they believed had been **revealed** to them through the Christ. No word in the gospels even implies that Jesus condemned the doubting Thomas. But Virgo is very discriminating, and in the discernment of the church, the attitude of Thomas met with grave disapproval. It was infinitely more blessed to believe what one was told to believe than to doubt and question and reason why.

"With this little digression into zodiac symbolism in mind, let us return to the Renaissance where our Piscean Age is in the throes of its mid-life crisis.

"The individual discernment and the concepts of reality that did not fit into the official dogma had been too long suppressed. Like the 'shadow' of Carl Jung's psychology, it was about to erupt.[18] The pendulum would hit the pole of Reason with a vengeance.

"In 1382, just about exactly halfway through the age, John Wycliffe had produced the first English translation of the Bible, believing that common people should be able to read scripture for themselves, rather than allow the Catholic Church, only, to interpret it for them. Wycliffe was condemned as a heretic for his efforts, and his Bible was forbidden. But by the 15th and 16th centuries, the printing press had spread new translations of the Bible all over Europe and the Protestant Reformation was a reality.[19]

"No longer could one church control what the people believed. By the time the Catholic Church tried to silence Galileo, the old dogmatic days were nearly over. Virgoan discrimination splintered Christianity into dozens of denominations, each bickering with the others over often minute details of difference in their interpretation of theology and scripture. Quite independently of the churches, great advances were being made in scientific observations; and there was a great revival of interest in all of the humanities and in long-suppressed

Greek classics.

"Yes, the Renaissance may have been a golden age, but a new dark age for astrology was about to begin. It has been called the Age of Reason, and it was the 18th century.

"In the cross that all of collective humanity bears in this Age of Pisces, religion tends to overemphasize the poles of Pisces [Vision] and Sagittarius [Revelation]; while science tends to overemphasize the opposite poles of Virgo [Reality] and Gemini [Reason]. They are out of balance. Good astrology properly synthesizes all.

"The first decline and 'dark age' for astrology came about because astrologers insisted on dealing with Reality and Reason. Astrology was therefore too scientific for the prevailing thought that was dominated by the early church. The second decline and 'dark age' for astrology came about because astrologers insisted on including Vision and Revelation. Now, in the 18th century, prevailing thought became dominated by materialistic science, and astrology was dismissed as too mystical, and scorned for insisting on intangibles that could not be analyzed under a microscope or measured in a test-tube--proved!

"The attention of nearly all the first-rate minds riveted on the material universe. The intellectual establishment discredited any assumptions about the nature of the universe that could not be supported by rigorous scientific investigation. Scientists had no time to consider unproven assumptions based on human experience or revelation. Interest in the intangible spirit waned to zero. Rationalism and materialism became the reigning philosophies.

"Astronomy and astrology split into two distinct camps. Astronomy became a science that deals solely with the investigation of the material universe beyond the Earth's atmosphere. Astrology continued to assume a correlation between the material universe and human experience. Most of the talented thinkers among the 'star-gazers' fell into step with the times and with the academic establishment and studied astronomy. Astrology was discredited by that establishment and dismissed from the universities. The talented minds who retained interest in astrology were forced to work in obscurity. As a consequence, little serious writing or research was accomplished. Only the 'pop' astrology as a fortune-telling device for the superstitious retained visibility; and eventually most people forgot that there had ever been a higher form of this now discredited 'Divine Science.'[20]

"The church and its biblical scholars also reeled under the onslaught of materialistic science. Darwin's theory of evolution, for example, called to question the credibility of the Bible. Genesis had been considered to be literally accurate. If it was not, then in what way was it accurate? Over the years, the now weakened religious authorities had to readjust to the now dominant thought of Reason. The plain fact had to be accepted that scripture could be interpreted in more than one way.[21]

"No longer did any one Christian denomination have the power to brutally persecute as heretics those who held dissenting views. Scholars sought ways to explain the Bible in a rational manner that would have at least some reasonable conformity to the 'proven' scientific facts that had won general acceptance.

"It is not surprising that modern biblical scholars neglected or completely forgot to consider the astrological traditions of biblical times in their translations and interpretations of scripture. After all, astrology was divorced from the church when the church rejected science way back in its first centuries. In the 18th and 19th centuries, science won out over the church as the new model for a generally accepted world view. But astrology was now also divorced from mainstream science--discredited by the establishment as superstitious nonsense. When one is trying to find ways to conform to an accepted world view, one does not usually bring up for serious consideration elements of a discipline that is held in disdain by the authoritarians of that world view. So even if biblical scholars knew enough about ancient astrology to spot an astrological structure behind a scriptural passage, they would be unlikely to point it out, because, after all, astrology is 'unscientific' and they would not want to invite any **more** problems from science that they already **had**!

"Now, however, in this latter half of the 20th century, it has become quite noticeable that the pendulum is swinging toward center. No longer does pure reason dominate the accepted world view. Scientists--at least many of them--are admitting that accepted 'proven' scientific facts have been **disproven**--and each apparent solution only provokes another question. The study of human experience has returned to respectability as a proper subject for scientific investigation. Such intangibles as human intuition are taken seriously.

"Along with the general revival of interest in humanism, astrology, too, has made a massive comeback in popularity. Many talented and well-educated people now consider astrology a worthy subject for serious investigation, and openly call themselves astrologers. Serious writing and research abounds.

"To the chagrin of many of the 'high' astrologers, 'pop' astrology has also never been more popular. The superstitious 'tell-my-fortune' brand of astrology screams out from newspapers and popular magazines to such an extent that nearly everyone is aware of it, and at least initially thinks that telling fortunes is what astrology is all about. This aggravates the formidable task of 'high' astrologers to win back the acceptance of the academic establishment. Old models of thinking die hard; and intellectuals like to think of themselves as being on a different level than that of the masses.   If astrology is popular with the readers of the scandal sheets, then what is it worth?

"But astrology at its highest level is the fulcrum for the pendulum swing of this 2700-year epoch, the Age of Pisces.   It can be a tool for the synthesis of science--Reason--and religion--Revelation; and synthesis of these two is inevitable and necessary in our path toward reconciliation of the Reality of our condition with our Vision of God.

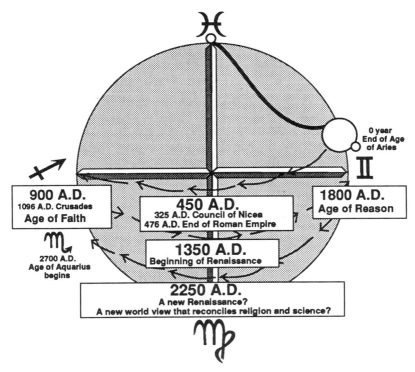

"It is in the quest of reconciliation that I propose through this work the reexamination of scripture for its positive links to the ancient science of astrology; and the reexamination by modern astronomers and astrologers of the scriptural evidence of a divine purpose for their investigations of the cosmos.

"The quest for connective links and synthesis and a wholistic view must go on in all fields of study if we are to achieve the golden age of peace and tolerance and humanitarian concern that is our vision for the future. To be sure, these pages present only a small part of that synthesis. But each of us must reach out from where we are, in the hope that our thoughts may blend with others into a new level of understanding."

When our class discussion returned to the Bible, it was suggested that perhaps Jesus' references to the "sign of Jonah" might be symbolic of the zodiacal Pisces. In Matthew 12:38-42, and in Luke 11:29-30, Jesus is asked for a sign, and Jesus says, "An evil and unfaithful age is asking for a sign, but no sign will be given it but the Sign of Jonah."

Well, a whale is not really a fish--but I had not yet studied the Book of Jonah, so out came the Bibles, followed by some delighted laughter.

"Hey! This whole book reads like a prophecy of the Age of Pisces!"

"Yes! In the light of all we've discussed, it's pretty obvious. It fits so well, it's funny."

"And no mention of a whale. That must be somebody's post-biblical afterthought because he couldn't imagine a man surviving inside the belly of anything smaller. The Bibles are clearly translating a 'big fish.' "

"All right," I said. "This is well worth going over in detail. I'll write it out."

Jonah and the Fish [22]

*O*ne day Jonah was told by the Lord to go and preach to the city of Nineveh. But Jonah, being quite reluctant, tried to flee the Lord and went aboard a ship to Tarshish.

The city of Nineveh is identified in the footnotes as being the arch-enemy of Israel. Jonah is being asked to take the word of God outside the ranks of his own people--to the Gentiles, even to enemies. This forecasts a prime concept of Pisces, and of the Christians who are to be the new "chosen people" of the Age of Pisces: Universal Love. Tarshish is identified as meaning "far west." **East** would symbolically relate to the ascending sign of the new age, or the ideal of God.[23] **West** is then its **opposition**. So Jonah chooses to oppose the Lord and nurture his own materialistic desires.

The Lord stirred up a great tempest upon the sea. So violent was the wind that the ship was on the point of breaking up. The frightened mariners cried out to their gods for help and attempted to lighten up their load by throwing cargo into the sea. Beneath the deck, Jonah snoozed peacefully, oblivious to what was going on. The captain awakened him, saying, "What are you doing asleep? Call to your God to save us!"

Pisces is a water sign, and the new age is coming, no matter how badly it shakes up the old order. In the turmoil of transition between the ages, some will cry out for help or try to do whatever they perceive might save themselves, but others will "sleep" through it, unaware that anything of a momentous spiritual nature is occurring.

In times of trouble, alas, most men must look for someone else to blame--even if their reasons are based on the irrational. The mariners cast lots to decide whom they could blame for their misfortune--and Jonah "lost." When Jonah, replying to their questions about his background, said he was a Hebrew who worshiped the Lord, the mariners were seized with fear. After all, Jonah had already told them that he was fleeing from the Lord!

Jonah, admitting his fault, offered the suggestion that they throw him into the sea. Still the mariners tried a little longer to get to land; but when the sea became even more turbulent, they gave up and threw Jonah in. The sea immediately quieted.

Jonah is symbolic of the resistant new order finally giving way to the necessity for change.

The Lord sent a big fish that swallowed Jonah. For three days and three nights, he remained in the belly of the fish; but from the depths of that belly Jonah offered a prayer of thanksgiving that the Lord had delivered him.

Jonah is consumed by the ideal of the Age of the Fish. Prophetically symbolizing the three days of Jesus' death and resurrection, Jonah expressed the ultimate ideal of such absolute faith in the mercy of God that he gives thanks for his deliverance even at the point of his greatest danger.

The Lord commanded the fish to spit Jonah out onto the shore, and again asked Jonah to take the message to Nineveh.

Jonah is saved by God, just as Christians are saved by Christ. But he (and we) must still live for a time upon this land, our material earth. And we are asked, in this age, to love **everyone,** even our enemies.

And so it was that Jonah went to Nineveh and warned the people that in forty days the Lord would destroy them all.

Forty refers to the temptations of materialism, and to the choice to oppose Divine Will.

To Jonah's great surprise, all of the people of Nineveh, from the peasants right up to the king, repented of all their errors, and fasted and wore sackcloth. So God forgave them all, and they were saved.

This, of course, foreshadows the time of Jesus, when people feverishly longed for a Messiah to save them from the expected end-time tribulations and destructions. Jesus urged them to repent and they would be saved, ultimately offering himself as a sacrifice. And the world was "saved" and a new age was born.

Jonah was very angry! "God! This is why I fled at first to Tarshish. I know that you are merciful, slow to anger, rich in clemency, loathe to punish. But now, let me die; it's better than to live." "Have you reason to be angry?" inquired the Lord.

Jonah is being quite narrow-minded and picky-- one of the worst expressions of opposition Virgo. He's not at all as ready as God to let his enemies off so easy. Let his **own** group, nation, church be saved--the rest of the world be damned. It's because of this attitude that he went to Tarshish (west/opposition) in the first place. He attributes to God a list of typical key words for an ideally expressed Pisces. And with typical Piscean innocence, God inquires why Jonah should have any reason to be angry.

Jonah left to reside in the east, and the Lord provided a plant to give him shade and comfort. Jonah was happy. But then a worm attacked the plant, and it withered. Then God sent a burning east wind, and the Sun beat down upon Jonah's head until he felt faint.

In choosing to live in the east, Jonah was trying to

follow the ideal of the Divine Order. In this he was happy and provided for. But the worm (the serpent of the opposition) is a constant temptation. The east wind and the Sun are symbols of the Holy Spirit and God. Obviously this tells of the eternal conflict in life between the spiritual and the material.

Said Jonah, "I would rather be dead than live like this." And again God asked, "Have you reason to be angry?" And Jonah retorted, "Angry enough to die!"

Jonah's whine could remind one of the long-suffering and negative expression of either Virgo or Pisces. In any case, the symbolism here is that death refers to spiritual death. Jonah would rather have material comfort, and eliminate conflict with this God who apparently wants to teach him something.

God admonished Jonah, "You worry about the plant which cost you nothing, which you did not raise. Why do you not think I should be as much concerned about Nineveh, a great city which repented, but in which there are many people who can't tell their right hand from their left?"

If God, in kindness, provided a plant for Jonah without any merit on his part, how much more would God be inclined to show love and mercy toward all men, regardless of nation or creed, or level of education, when they repent and ask for forgiveness. Again, this obviously foreshadows the new concept of God that would be taught by Jesus as the ideal of the Age of Pisces.

* * * * * * * * * * * * *

After class I went to the library to see what the

New Catholic Encyclopedia had to say about the Sign of Jonah. In more than a page of speculation, that contained not a hint of a mention of Pisces, the conclusion stated was that **nobody knows** what Jesus meant by the Sign of Jonah. The reference, it said, remains a big puzzle.

Intrigued, I looked up "fish" to see what the Catholic scholars had to say about this symbol that was used by the early Christians as a sign of recognition, and is **still** used frequently to decorate missals and church brochures.

Several pages were devoted to "fish," including a double page of photographs of fishes in Christian art. The text debated on whether the acrostic is older than the symbol, or whether the symbol came before the acrostic. The "acrostic" is the Greek word for fish, the Greek letters of which form the first initials of each word in the phrase, Jesus Christ Son of God Savior. The text mentions that the acrostic probably goes back to Gnostic circles. Of many paragraphs of various speculations on the

origin of the symbol, a possible link to the zodiacal sign of Pisces is dismissed as "not deserving of confidence," without **any** explanation of why it does **not** deserve confidence. The last sentence of the text states "*though both the acrostic and the symbol appear at almost the same time in the sources, it seems that the symbol, fish = Christ, originated before the acrostic.*" [emphasis mine][24]

Christ came at the dawn of the precessional age of Pisces the Fishes. This was well known at the time. There are plenty of scriptural references to the ages. Astrology permeated the culture at the time of Christ.

Jesus was the Messiah who would save the world from the old order and bring in a new age of peace and love. He was born of a mortal virgin (Virgo). He chose his first disciples from among fishermen, and made them fishers of men. He fed his followers loaves (symbols of Virgo) and fishes (symbols of Pisces). When asked to give a sign for the age, he referred to Jonah and the "big fish."

Why would the scholars of the *New Catholic Encyclopedia* deny such a blatantly obvious zodiacal symbology as "fish = Christ"? I can only think that our modern scholars are so influenced by the scientific world view that disdains astrology, that they just do not want to think the earliest church fathers could have found anything good enough about it to merit the choosing of a zodiacal symbol for Christ. After all, one would think, to admit to a zodiac connection just might support a scientist-skeptic's opinion that all of religion is just so much superstition.

I reported what I had found at the next class meeting--but the discussion that evening focused on the Virgin.

One student suggested, "In our discussions of the earlier ages based on the stories of Genesis, you made much of the shift of dominance from masculine to feminine and back. Pisces should be a feminine age, but we still have a male God-figure and we don't hear much about ERA anymore. Let's talk about that."

"O.K., so God is still called 'he.' Guess we could blame that on Eve being the first one to throw the scales out of balance back at the beginning of this Great Year cycle. But seriously, let's look at how clearly the gospels shifted the emphasis back to the matriarchy and the elevation of the female. God came to Moses and the Age of Aries in a burning bush and in a pillar of fire. But God came to the new age as a human baby, born of a mortal woman. Jesus loved and respected his mother, and provided for her even as he died on the cross. He pointedly set up ideals of gentleness, compassion and meekness. It was a woman, Mary Magdalene, who became the first person to discover and tell the good news that Christ had risen.[25] Mary Magdalene, by the way, is believed by many--and preached from pulpits--to be a sinner and a prostitute. Try to find **anything** in the gospels that validates that idea! I've looked through all four of them carefully and there is nothing. From the gospel accounts she could more likely be taken as a woman of means who was supportive of Jesus' ministry.

"The early church reflected the shift in its elevation of Jesus' mother Mary to the status of Queen of Heaven and Mother of God. Really, it is Mary who should be carefully reconsidered as the symbol of the proper example for humanity to follow in reaching for the ideals that were taught by Christ. The church has made of Christ a God, forever set apart from all mortals, one and the same as God since before the Creation. Recent catechisms try to modify this approach, placing more emphasis on the humanity of Jesus; but the result is still a confusing issue to many. Christ, to students, still too often comes off as detached, set apart and out of reach. They ask, 'If he is and was always God, then how can he possibly also be human in the same manner as the rest of us?' The compassion of Mary is easier to understand. She was mortal, just like we are--yet she was elevated to immortality. With her we can identify. She shows that it is possible for a mere mortal to attain immortality."

A student added, "It would be even easier to identify with Mary if the church could rise above its insistence on interpreting 'Virgin' only as a literal sexual technicality and reexamine what the symbol Virgin really means."

"True! Just think of the time that has been wasted arguing over the totally unprovable assumption that Mary was a technical virgin and Jesus was conceived without the help of a mortal father. In the final analysis, why should that really matter? Would it make the lessons that Jesus taught any less valid if Joseph were someday proved to have been his natural father; or even if Jesus himself, were proved to have been married and fathered children?[26] If one's faith in God is anchored on literal interpretations of the Bible, one is very vulnerable to the possibility of shattered faith when scientific evidence is offered that disproves that literal interpretation.

"But if one's faith is based on the concepts that the stories and the people of the Bible symbolize, then one's faith is much more likely to grow and evolve with each new discovery. I've no doubt that the earliest Christian writers used the symbolism of the Virgin and the Fishes, polarities of the New Age, in their narratives. Too bad the connection has been forgotten. A review of the meaning of the ancient zodiacal symbols could bring a new perspective of great value to these times in which we live."

"O.K.," the student agreed." according to your theme of opposition, Virgo symbolizes, in this Age of Pisces, the ways in which we are bound to matter."

"Yes," I added, "And by the negative manifestation of Virgo, humanity remains separate from its vision of God; while by the virtues of Virgo, great growth in civilization and greater harmony with the collective ideal is achieved.

"What, then do we have in Mary as a symbol? Certainly she epitomizes the key phrase for Virgo, 'I serve.' In Luke, Chapter 1:26-38, we learn that the archangel Gabriel appeared to a virgin named Mary, who was betrothed to a man named Joseph of the House of David. Gabriel informed Mary that she was to bear a son who would be called 'Son of the Most High,' and that God would 'give him the throne of David his father.' Mary questioned the angel as to how this could be possible, and was given the example of her kinswoman, Elizabeth, being in her sixth month of pregnancy even though she was long past childbearing age. With that, Mary accepted the message of the angel, saying, 'I am the handmaiden of the Lord. Let it be done onto me according to thy will.'

"One can interpret these verses in a way that totally supports the early church emphasis on absolute faith and obedience to the revealed word of God. Thus we have been given, through religious art and through elaborations on the gospel story, a picture of a very young and completely innocent girl, who, with only one small, frightened question, believed the miracle of the angel's message and humbly agreed to serve as she was told. Out of this grew an image of Mary that defines Virgin--and the prime ideal for womanhood in the teachings of the church--as pure, set above the lusts of the flesh, and absolutely subservient.

"Now, I propose that this interpretation short-changes Mary and all of womanhood with her. Let's take another look at Mary-of-the-Gospel. Are there really any words of Luke's that portray her as the least bit meek or overawed by this person who claims to be a messenger of God? No, she speaks right up with true Virgoan discernment, saying, in essence, 'What you are telling me sounds pretty incredible. Prove it to me.' Gabriel sounds quite sure of himself, so she accepts his mission verbally while probably thinking to herself, 'That is, if what you say is true, **then** I'll accept it, because I do want to be of service to God.'

"Now does she go to her mother, or to her betrothed, with this fantastic story? Does she dreamily fantasize to them about her new spiritual glory? Maybe a Pisces might do that, but not our Virgin! As is stated in the very next verses of Luke, she sets out 'in haste' to visit Elizabeth. Why? It seems to me that the most likely reason is that she needed to find out if Elizabeth was truly pregnant. It was only after Elizabeth's greeting to her 'proved' the angel's story that Mary rejoiced in her own blessing with the words of the beautiful *Magnificat.* "

"For sure," agreed a Virgo, "No true Virgo type would have swallowed the angel's story without analyzing the evidence."

"A reconsideration of the image of Mary as the primary carrier, in this age, of the archetypal Virgin of the zodiac would give a healthier perspective on womanhood in general and on the struggle for equality of the sexes that is an issue of our times. Even the astrological interpretations of Virgo have suffered in reflection of the position of Virgo as the opposition to the Piscean ideals of this age. Astrologers, too, have apparently been influenced by the same unconscious 'force' as the church that has cast the Virgin in her sterile role of pristine chastity. Tell me, is the Virgin of the ancients the critical, discriminating, fussbudget that many of our astrology books would describe her?"

A listener pointed out, "Geraldine Thorsten, in her book, *God Herself,* says that our word for virgin originally meant 'independent.' The virgin was free, her own woman, property of no one, with full control over her own life."[27]

Another added, "And Rabbi Dobin's book says that in the near east, where astrology developed, virgins were not interested in prissy celibacy, but instead were so anxious for new experience that their fathers locked them up in harems to protect them from themselves."[28]

"Good points!" I said. "Actually, the Virgin of the constellation is mythologically the earth mother from whom all life emerges. She is the womb of time through which humanity must work out God's plan. She represents the seed that is planted, and the labor and struggle of growth. And she is the bounty of the harvest, pictured as she is with a sheaf of wheat or an ear of corn. In this age, we call her 'a barren sign,' but the virgin earth bursts with all the potential of life and creation!

"Virgo is the zodiacal symbol of the Mother Goddess, and the most ancient personifications of deity were surely Mother. Long ago, childbirth was a major mystery. No one had figured out that men had anything to do with it. Women, who could reproduce not only their own kind, but also the opposite gender, males, were regarded with great awe. It was only natural that the first deities were goddesses. Fertility figure relics of the most ancient religions attest to the matriarchal emphasis. The main function of men was to use their superior strength for the hunt and for the protection of the women and their children. The women were the wise ones, the keepers of the mysteries, the priestesses, the nurturers of their children and of communal life. Earliest astrologies were primarily lunar, as the phases of the Moon guided the seasons of planting and harvest and the hunt. And woman was associated with the Moon, who gave birth anew each day to the Sun. Ancient representations of goddesses often included lunar symbols--even Mary in some Christian art is portrayed standing upon the Moon. The Goddess reigned supreme throughout the world as the feminine sign, Taurus, became the Cardinal Ascendant. During the short Age of Aries, conquering patriarchal tribes enforced the new order by the brutal slaughter of many goddess-worshiping populations. Still, many clung tenaciously to worship of the Mother right into the transitionary period of the Arian to the Piscean ages. The only way that the Christians could make their new religion with its god-man palatable to conquered people, such as the Celts, was to offer Mary, Mother of God, as a substitute for their goddess. This is largely the reason for the extreme veneration of Mary in the early church.

"Even the name, Mary, has an interesting history. I wonder if those who wrote the gospels really knew the actual name of Jesus' mother, or if the name was chosen for its symbolic meaning?"

"What do you mean?"

"Mary comes from the root 'mar,' which in Indo-European languages is 'the sea.' The pre-Christian goddess Mari was Goddess of the Sea, the Great Fish who gave birth to the gods, sometimes pictured in the form of a mermaid. The Latin form of Mary, Maria, means 'the seas.' Even the name of Mary's mother, Anna, is a form of the pre-Christian 'grandmother goddess.' She was the crone of the female trinity: virgin, mother, crone. As Di-Ana (divine Ana), she was mother of Mari. In other language variations this creatress-goddess was called Anu, Nana or Inanna."[29]

"I just had an interesting thought!" a listener exclaimed. "Christian doctrine may preach a man-god, but Christian **intuition** must be more comfortable with the Mother. Think of all the notable visions and miracles of Mary--like at Fatima and at Lourdes. I can't think of any comparable visions of Jesus. When supernatural visions of deity appear in this age, they are female!"

"You're right! I hadn't thought about it that way before. Fascinating--"

"Why, then, in this age of the Pisces-Virgo feminine polarity have women been so severely suppressed by the church? Why has the full potential of womanhood remained so repressed and distorted in our culture?"

"One reason is probably that our action principle in this age, our Cardinal Ascendant, is Aries. Our ideal, the Word that must be spread (mutable), is Piscean; but action is initiated (cardinal) with the expression of Aries. Jesus, a key teacher for this age, understood and exemplified the highest expression of Aries, and Pisces, and of all the other signs for that matter. But the end of the Arian Age found most of humanity entrenched in a world view that expressed Aries at its macho-masculine worst. The struggle for patriarchal dominance was won and God was unequivocally male. Only **man** was created in **His** image. Jesus tried to soften people's concept of God into an always forgiving father figure, but the new religion was rooted in the fiery, masculine, punishing God-concept of the Arian Age. World views change very slowly. A new concept (like the teachings of Jesus) may be accepted in theory, but those who must act to spread the new concept have unconscious motivations carried over from the old ways. Witness the un-Christ-like wars, slaughters and heretic burnings of the early churchmen's actions that they claimed were done in the name of spreading the teachings of Christ. Women were little more than pieces of property by the end of the Arian Age, so despite the prominence of the Marys in the gospel, women were given only the most subservient of roles in the organization of the new religion.

"Probably the main zodiacal explanation, though, for the suppression and distortion of feminine potential is because it is the Virgin, herself, who is now the symbol of **opposition** to our Pisces vision of deity. Once upon a time a Goddess, she is now only a mortal and fit to be saved only by the benevolence of a Father God. However virtuous the maiden might be, she is still the descendant of Eve, who according to the authors of Aries-time, led man to his downfall. If Pisces, in the form of the Fisherman [Christ as avatar of Pisces] is **all good,** then his opposite, Virgo the Maiden, must be bad--or even if she is virtuous, she must certainly be kept in her place!

"Remember the prophecy of Simeon at the circumcision of Jesus; when he said to our Virgo, Mary:

> *This child is destined to be the fall and*
> *the rise of many in Israel.*
> *His sign shall be opposed.*
> *Yes, and a sword shall pierce even*
> *your own heart--*
> *That the thoughts of many hearts*
> *may be revealed.* [30]

The sword must pierce the very heart and image of the Divine Mother, who must now take her turn as the opposition symbol to the deity of the age.

"The baby avatar of Pisces will grow up to symbolize God. The opposition sign, Virgo, symbolizes notgod: collective mortal humanity. The Virgo-mortal can 'fall' or 'rise,' as the message of this child is revealed in the heart. Whatever have we done to our Virgo-selves?

"Astrologically, the characteristics of the Virgin became distorted at the dawn of this age when Ptolemy, in classical Greece, assigned his planetary rulers for the constellations. The association of the Virgin with her natural 'goddess,' Moon, was not to be. Instead, dominion over her was assigned to Mercury. The assignment was apparently quite arbitrary. In Ptolemy's *Tetrabiblos*, Sun and Moon are assigned to Leo and Cancer for the reason 'that they approach nearer than the other signs to the zenith in this part of the world, and thereby cause warmth and heat.' Mercury is given rulership over Gemini and Virgo only because it is the planet closest to the sun, and Gemini and Virgo are adjacent to Cancer and Leo. [31] So it was that in our time Virgo became associated with the sexless, intellectual Mercury instead of womanly, nurturing Moon. It is an interesting bit of synchronicity that Mary-of-the-Gospels was also assigned her destiny by the Messenger of God. Mercury of mythology is also known as a winged messenger of God.

"For centuries, the collective society of mortals

acted out its distorted and suppressed and misunderstood Virgo. Her earthy sensuality was considered an evil rather than a virtue. Her ability to think with creativity and wisdom was devalued in favor of the emphasis on unquestioning faith. Her capacity for discernment was distorted into a nit-picking, fussy-with-details intolerance that caused the splintering of the religion her son founded into hundreds of quarreling sects. It was as if she was bound in slavery, rather than in service. When the symbolic pendulum swung from the pole of Revelation/Faith to the pole of Reason in the 18th century, the suppressed slave began her escape.

"One who is suppressed for all that time is likely to emerge a very angry lady! Her intellect so rebelled against the old requirement of obedient faith that spiritual values were denied in favor of total dominance by materialistic science. Society still suffers from the effects of her rebellion, though in this latter 20th century, some signs of movement toward balance are beginning to be seen, particularly in the new consideration by scientific leaders of matters of the spirit and the intangible. Also very hopeful are recent ecumenical movements among Christian denominations; and tolerance--even interest--in blending some of the ideas of Eastern religions with those of the West.

"The problems caused by the severe repression of sexuality, and of women in general, are still very much with us. Suppressed sexuality erupted into an overblown, overemphasized pornographic version of sex that denies its spiritual nature and purpose.

"In their zeal to attain equality with men, some feminists have tried to **be** men rather than to attain their higher identity with the full and rich womanhood that was the Mother Goddess before her fall into the suppression of this age. Much will be gained in the spiritualization of Virgo that is necessary to reach for the ideals of Pisces, when we collectively realize that society must place the highest priority values on the functions that are of the nature of the Mother Goddess. No material concern, no mark of status, should ever be placed before the nurturing and education of our young, and the feeding of our hungry!"

"You're really on a soapbox, aren't you?"

"Yes, I suppose so. But one of my pet peeves is the low status accorded to the full-time mother and the elementary schoolteacher, when the work they do is more important than anything else to the future of society. Mark my words, great changes will take place before this age comes to a close. Pisces/Virgo is a feminine polarity. The Holy Mother will yet see her daughters returned not only to equality, but to positions of great respect. And take heed, fathers of the church. The church is, in truth, our Holy Mother. You've denied her daughters the right to serve as her 'high priestesses.' This will change and **must** change. Your ability to recognize this, and to welcome female priests, may well be a major deciding factor on whether the church as we know it will fall, or move forward into the Age of Aquarius and lead the masses to a truly "**catholic**"--meaning **universal**--faith!"

Cheers from the women in my class--and good-natured boos from the men. Well, we have several hundred years left, sisters, before the end of this age. Guess we can be patient a little longer. I changed the subject.

"Back to astrology. I must say that with respect to all those who have written in terms of Aquarian Age symbolism to describe the current signs of a shift in the models of collective thought, all of the conflicts of our time can be as well or better described with the symbolism of Pisces/Virgo. It will be hundreds of years yet before the vernal point enters the constellation Aquarius. What we are seeing now, symbolically, is the return of the pendulum toward the center, and the consequent restoration of some sense of balance between Faith/Revelation and Reason, and between Reality and Vision. The pendulum will return to center at about A.D. 2250. It was last at center at the dawn of the Renaissance period, A.D. 1350. Perhaps the next 'centering' will bring a new Renaissance, and a new paradigm that will reconcile religion and science."

A listener remarked, "All this discussion makes it easier to relate to how we mortal humans are linked to the Virgin in this epoch; and how far we have yet to go before we can collectively realize her and our full spiritual potential."

"Now let's talk more about the Fishes," I suggested. "We've discussed some of the characteristic virtues of the zodiacal sign, Pisces, that are ideals of the teachings of Jesus. And we've mentioned some of the ways in which the fish has been used as a symbol."

"I still find it difficult to relate to a fish as the symbol of our deity."

"But Christ didn't call his disciples fish--he called them fishers of men. Man, then, must be the symbolic fish they are trying to catch."

"We are the fish!" exclaimed one, in a flash of discovery.

"Yes. In each epoch, humanity deifies, holds up as ideal, the virtues of one of the twelve expressions of God. But there are also twelve expressions of humanity in the image of God. It is in reaching out for the highest ideals within ourselves that we become reunited with God.

"Peter Lemesurier's book, *Gospel of the Stars*, contains an excellent explanation of Pisces symbolism.[32] He says that water is the womb of Mother Earth, and fish are the unborn. It makes good sense. We know that the unborn child lives in uterine waters, and the fetus, in its early stages, does resemble a fish.

"Lemesurier points out that water was a symbol

for death and mortality in the Hebrew scriptures. The world was destroyed by flood and reborn anew after it. The Hebrews had to cross the Red Sea and later the Jordan River in order to reach the Promised Land. The ritual of baptism is a symbol of rebirth. First immersed in the waters, one emerges reborn into a new life.

"The Fishes of the constellation, then, are symbols of the unborn.[32] They are bound by a cord, reminiscent of the umbilical cord, that holds them prisoners of their mortality. As the baby must leave the womb in order to be born, so must the fish that represents the mortal human leave the womb of Earth to be born into spiritual life.

"There are two fishes in the constellation, and they swim in two different directions. One struggles to swim free of the ecliptical current, but the other swims right along with the current, preferring to remain 'in the water.' These two represent the two decisions of Pisces, and either decision requires a death. To drift with the current and remain in the dark waters means spiritual death; to come out of the waters into the air means a physical death."

"Most fish seem to find it more comfortable to evade the fisherman and stay in the water!"

"Yet many are caught by the bait of the bread of enlightenment--the bread of the bounty of the Earth Mother, Virgo. It was with loaves and fishes that Jesus fed the people. But in feeding their physical bodies, he was symbolically nurturing their spirits--teaching them--offering them enlightenment. The Christian church has transformed the bread of the earth into a spiritual eucharistic food and called it the Body of Christ. And Christ is symbolized not by the two bound fishes of Pisces, but by **one fish**--the one who has been **caught**--who has left the waters of earthly mortality, has died a physical death, and has been reborn into an eternal life."

"So Pisces symbolizes death and rebirth, too. Why then, do you not think that this is the end of the cycle instead of Scorpio? Could it not be that Christ will return at the end of this age as many Bible interpreters think he will, and cast his net for one last time to catch up all the 'fish' he wants --as in the stories of 'rapture'-- before the final destruction of Armageddon falls upon the Earth?"

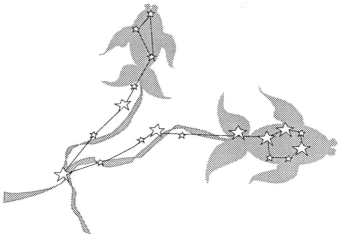

"I've thought a lot about that. If Pisces is the end time, then Aquarius and Capricorn would have to be at the beginning of the Great Year, and I just can't think of how they would fit that symbolism nearly so well as does Libra. Libra, the one inanimate object in the zodiac--the Scales of Balance--seems a natural fulcrum for the wheel. Also, the numerical clues in Genesis, that I've already pointed out, wouldn't fit with an Aquarius beginning. There are numerical clues in Jesus' story, too, that could be interpreted to carry out my theory of the sequence of the ages."

"Tell us about them."

"First, let's review that Jesus is born at the end of the Age of Aries, to be sacrificed as the Lamb of the old order, and to be the bearer of the Piscean message of death and resurrection. Aries is the seventh age from Libra.

"Jesus said, *'Destroy this temple and in three days I will raise it again.'* [John 2:19] The temple meant his body. The destruction of that temple, as well as the actual destruction of the temple of Jerusalem not long after Jesus' death were symbols of the end of the Aries Age and of the old order.

"Jonah was in the belly of the fish for three days. Jesus said that the only sign he would give for this age was the Sign of Jonah.

"Jesus was crucified and on the third day he rose again.

"Let's examine this symbolism of three. Does it only mean the three actual days from cross to resurrection? Or could three days also symbolize three ages? Could it be that humanity is to be given three ages to assimilate the message of the Christ before the time of the Revelation?

"Sagittarius is the sign of Revelation. Now, tell me, how many ages are there between Aries and Sagittarius? And do their symbols have any common link?"

"I know! It's fish! Pisces introduces the symbolism of the fish. Aquarius is pictured pouring water out of an urn. That could be correlated with baptism. Below the constellation Aquarius is another small fish constellation, *Pisces Australius*, positioned almost as if it had been poured forth from the Aquarian urn. Sometimes Aquarius art shows fish in the water that pours from the urn. Capricorn is the sea-goat, pictured with a fish tail. None of the other zodiac symbols are fish-like--only these three."

"So then there's hope that we are still a long, long way from final Armageddon. But what does all this mean for the future?"

"That, my friends, is another chapter."

15

A Spiritual Interpretation of Numbers

Shannon had been thinking about the things I'd told her on the symbolic meanings of numbers. "I still don't really understand how three can be one. It seems to work and then it seems like double-talk. And if you make so much of 2 and 3 and 4, what about the other numbers? Like do 5 and 9 mean anything?"

"Yes they do. I've thought a lot about this and I've read the ideas of quite a few others on the subject. By now, I've thought myself around in some pretty frustrating circles. But I think I've sorted out a somewhat comprehensible system, if you are patient![1] Anyway, thinking this through was more fun than plain old mathematics. Makes me wonder, too, just what came first--our present numerical system--or philosophy of numbers. Pay close attention--here goes!

"This is a circle. This symbol also represents, in our numerical system, zero. Our largest single digit is 9. Nine is the completion of the cycle. After nine we go back to the zero again and add one to form 10, then 11, 12 and so on. Now I want you to understand that 9 and 0 are **equal.** They are one in the sense that one means **unity** or **wholeness.**"

"That sounds crazy. How can that be?"

"Nine is like an absolute--a complete cycle. I can demonstrate that with a little trick used by numerologists to reduce all numbers to a single digit. Let's add up a random series of numbers like:

3 + 2 + 4 + 9 + 5 + 1 + 7 = 31, and then 3 + 1 = 4

If we add the series and **leave out the nine,** we get 22, and 2 + 2 = 4.

"Now add the series and eliminate all values of nine, like 3 + 2 + 4 = 9, cancel that nine, and also the original nine, and we're left with 5 + 1 + 7 = 13. 1 + 3 = 4. Nines in or nines out, the result is still four. You can do that with any series of numbers. The result will always come out the same whether you add in the nines or take them out. In other words, the nine might as well be zero, so far as the end result is concerned, using this system. Also, no matter what you multiply nine by, you can always reduce the final result back to nine."

$$9 \times 2 = 18 \qquad 1 + 8 = 9$$
$$9 \times 3 = 27 \qquad 2 + 7 = 9$$
$$9 \times 4 = 36 \qquad 3 + 6 = 9$$

"O.K. Neat trick, but so what? What does it prove?"

"It's another example of the **nothing** and the **everything.** The circle symbolizes nothing, zero, but it contains everything--completion of the cycle, nine. Even the 360 degrees of the circle reduces to nine: 3 + 6 + 0 = 9. Nothing and everything are in a state of unity or **one**ness. **Anything**--any other number--can only be perceived if you separate it from the unity. Now, how can we separate something from zero/nine?"

"Nine plus, minus or times zero still just gives 9 or 0. Can't do anything with just zero. But nine divided by nine is--aha!--one!"

"The first manifestation, then, is **one.** But in this sense, one has been divided. It has been **separated** from the unity of nothing/everything. In the beginning, we are told, everything concentrated into one seething center--sort of like God inhaled, perhaps. This pulling into the center, we can symbolize by the dot within the circle. The dot represents **origin.** It is **one,** but it is still the one of **unity.** It is ready to begin, but it has not yet begun. It is nothing--0, it is everything--9, it is all one--all the same whole, complete in itself.

"The dot within the circle is the astronomical symbol for the sun. Thousands of years ago many people believed that the sun was God. The very first monotheistic religion known to history was the sun-cult of Akhenaton that arose in Egypt around 1450 B.C. It is quite likely that the concepts of this religion influenced the mind of the young Moses in his education as a prince and priest of Egypt.

"Now our dot, the center, explodes--or we could say, exhales, and lo--the "Big Bang." The dot moves. Waves and vibrations expand out from the center. Imagine this movement symbolized by the **line.**

| "The line is our symbol, our numeral, that stands for one. **This** is the **one** that is defined by **dividing.** It has separated from the unity of nine. It has manifested. One, in this definition, is unique--individual. It is the something that has become separate from the unity of everything contained within nothing. In the act of separation from unity it has given birth to the concept of two. We have that which has manifested and that which has not manifested--the principle of opposites."

"This is a little different way of saying what you already told me before--"

"Yes, it is; but I've developed my thinking in a little more detail now. As I thought through this number symbolism, I wrote it down. I'd rather give it to you to read at your own speed. Here's the number theory-- start right here--"

"O.K., I'll give it a try--but it better **not** be like boring math."

A line has polarity. The dot where it began is its active, or positive pole; the point where it stops is its receptive, or negative pole. The line symbolizes the birth of the principle of opposites. That the principle of opposites is only an illusion of material manifestation can be seen when we realize that the apparent two is really three. The line has a beginning (an origin point), an ending point--and the line, itself, in between. It **was** unmanifested; it is *past.* It **is now** manifested; it is *present.* It is easy now to see the potential that can be added on in further manifestations; it is *future.*

All apparent duality and opposition is resolved in the unity of Three-in-One. Union or balance of the opposites is the first step toward realization of Divine Unity. The insistence that reality is opposition, that one side is 'positive' and the other is 'negative,' and 'never the twain shall meet' keeps us out-of-balance and **separated** away from the awareness of that Divine Unity or Absolute that is God.

There is no single shape that we can draw that symbolizes two. **Two can only be illustrated with separation: ||**

The first enclosed shape is that which can be made from **three** lines: the triangle. The upright triangle is another ancient symbol for God in three aspects. The inverted triangle symbolizes the three aspects of the soul, created in the image of God. Each triangle contains 180 degrees, and $1 + 8 + 0 = 9$ and is complete within itself, but the triangle contains only half of the 360-degree *All,* everything--whole truth--that is the circle. The whole truth now includes the soul, and can only be realized in reunion with God.

The well-known symbol of the Star of David interlocks the two triangles and has been interpreted "as above, so below," meaning we are created in the image of God. Other researchers have said that the Star of David is based on the actual horoscope of King David, which had two interlocking grand trine aspects of the planets.

Now our circle, which is nothing (0) and everything (9) has drawn into itself to form a center (dot, or One.) We have demonstrated in earlier chapters the various ways that the basic qualities, or aspects, that it contains are three: It is fixed; it always was and always will be **spirit.** It is cardinal: it can act or create anything out of nothing with **mind.** It is mutable: it has the capacity for change and the expression of **individuality.** The circle contains three in one, and now it is easy to see how another number can manifest: 3 + 1 = 4. Once one is manifest, it can be repeated--added on-- into infinity.

The fourth aspect of the circle is the number of the material world. It is matter; it is **body.** We can demonstrate that the three-in-one always had the potential for four in that the equilateral  triangle contains within itself four equilateral triangles.

 We speak of matter, earth, as being 'solid' and 'three-dimensional.' If you fold up the corners of the equilateral triangle, you can make a tetrahedron, which is the very first three-dimensional object (length, width, depth) that can be formed from separate planes. It has four faces. God, or the soul, manifested into matter is **four.**

To return to our basic shapes: now that four aspects have manifested we can enclose a shape made of four lines, and our triangle can become a square. The sum of the angles of the square is 360 degrees, the same as the circle. This suggests that the whole truth can be realized by the soul (3) within the material world (4). But this truth must include the knowledge that the square can only exist in **separation** from the eternal, timeless circle. We perceive matter, or "anything" in the material world (symbolized by the 4 or the square), only as it exists separated from the perfect unity contained within nothing that is symbolized by the circle. The circle is perfection; the square is imperfection. The circle in infinite; the square is finite. The circle is timeless; the square is locked in time and space. Four, or the square, then, represents the suffering and the limitations of humanity's existence in separation from Divine Unity.

Another graphic symbol for 4 is the cross. Here we have the vertical line, symbolizing the descent of the souls, entering the horizontal line (horizon), symbolizing the earth. The souls are thus bound on the cross of time and space.

As I said before, the ancients taught that the basic elements of matter are four: earth, air, water and fire. Of course, now, through science, we understand the word 'element' in a different way. But allegorically we can still validly speak of four aspects (or elements) of creation. Before there was **earth** (matter), the 'wind' or **air** (the **mind** of God) acted, moving over the **water of spirit** that was always there, and expressed **individuality** in a sudden incredible flash of light--**fire,** and the universe came into existence. **The entire universe is the body of God.** We humans, with our limited perception, named our small piece of the universe Earth, but in a larger sense "earth" symbolizes the entire material universe.

Each of us humans reflects the image of God-in-the-universe in that we have a soul that is mind, spirit and individuality and we have a body--**as above, so below.**

Four, or the square, **solidifies** the illusionary 2 that was suggested by the line. This is the **principle of opposites.** Four is the two doubled. **In order for there to be perception, something must manifest.**

Only then can we perceive that which has **not** manifested. We perceive God through the workings of the universe. **In order to perceive, or work within the universe, the soul must have a body.**

Yet, within the square is contained the triangle. Three comes before four. Four is totally dependent upon three. Four cannot exist without three. **The universe cannot exist without God!** The human body cannot exist in the image of God without the soul.

Four represents the pain of separation from the harmony that is Three-in-One, but it is also the means through which we must work within the universe and search for the truth that will ultimately allow us to return to the unity that is God.

Four plus one more brings us to five, the next numeral in sequence. Four can also manifest from 3 + 2. Three, the soul, must learn the experience of two, the principle of opposition. It is through our perception of opposites and through our relationships with others that we learn and communicate what we are learning. Five is one step up from the limitation and difficulties of four, and in that sense five represents the beginning of freedom. It is through **learning** that our soul can begin to become free of material bondage. A five-sided shape that is familiar to all is the pyramid, which is made up of four triangles atop a square. The Great Pyramid at Giza communicates to all ages the highly advanced mathematical and astronomical knowledge of its architects.

The association of the number five with higher knowledge goes back to antiquity. Five was considered to be the fifth element or essence that was of the heavenly spheres, and therefore above the four elements of the material earth. It was called "quintessence" and this word survives in our language to define a pure or a perfect embodiment of something.

In the 6th century B.C., Pythagoras and his followers built a religion out of his mathematical theorems. One of the main tenets was the proof that there can be only five regular solids (three-dimensional objects that have all faces of the same shape of equal sides). The most familiar of these is the cube, composed of six square faces. The others are the tetrahedron (4 equilateral triangular faces), the octahedron (8 equilateral triangular faces), the icosahedron (20 equilateral triangular faces) and the dodecahedron (12 faces that are pentagons).[2]

The dodecahedron, which combines the 5 (pentagon) with the 12 of the zodiac, was mystically associated with the cosmos. The knowledge of its formula was withheld from the uninitiated.

Five symbolism to denote the awakening of knowledge and the ability to rise above the four of material bondage and comprehend the spiritual is used in the New Testament in Mark 8:18-21. Here Jesus admonishes his disciples:

Have you eyes but no sight? Ears but no hearing?
Do you remember when I broke the five loaves for
the five thousand, how many baskets of fragments
you gathered up?" They answered, "Twelve."
"When I broke the seven loaves for the four thousand, how many full hampers of fragments did you
collect?" They answered, "Seven." He said to them
again, "Do you still not understand?" [3]

The loaves of bread symbolize the spiritual food, or the teaching with which Jesus offered nourishment to the people. The five thousand people were awakened to a level of knowledge above that of materialism. Jesus offered them the five loaves of knowledge, as well as the two fishes (Mark 6:41) that symbolized the advent of the Age of Pisces. They assimilated his teaching, but twelve baskets of fragments remained. Even with knowledge, still humanity must experience the full cycle of twelve lessons in the Divine Plan before the souls will be fully redeemed.   The four thousand people were not yet awakened in consciousness above the material plane. Jesus offered them seven loaves, symbolic of the seven "days" of creation, and God-in-the-world. They assimilated this and seven hampers of fragments remained. They were not yet ready to comprehend, so he sent them away (Mark 8:1-10).

Six is 3 + 3, or 2 + 4, or 5 + 1. The doubled three relates to the Star of David, which has six points. Three and three are balanced and harmonious; but six is also related to the two series, the principle of opposites. The solid form derived from the square, the cube, has six sides.   If you open up the cube and lay it out flat, it forms the cross of matter.

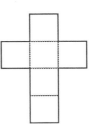

Six symbolizes, in a step up from five, the opportunity to **learn** harmony, peace and love through striving for **balanced relationships.** True love must come through realization of the three and three (as above, so below), for the 2 + 4 and the 5 + 1 are out-of-balance and thus present conflict.

The Bible tells us that God created the world in six days, and on the seventh rested. The seventh day, then, is the Sabbath, a holy day. Seven is frequently used in the Bible whenever holy or mystical events are being described. That seven has come down from antiquity as a mystical symbol is derived from the fact that there are seven "wanderers" in our solar system that are visible to the naked eye. These are the lights and planets of ancient astrology that became the basis for myth and esoteric philosophy. As viewed from Earth, they are Sun, Moon, Mercury, Venus, Mars, Jupiter and Saturn.

As the cycle of creation is seven, so is our week made up of seven days. The days are named for the planets: Sun-day, Moon-day, Tuesday (Tiw, a Teutonic god of war corresponds to Mars in Latin), Wednesday (Woden's day, translated to Latin as day of Mercury), Thursday (Thor translated to Jupiter), Friday (Freya, the Teutonic goddess of love, corresponds to Venus), and Saturday, which is Saturn's day.[4]

The cube is said to be the basic form of matter-- the solidified four. Salt crystallizes in cubes, and this could be the basis for the saying "salt of the earth." We have seen that the cube is made up of six sides. Six manifested planes make up the cube, but there is also a seventh unmanifested factor--the cubic content. In this sense, seven has an intangible quality about it. It calls for us to pause in our cycle of busily creating our own world and think about **why** we are doing it. What is the **content**?

Seven has been called the number of destiny; and on a lower level, it has been called the number of Lady Luck.

The three aspects of God and the four elements of matter add up to seven, therefore seven is said to be the mystic number of the Cosmos: God + the world.

Eight is the doubled four, which in turn is the doubled two. Here the struggle of the opposites reaches its peak. If six is the symbol of the creation of the material world, and seven is the symbol of reflection on the mystical purpose, then eight has a sense of begin- ning anew, and we can visualize evolution continuing in a spiral. The baptismal fonts in many churches are shaped like an octagon as a symbol of rebirth. Before Christianity, eight was a symbol of the Egyptian god, Thoth, who poured water of purification on the heads of initiates. Ritual circumcision, as a mark of the new covenant with God, is performed on the eighth day of life.

But in its symbolism of the multiples of two, eight is still very much mired in the problem of balancing the opposites. Two is brought to its highest power within the single-digit cycle, and eight has great energy and power. But how shall this power be used? If one's concept of reality is locked into the principle of opposites and based on two, then in eight the swing of the pendulum from one side to the other can be at its most extreme. How can this dilemma be resolved? The doubled 8 is 16, and 1 + 6 = 7. It is only through true understanding of the message of 7 that 8 can take the next step up and realize the unity of 9.

Nine, the completion of the cycle of single-digit numerals, symbolizes the everything that is contained in perfect unity within nothing. Nine is the mystic three multiplied by three, and the three interlocking circles is a well-known symbol of unity. In order to truly comprehend the meaning of nine, we must try to think in circles. So long as we think in terms of lines that begin and end, lines that are boundaries for planes that form triangles and squares, that in turn form cubes and tetrahedrons and pyramids, we remain locked into the three-dimensional world of time and space. We try to measure the universe linearly and we cannot find an end. Are there any square planets? Do any move in triangular orbits? No! Although in the material universe of separation from perfection, most orbits are imperfect circles (elliptical), still, all goes "round and round" in endless circuits. Perhaps through the symbol of the circle, then, we can imagine a whole new dimension in which there are no limits of time and space. Is there a dimension in which the trinity of past, present and future is **one** and is experienced simultaneously? Is there a dimension of one wholeness where no separate parts exist in separate spaces from each other? Is **this** the **Oneness in Being that we call God?**

In Christianity we say that Christ is "one in being

with the Father." This is the meaning of the Ascension. Perhaps where many of us fall short of full understanding of the Ascension is that we perceive Christ-one-with-the-Father as being **out there,** always and forever **separated** from our own potential. Through Christ, we are told, we can be saved from death. If we give ourselves to Jesus and accept the gift of salvation, which we can never hope to earn because we are hopeless sinners, then we will go, after death, to a vaguely defined place called Heaven where God will be seated on a throne with Jesus at His right hand, and we are somewhere there in His presence, freed from all cares and therefore happy. In this linear type of thinking, God is still **out there,** even in our imagination of paradise. As a natural consequence of our linear thinking, the principle of opposites must take effect. God must have an opposite and so we imagine a Satan that is also "out there." God becomes the personification of all that we have been taught through our social mores and religious background is "good," and Satan personifies all that is "evil."

So long as we project God outside ourselves, we are **separate.** Jesus did not just show us the way; he said, *"I am the Way."* (John 14:6) And he said he would be with us always. Should we not understand the Ascension as our own potential for oneness in being--for being one with Christ, as Christ is one with us? In the dimension of oneness with God, the principle of opposites is resolved. There are no opposites. Satan does not exist. Satan can only exist in the perception of separation from unity. If we perceive ourselves as one with God, if we bring God into the center of our being, instead of projecting God "out there," then we must perceive that **all** souls are one with God, We have eliminated the line of polarity and have become the **One,** the center of the circle. We have found our soul, and we realize that the responsibility for our perception of the universe rests within. We are the creators of our reality, and the extent to which we hold ourselves in separation is a matter of personal choice. If we choose to separate ourselves from the Whole (that we call God), then we become unique--an individual-- and we can then experience all the pain and the pleasure of polarity.

When the self becomes **unique,** then everything else is "out there," and we perceive what's "out there" in terms of opposite extremes that are separate from self, and over which we often have no control. No wonder so many feel helpless to do anything but pray to God who is "up there" to save them from the devil who is "down there."

But if we can bring all into the center and perceive Oneness defined as a Whole made up of all that is of the same nature (God **is** the universe), then we can experience a glimpse of the Oneness in Being that is the lesson of the Ascension and our hope for salvation.

Nine is a trinity of trinities. Three is the only equal division of nine; 3 x 3 or 3 + 3 + 3 = 9. Yet it is only in the linear thinking of our three-dimensional world of time and space that the mystical three-in-one of the trinity emerges. We divide the Absolute into the Trinity because it is the nature of our three-dimensional existence that we should do so. Each "person" of the Trinity is also a trinity: "Father," who creates, is also the sustaining spirit that is, was and always will be; expressing "himself" in an infinite variety of ways. The always sustaining "Holy Spirit" is creative, and expresses "herself" through individuals. The "Son," who is our primary expression of the individual uniqueness of the Absolute, is also of the sustaining spirit who creates: *"In the beginning was the Word . . . and the Word was God."* (John 1:1) It is only in the Wholeness of nine that we can contemplate the everything contained within nothing, the Eternal Now, that transcends this dimension.

But here we are. We are in this dimension--the third dimension. We dwell in the body, and the qualities of the body are also triune; the body is created out of the material of the earth and it will return to earth-- "ashes to ashes, dust to dust." The body is thus **sustaining.** The body has a mind, with which it is **creative.** The body is **individual,** unique, not like any other. Within the body dwells the triune soul. With the fourth trinity our nine becomes twelve. Twelve is the number of the full cycle in the Divine Plan for life in the world of three dimensions: 3 (the triune God) x 4 (God manifest) = 12.

But there is one more significant number still to be considered. While in the Old Testament much is made of the symbolism of twelve, in the New Testament totality is an implied **thirteen.** Jesus made a great point of selecting twelve disciples. This is a fact agreed upon by all four gospel writers, even though they do not agree exactly on just who the twelve were. So the twelve, carrying on the symbolism of the twelve tribes of Israel, plus Jesus, himself, make thirteen. Since early Christian times, a superstition of ill luck has grown up around the number thirteen, traceable to the idea that thirteen were present at the Last Supper, and one betrayed Jesus. Yet we are taught that the Last Supper was a necessary part of God's plan. Let's probe beyond the mystique of superstition for a more philosophical significance.

The dodecahedron of Pythagoras was supposed to hold the secret mysteries of the cosmos. It is a solid made up of 12 in 1. Twelve plus one is, of course, thirteen. A few years ago, contemporary astrologers rediscovered the dodekademoria, or the thirteenth harmonic chart, in which each planetary position in the horoscope is multiplied by twelve and then added to the original position. The origins of this technique have been traced back to Babylonian times. It is said that the thirteenth harmonic chart magnifies the hidden or inner side of the personality. So both the dodecahedron and the dodekademoria unveil a mystery.[5] But is this twelve-in-one = thirteen really so mysterious--or is it like the proverbial nose-on-your-face?

If God is everything-contained-within-nothing, and that is symbolized by 9; and if Jesus plus the twelve-cycle of the Divine Plan equals 13; then what has happened? Thirteen minus nine equals **four.** Thirteen reduced, or $1 + 3 = 4$. Four is the symbol of physical manifestation. God (9) plus 4 (manifestation) = 13-- **Christ!**

God in the **un**manifested state can be symbolized by nine or zero, but **God is manifest.** And God manifested is **four.**

Can we break the boundaries of our three-dimensional world and reach the elusive **fourth** dimension? And if we do, what will we find there? That four-in-one is five, and **we have only begun to learn the whole truth?** Conjecture on and on, round and round in circles--but still, we are in the manifested three-dimensional world of the symbolic *four,* and we must remain here for our allotted *time* and in our alloted *space.* How shall we consider this state?

If we regard our condition as a "valley of tears," and are able to identify only with the suffering Christ, dying on the cross of matter; if we think that the things of the material world are **all,** and that we die with our very vulnerable bodies; then it's little wonder at all why we might regard thirteen with suspicion of bad luck.

But if we pause, even for a fleeting moment, and identify with the Risen Christ, if we can experience our essential **oneness,** then perhaps we can grasp the meaning of the Divine Plan and our true nature and purpose within it.

Thirteen is Jesus, and Jesus is *The Way* of life through which we must fulfill the Divine Plan and reach for the unity with the Risen Christ that is our release from time and space. In this truth is the paradox of fate and free will, which we perceive as opposites but which are, in truth, one and the same.

Remember that opposition, or two, is an illusion that is created by separation from Divine Unity. An individual might reason that life is either fated, or that one has free will. Or one might say that some things are fated, but in others we have free will. But is this the whole truth? Let's look at it.

As we live our daily lives, we make a myriad of decisions. We think that these decisions are of our own free choice. But how free are we, really? The human mind is very complex, and for most of us, most of the time, that part of our thinking which is consciously directed is only the tip of a very large iceberg of unconscious motivations of which we are only dimly aware. Our choices are influenced by our basic character, which is made up of inherent qualities that we bring into this life (symbolized by the birth horoscope), and which is influenced by heredity and environment. Anyone who has even taken the trouble to really study an individual life in the light of a birth chart, heredity and environment knows that people, for the most part, are usually quite predictable. And the more ignorant an individual is of his/her unconscious motivations, the more predictable that individual is. In this sense, there is truth in the adage, "character is destiny."[6]

As an individual becomes increasingly aware of the unconscious, of his/her own true nature, that individual becomes much less easily predictable. Birth chart, heredity and environment can all be, in one sense or another, transcended. Astrologers often say that those who are spiritually aware do not behave as conventional delineations of their charts would suggest. Adverse aspects have been transmuted into strengths. And the person who is in touch with and aware of his or her spiritual nature is most unlikely to be found seeking the advice of a psychologist. So we could say that awareness gives us freedom from our character/destiny.

Now, does spiritual awareness really mean free will? It may seem so, in the beginnings of awareness-- and this is what we preach, because through the concept of free will we learn to accept responsibility for our decisions, our attitudes, and our condition in life. This is a higher level of development than to feel a helpless victim of fate, and to blame our stars, our parents, or our lack of fulfillment of some material desire for our sorry state in life.

But as we continue to grow in spiritual awareness, we must ultimately come to realize the truth of the paradox. There is no freedom from the limitation of time and space other than in acceptance. Freedom of choice, or will, only increases our bondage to this world. We have no power to change the one divine law of Love. We can only grow (or resist growth) in our capacity to consciously understand it. Only in total transcendance of personal will, or ego, can we free our souls from matter--only in total acceptance of the Divine Plan can we be free. This is the meaning of the crucifixion--of Jesus' sacrifice of his **self** on the cross of time and space. He freely chose to fulfill his destiny, as he came to understand it. As a man, he died; but as the resurrected One-with-God, he transcends all limitations and resolves the paradox. Freedom is destiny.

Shannon's comment as she returned the manuscript: "Mom, does anyone but me ever tell you that your ideas are strange?"

16

The Future of Pisces, and Ages to Come

On Earth, we are bound to the cross of time and space. We must live in our space for our allotted time. The zodiac and the motion of our planet Earth combine to form a huge Cosmic Clockwork that marks off the ages and years of our time.

If we could imagine an illustration of the clock of the precessional ages, it might look like this:

A strange-looking clock it is for us, accustomed as we are to evenly spaced symmetry in our timepieces. But the constellations are not the same size. Perhaps because some lessons require more time than others.

The time is now **eight.** The eighth age; the eighth constellation since our planet emerged from its last major world-wide destruction in the ice of the glaciers. The hand of time has passed almost through the eighth sector, but it is not yet nine.

Let's imagine a faster-moving clock for the time span of the eighth constellation only. It takes about 2700 years for the hand of time (the vernal equinox) to pass by the eighth constellation of Pisces. Let's divide this clock into twelve equal sectors in order to see where we are. At the present we are **still** at "eight o'clock"--more than halfway through sector eight, but not yet at nine. Not until the second decade of the 21st century will we reach nine, and be three-fourths of the way through the eighth age. I, the writer, and you, the reader, will spend all or a large part of the rest of our short lives in a time period that we could say is symbolized by double eight--**eight of the eighth age!**

Do you recall the symbolism of the numbers? Eight brings the symbol of opposition, two, to "its highest power within the single- digit cycle, and eight has great energy and power." Certainly there is great energy and power at work in our time. But how shall that power be used? Shall we build bigger and better weapons to protect ourselves from fellow humans whom we perceive to be our opposition? Shall we flaunt our

"white hats" of good against their "black hats" of bad--
while "they," no doubt, think the color scheme is quite
reversed?

If one's concept of reality is locked into the principle of opposites and based on two, then in eight the
swing of the pendulum from one side to the other can
be at its most extreme. How can this dilemma be
resolved?

The doubled eight is 16, and $1 + 6 = 7$. What **is**
the message of seven that can help us resolve our
dilemma?

Seven calls for us to pause in our cycle of busily
creating our own world and think about why we are
doing it.

What are our collective ideals? Our true spiritual
leaders, of all faiths everywhere, speak of love of neighbor, compassion, selflessness, sacrifice--Piscean virtues
all.

Virgo symbolizes our reality and Virgo is notorious
for "missing the forest for the trees." Are we so caught
up in mountains of trivia, in narrow fields of specialty,
in details of living in our own small space on the planet,
that we have lost sight of the wholeness of our vision?

An astrology text might describe the faults of
Pisces as lack of firm principles, vacillation, self-delu-
sion, escapism, and a superficial sentimentality in place
of true empathy. Do these not sound like familiar ills of
society in these times?

Our most technologically advanced civilizations
express materialistic Virgo at the height of efficiency.
But in the process, our very humanity is reduced to a
computer number. A vast proportion of our technology
is used to build weaponry that threatens to reduce our
humanity to ashes. Small wonder that escapism is
rampant.

In this time period, as never before, it is important
to pause and reflect upon why we are building these

things--or permitting them to be built by our silent acquiescence to those who hold positions of power. Our technology should serve the spirit and vision of humanity, not threaten to destroy it.

In the reality of our physical world, we humans come in many varied kinds--and how our Virgoan minds love to categorize and discriminate and criticize others' differences! We differ in color, in nationality, in religion, in education, in language, in size, in taste--the list could go on and on. But suppose we were actually visited by a race of extra-terrestrials? Would we seem as different from each other to **them**--or would they simply regard us as all members of one species? Should we not concentrate our energy into discovering the ways in which we are **similar**? Perhaps, then, empathy and compassion would come more easily, and fears would diminish.

The fate of the remaining years in this our present life span may well lie in our collective ability to deal with the dilemma of eight, and to answer the **why** of the double eight.

Within this time will we have the war to end all wars, or will we decide to end the potential for a war of total world destruction by disarming? Either alternative would mean a rebirth--a new beginning. Let us project that the decision to disarm can be reached through initiative, rather than through response to the devastation of a third world war.

We live in a time in which change and upheaval on a massive scale is truly to be expected. Our technology has made this so. Events in any part of the world can be instantly transmitted throughout the world, touching the lives of billions. Most of these events pass in and out of our consciousness, having only a passing effect. But we are vulnerable now, and far more linked to everyone else than ever before in history. The economic collapse of one country, even a small one, would domino its effects all over the world. A nuclear attack-- or accident-- anywhere could start a chain reaction that could threaten everyone. The health of present and future generations of millions could be threatened by a mistake, an accident, or an irresponsible use of chemicals. There is no question that our attitudes of separateness, of opposition, of "us vs. them" must change. The only question is how much punishment we will bring upon our world before we realize that **we are all in it together.**

In any case, by about A.D.2025 , the clock of our Piscean Age will be at **nine.** We are still in the eighth age, but now with the opportunity to realize a larger, mass awareness of the wholeness, the everything, that is symbolized by nine. This will be a time in which great masses of people can rise out of the mire of separatism and opposition that has characterized this epoch, and then begin to realize the aspect of eight and Pisces that means rebirth and renewal.

I see the 9th and especially the 10th time periods of this age (2025-2250 and 2250-2475) as a kind of New Renaissance, but more glorious than the last. Science will continue to advance, but now with a new sense of humanitarian purpose for its progress. New emphasis will be given to all of the humanities--to all fields of study that nourish the spirit of humanity. The arts will flourish as never before. Chastized by the past upheavals that were caused by greed and separatism, those of us who still remain, and those who were born and brought up during the upheaval, will have new values--and renewed vision. The practical realities of Virgo will again be given balance by the mystical vision of Pisces. The pendulum is at the fulcrum--but soon to swing out again.

The last sector on our clock of this age begins with the number 11. The time period is 2475 to 2700. As the clock strikes 12, the new age will be emerging.

Our imaginary pendulum has again reached an outermost point of its swing--but now that point is Scorpio, and the top of the cross is Aquarius. It is the Age of Aquarius.

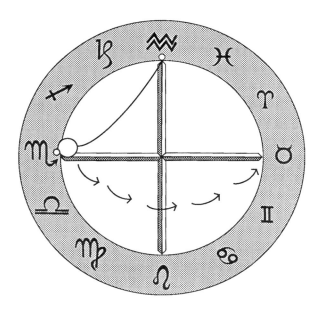

The time periods that begin with 11 and 12 on our "clock" are times of transition. The symbolism of the numbers suggests a pattern that is probably common to all transitionary periods between the ages. Eleven, in the ancient lore of numerology, is called a "master number." Mastery, then, of the lessons of the closing age, must here be possible. Our numeral for eleven is double 1, two ones side by side: 11. In that form, eleven could also be taken as a representation of two-- the Roman numeral II, or 1 + 1 = 2. So "two-ism" is a possible manifestation of the "eleventh hour" of an epoch. A final conflict between opposing concepts takes place.

But is it not an illusion that eleven is two? If we mark it out in quantity, there is no even division.

We can conceive of our universe in arrangements of harmony and balance,

but we cannot split it in two (like "good" and "evil") without throwing it out-of-balance

and dividing and weakening our very center. (God and Satan?)

If our center is to be whole, and not divided, then we must realize our essential point of unity with all other beings. Love thy neighbor? Yes. And **everyone is thy neighbor.** Synthesis. This is Pisces! This, indeed, is the wholeness of the 12, not the separate compartments of Virgo into which we have placed ourselves. Virgo's path must be to find practical, workable methods to **serve** the vision of "love thy neighbor."

The clock strikes 12. The end of the old order overlaps the beginning of the new. By the time the clock strikes one, the identification of the vision of the new order will be firmly established. And the seeds of conflict with its opposing forces will be planted. For now, those who have mastered the lessons of Pisces will have already accepted the highest ideals of Aquarius, and will be at peace with their universe. For those still struggling with the illusions of two, all is chaos.   If peace with one's fellows cannot be found on this small planet, how will one ever deal with Aquarius?

Aquarius symbolizes the breaking of boundaries. The Waterbearer pours out the waters and sets the fishes free.   The fish that swims in the waters of the constellation Aquarius is not bound by a cord as were the fishes of Pisces.   It is free--physically free to leave the circle of the ecliptic and explore the entire cosmos!   In the Age of Aquarius, travel in outer space will no longer be just the experiments of a few.   It will be the experience of many.   The cycle of time for our earth and its passengers will still be marked by our cosmic clock of the zodiac--but now many humans will break free of that clock and move on to places where other zodiacs and other concepts of time will prevail.   How naive to think that the faces of God (the Whole) are twelve.   God has **infinite** expressions--yet all belong to the Whole. Aquarius is the ninth age, and nine symbolizes everything.   Now the inhabitants of Earth will begin to get a true glimmer of what **everything** really means.   Still "fish," still swimming in the waters of Earth-ly mortality, the children of Aquarius will find that the outer limitations of that mortality are far more distant than their ancestors ever imagined.   Boundaries will be broken for those who remain in residence on Earth, too, as the potentials of the human brain are explored and expanded.

New archeological finds will unlock ancient mysteries.   Visitors from other worlds will bring new concepts.   The capacity of the human brain will be found to encompass phenomena now thought to be supernatural.   Astral projection, levitation, telepathic communication will be so commonplace that they will be routinely taught to school children.

All of these new developments will assist the spiritual teachers of Aquarius to **prove** that all gods are

One. Not just one Messiah will come to the Age of Aquarius, but many--the caught fish who are now the Waterbearers. In equal proportion the teachers will be men and women of every race and of every ethnic background. They will bring the same message. They will point out the same Truth that underlies faiths of ages past. In unity with each other they will cause all religious boundaries to melt away--and all ethnic and nationalistic boundaries as well. All, in the center of Being, are One.

With Pisces rising, as the Cardinal Ascendant, Mary as Mother Goddess, could well be the most popular personification of deity, but no violent struggles will enforce that choice. In the new enlightenment of the masses in this age it will be understood both intuitively (Pisces) and intellectually (Aquarius) that all gods are One. Christ will be revered by all, but not in a manner forever set apart from human potential, but as a personification of the fulfillment of every soul's destiny to return to unity with God. A new name will be chosen to express the universality of the new world religion.

The new religion will so influence the mass consciousness that discrimination based on one's heredity and cultural environment can finally vanish. No longer will sex or color or background be a factor of acceptable limitation to one's achievements. Only excellence of the mind (an ideal of the new "airy" paradigm) will count.

The scene just painted may sound like Utopia to many readers, but a nightmare to others. In either case, it is only a part of the potential expression of Aquarius. It is fashionable, in our present day, to look toward the Age of Aquarius as a Utopia--a golden age-- in which peace will reign and love will rule us all. Even those who do not identify with Aquarius at all speak of a golden age after the millenium when Christ will return to rule and resolve all conflicts.

Perhaps it is an irresistable facet of human nature

to place at least the dream of Utopia within the framework of one's own life expectancy. Search out the writings of prophecy by either psychic or scripture interpreters from nearly any century and you will find the prediction of disaster followed by a golden age to be just a few years ahead--at the turn of the next century, perhaps. Christians have hopefully anticipated the Second Coming since before the fall of the Roman Empire.

One individual human lifetime, however, is but a split-second of God's time. It is unreasonable to expect that even the scope of one entire Great Year, let alone one age, would be enough to bring the whole of the Divine Plan for humanity to fulfillment.

Aquarius, no more than any other constellation, makes a wonderful ideal if we speak only of his virtue--of freedom, of humanitarianism, of universal truth. Aquarius is an air sign, associated with the intellect or Mind. Yet he bears water, associated with the Spirit. So, we could imagine a blending of Mind with Spirit, as the highest human intellect, having discovered Universal Truth, pours out the waters of Spirit to nourish all.

Certainly, these ideals will be presented to humanity by the great teachers who will emerge during the centuries of transition.

But Aquarian ideals, no less than those of other constellations, can be corrupted. The faults of Aquarius, and the characteristics of Leo, its opposition, as well as the extremes that might be characteristic of its "insurgent" squares, Scorpio and Taurus, can provide clues to the ways in which the Age of Aquarius will fall short of Utopia.

As the Age of Aquarius begins, the wheel will have shifted and our imaginary pendulum will strike the Scorpio arm of the new cross that humanity must bear.

Scorpio is the sign of death and regeneration. Among its characteristics are a capacity for deep, probing research and a tendency to be manipulative and a need to control. Scorpio will sacrifice personal possessions to take care of others--often whether the others want that kind of help or not.

Aquarius is a revolutionary that breaks boundaries of the mind and idealizes Universal Truth. But Aquarius Truth is for **all**--for the humanitarian needs of the group. Aquarius can be quite detached from the feelings of the individual. So what is right for the group? And who will decide?

The birth pangs of the Age of Aquarius will include the new reality that in order to achieve the vision of Equality of rights and liberty for all, somebody has to organize the masses. The new reality is symbolized by Leo the Lion of Dominion. A government will emerge that will organize all of the people of the world into one democratic unit. The new government will not come to power through nuclear war as that threat will have been resolved centuries before. This government will be given power by acclamation of the people because its leaders will have demonstrated an ability to improve the lives of the people. So many and extensive freedoms will have been achieved in the New Renaissance and transitory centuries that anarchy will prevail all over the world. Not enough people will grasp the Pisces vision of "love thy neighbor."

Too many people will accept the new religion on a superficial level only. Bound by material values, society will discover that too much freedom means that no one is free. Weary of the struggle to survive against others whose idea of freedom infringes upon one's own, the people will be ripe for Scorpion manipulation and control. An Aquarian oligarchy will be ready for them and ready to use all the powers of Scorpio; just as over two milleniums before, the church leaders of the Age of Pisces had used the dogmatism of Sagittarius to establish their vision with the masses.

Scorpio issues of death and birth and genetics will be researched extensively and manipulated toward the goal of equality that represents the ideal of the oligarchy and of the people who elect it and give it power. Individual creativity (Leo) and the right to individual possessions (Taurus) will be suppressed, perhaps severely, for the sake of the needs of the whole group. No one must be hungry, everyone must have a job, a place to live. How can this be accomplished? *Brave New World*? Huxley's vision will be scientifically possible by this time.[1]

But the cosmic clock will move on. Individual freedom cannot be suppressed forever. And this is not an age of eight--of extremes of opposition. It is the ninth age--and the fishes have been set free. And the fishes will find a way to **be** free--in the mind and in the spirit, even if some material limitations must be accepted. The oligarchy will be stopped before the nightmare of *Brave New World* can be achieved; and the problems of burgeoning population will be solved by the colonization of other worlds. Taurus can again acquire and take root and build. And Leo will be encouraged to create with joy and bring up an abundance of children to populate the universe. And so many people will still teach the Piscean message. Love thy neighbor? Did the disciples of Jesus ever dream how vast that concept could be?

Capricorn, the tenth age, is symbolized by a creature that is half-goat, with the tail of a fish. The goat is a climber of mountains, but the fish's tail relates back to the two previous ages. In Pisces the fishes were bound by a cord to the womb of mortality, and the fishermen sought to catch them in order to teach them of the resurrection into immortality. In Aquarius, the fisherman sets his fishes free, so that while still mortal, they might learn with their minds more vast realizations of Truth. In Capricorn, the fishes have half-emerged from the dark waters and are attempting to climb the highest mountains of responsibility for their own freedom. But they are still mortal.

Most of the creatures of the zodiac are animals. With the exception of the Twins, who as number 5 (fifth age) represent the intellect that enables humanity to rise above the animals, the only humans are the Virgin and the Waterbearer. After the divine scales of Balance, the Virgin begins the evolutionary cycle. She is Mother Earth and she is the Divine Mother, the Great Goddess, through whom the Holy Spirit sustains all life. She is an image of God (Goddess--all is One). She gives birth to humanity, and is the channel through which the God-Man comes to Earth. The number of her age is two; she is mortal and yet divine.

In the age of the Waterbearer, the "everything" that is 9 is open to humanity. One can know not just by faith alone, but by intellect, that one is immortal, that physical death is only a transition. The resurrected God-Man sets the fishes free.

But regardless of what one knows through mind or spirit, while one occupies a physical body on earth, one is still bound to matter. One is still an "animal." But one can strive to climb the highest mountain, like a goat.

This is the tenth age, and 10 suggests a new beginning, a new 1, but with the wealth of history and experience of the previous 9 to build on.

Capricorn belongs to the element family of earth, and 10 is a new beginning, based on a past cycle of evolution to maturity. Thus the ideal might be stated that the fully aware individual now takes full responsibility for both material and spiritual evolution of the **self.** Now enough people should have advanced in awareness and acceptance of their responsibility that the collective consciousness is finally prepared to deal with the preservation of our earthly home. Attention that was previously focused on the outer space of the universe, and on the inner space of the mind, will now be refocused upon Earth, and upon the experience of the life span of the soul within the earthly body.

Transitions between great epochs, however, are always accompanied by great upheaval. A major refocusing of thought must take place at this time, so the motivating upheaval is likely to be spectacular.

In the Aquarian centuries, the problems of environment are diffused by the exodus of colonists to other worlds, and by the full development of solar energy (Leo). Advanced scientific techniques solve chemical problems with more chemicals.

The Aquarian fish are set free to escape, if they wish, the cross of earthly time and space. They can move on to other worlds, where other dimensions of time, and other symbolic systems, other zodiacs, will influence their paths toward Universal Truth. Most of the finest intellects of Aquarius choose to explore these newer paths. They choose a path toward outer space; or even if they remain on planet Earth, they choose a path of inner space, removing themselves in remote groups devoted to contemplation and the expansion of the mind.

Of course, all must eventually experience physical death, in spite of advanced scientific techniques that have increased the life span. But the souls of Aquarius, who have advanced to full spiritual enlightenment, know that their death will only be a passing over into a new dimension; and they will not return to Earth again within this cycle. Their lessons here are completed. Other dimensions must be explored. The time that remains in this Great Year on Earth is for the continued development of those resident souls who are still entangled in the sensations and desires of the material world.

The Aquarian leaders will assume that their science and technology can solve anything. But now, in

this fifth millenium since the time of Christ, Mother
Earth is quite worn out from constant attempts to
change her natural laws to suit human desires. She
announces her exasperation with her children by bringing in the Age of Capricorn with catastrophic earth-
quakes and Arian (Aries, the "insurgent" square) volcanic eruptions at "Mount Sinais" all over the world.
Weather conditions wreak havoc everywhere. Land
ruined by accumulated chemical manipulation will no
longer bear healthy crops, and the contamination of the
land affects animal life, too. Some species of insects,
birds, and animals that were once thought harmless,
mutate out of control and become dangerous. Insect
infestations cause people to again think of the ancient
biblical prophecies and wonder if the tribulation is
finally at hand. Even the ever-purifying oceans have
become dangerously polluted. The people are forced to
much greater use of chemical substitutes for the ruined
natural food supply; but the extensive unnatural
manipulation of nutrition results in new diseases for
both humans and animals.

The world government oligarchy will acknowledge,
too late, that massive changes must take place. Earth
may have to be abandoned completely, they speculate.
But that is impossible--there are still billions here. The
cost! It can't be done! The people clamor for protection;
the leaders bicker among themselves about what to do,
who is to blame, whose ideas should prevail. The oligarchy will collapse and a dictator will take control, and
raise a powerful police force to try to bring order out of
chaos.

But for the first time in many centuries, the
instant communication all over the world that made
central government possible will be broken down by
Mother Earth's rebellion. Natural disasters will cut off
groups of people from the rest of the world, with too
much happening too fast for the central government to

handle.   In the absence of tight central control, rival leaders will take charge in various areas and challenge the central dictator.   As people gather into groups for protection, separate nations will gradually begin to emerge.

Some people, previously reluctant to immigrate to other worlds, will now try to leave and escape the chaos on Earth, and some will succeed.   But with the breakdown of central control, and the extensive cost of dealing with the problems of Earth, space travel will decrease.   And Earth's colonies on other worlds will lessen their contacts with their former home, choosing to avoid risk at the hands of rival dictators and their police forces.

Some groups will gather under truly responsible leaders who will be able to organize the people into efforts that will restore the natural resources of their area.   This will be a true "back-to-nature" movement, as people research and rediscover how to live off the land. Life will be difficult for people accustomed to the push-button, automated world of Aquarius, but in many areas, there will be no choice.

Leaders are likely to use a revival of a pantheistic type of religion to encourage unity among their people. On the higher level, this will be the realization of each one's own Oneness with the universe.   On a superstitious, popular level, the ancient goat-footed god, Pan, may re-emerge.   Great interest will be given to history, for practical research into how to restore the land, but also for ways to understand the **why** of what is happening in the world.   The similarity of current events to some of the ancient 20th century writings of interpretations of the biblical Revelation will cause renewed speculation of the Second Coming of the Christ.

Astrologers, who in the Aquarian Age were mainly concerned with heliocentric and galactic-centered concepts, and detailed mathematical abstractions, will now return to Earth-centered basics. Deprived of their computers in many weather-ravaged areas, they will relearn how to look at the sky; and they will research ancient writings on dusty shelves of neglected libraries, and try to piece together their heritage from a human and a religious perspective.

The cosmic clock will turn onward, in this time of the cross of Capricorn. Eventually, the Arian square that brought a return to aggressive conflict will find its Libran balance and become the pioneering spirit that helps meet the challenge to protect the home (Cancer) with the ideal of Capricorn responsibility. The goat can climb the mountain.

In the seventh millenium of the time of the Christ, the vernal point will pass into the constellation of Sagittarius. The symbol is the Archer, a centaur, half-man and half-horse, who shoots his arrow toward the heavens. The ideal: that humanity is ready to rise out of its material (animal) nature and become truly one with the God whose image it bears. The centaur has half-emerged, and shoots his arrow toward the final Revelation, in true faith that he will reach his destiny.

The number of the Age of Sagittarius is 11. This is the time of final choice: mastery (11) or separation (2).

The souls in matter are symbolized by Gemini the Twins, who always see two sides to everything, and must approach all matters with pure reason and logic. "Present me with a good logical argument," one might say, "and I'll believe you. But then, if someone else gives me a better and more logical argument, I reserve the right to change my mind and believe that person!"

The squares, Virgo and Pisces, bring back all the old conflicts of the eighth age. The people of Earth are divided again, into different nations and different concepts of how the world should be managed and how God should be worshipped, or if there is a God at all.

Many generations have come and gone since the centrally controlled advanced educational techniques of the Age of Aquarius. The vast body of acquired knowledge was retained through all the earth upheavals of the Age of Capricorn, but inconsistently. Yes, all of the old conflicts return, even the threat of total destruction, either at the hands of an earthly intellect who has revived the old technologies of nuclear war; or perhaps at the hands of citizens of another world who, impatient with Earth's squabbles, decide to take over. The masses are ripe for a new leader--not just a conqueror who can restore world peace--but also a spiritual leader who can restore meaning and purpose to lives grown cynical and void of dreams.

Sagittarius is a sign of Revelation, and this is a time in the history of humanity (as much as any other) in which perhaps some of the circumstances from   the old 20th century stories based on the Bible's Revelation might indeed come to pass. Let's fantasize that at this time a new leader might capture the imagination and the allegiance of the masses by recreating in detail, the elements of the Jesus story, so that he is thought to be Christ returned--the Antichrist!   But remember, scripture tells us that it is not meant for us to know the hour.

The future is a mystery--shrouded, deliberately perhaps, by a veil of mercy.[2] But this chapter is fantasy based on symbolism, and in that light it seems fitting to associate our Centaur with the Four Horsemen of the Apocalypse.[3]

The first horse is white. His rider has a bow and is given a crown. He rides forth victorious, to conquer. He, like the Sagittarian Archer, could symbolize the capacity to "shoot for the stars" (Heaven), rise out of matter, and win the "crown."

The second horse is red, and his rider is given the sword of opposition. He symbolizes material bondage in opposition to God.

The third horse is black and his rider carries the Scales of Balance, and proclaims the need for equal measure.

The fourth horse is sickly green and his rider is Death, the destiny of all mortals.

Sagittarius is the stage upon which will be enacted the Final Conflict for all those who believe in conflict--who believe that opposition is an eternal fact of life.

For those who master 11, and realize their essential point of unity with all other beings, and the Oneness of all beings with God, no conflict will be perceived--only a passage.

The great Cosmic Clock strikes 12, but 12 is 3 and 3 is One. It is the Age of the Scorpion. The cycle nears completion. The Day of Judgment is at hand.

The constellation Scorpio has long been associated with death, at least as far back as the ancient Egyptians, who called the constellation Selket the Scorpion Goddess. Selket was closely watched in order to make preparation for the hordes of Scorpions that she released during the annual sandstorms.

Just off the ecliptic, but very near the constellations Scorpio and Libra, is Serpens the Serpent. Serpents, as well as scorpions, are symbolic of the lowest materialistic manifestation of the Scorpio character. Perhaps in this close association of signs in the heavens lies the reason for the serpent's appearance in the Age of Libra's Adam and Eve story. After the judgment, the destruction and the beginning of the new cycle, the serpent remains, as the symbol of earthly desire, to tempt the newly arriving innocent souls.

The esoteric symbol of Scorpio has always been a bird. Most often an eagle is portrayed. In scripture, written at the time when Taurus was still considered the Ascendant of the cardinal cross. the living creatures of Ezekiel's wheels and of the Revelation were composed of the Bull (Taurus), the Man (Aquarius), the Lion (Leo) and the Eagle (Scorpio).[4]

In the time of ancient Egypt, the regeneration from death was portrayed as a phoenix rising from the ashes.

The dove, since remotest antiquity, has been associated with the Holy Spirit, only recently thought to be male, but originally the spirit form of the Divine Mother. One of many myths (one that has a very familiar ring) is that of the ancient Assyrian goddess, Ishtar (who was also called Nu'a). She was so angry at the evil on Earth that she caused a mighty flood to drown all her children. But then she grieved and hoped to begin again, so she sent out her spirit in the form of a dove to see if the flood had receded. When the dove returned with an olive branch, she sent more children to Earth.[5]

The eternal human hope to find a release from death surely caused the bird symbols to be added to the Scorpio symbology. They became the emblem of one who rises above materialistic desires and is reborn into a higher level of spiritual consciousness.

I have not been able to discover exactly when and why Eagle became a specific Scorpio symbol. Perhaps someone, somewhere knows, but all the books I have read just say it **is.** The eagle seems to be somewhere between the level of scorpion/serpent and phoenix/dove. It is still a bird of prey, attacking with talons instead of a scorpion sting. Yet it has the ability to soar above the earth. It seems to symbolize a level of consciousness that is more evolved than the scorpion, aware of its higher self, but still not yet ready to relinquish its earthly pleasures and pains. Perhaps it realizes that only in death can it truly become Phoenix, and Eagle is not yet ready to die. It first wants to soar to the heights of its earthly potential.

Just maybe, the eagle idea could have come from someone long ago who speculated, as I have, on the cycle of the ages. Perhaps that person also saw Scorpio as the death and the end of a cycle; and also saw the period of the Age of Sagittarius as the Revelation. The eagle constellation, Aquila, lies above the ecliptic between Capricorn and Sagittarius. The Eagle, then, could represent the souls who through a high level of enlightenment are able to **rise above** the Final Conflict. Eagle has left the ecliptic--left the current of material evolution. It will become Phoenix without having to suffer the ultimate pain of Scorpio's sting.

In the Age of Scorpio, a cataclysmic event will occur that will make the earth upheavals of the Age of Capricorn seem but minor rumbles. Some intellects will be able to scientifically explain the cause of the event; but most people will call it the Judgment of God, and perhaps as the ancient prophets described, mass visions will be seen of a Christ figure in the clouds. The infamous polar shift? A new and massive movement of glaciers? A devastatingly large meteor shower?

Whatever the events, the entire face of Earth could be changed forever. Humans and animals will die by the billions. Continents may sink and others will rise. Entire civilizations will be reduced to rubble. Should the movement of Earth be slightly altered, even the signs in the sky would seem changed, and a new zodiac may greet the souls of the next cycle.

Once-fertile lands will now become the deserts of the Scorpion, and life on Earth will truly be a hell. The few humans who survive will be deprived of nearly all of the fruits of advanced science. None who remain will know the whys and hows of technology. All who still live are only scattered remnants of humanity, totally bound to material comforts they took for granted but did not understand. What is left of civilization will literally regress back to the Stone Age, as knowledge of the way things were becomes distorted and lost through successive generations who will know only the "myths" and "legends" told by their elders around the campfire.

Centuries pass and Earth's upheavals quiet. A slow healing process begins, restoring her elements to Balance. Once again her beauty will return and become a new Garden of Eden to attract new souls in search of a path of enlightenment.

And once again God will say, "*Let there be Light!*"

17

Twelve Wings of the Eagle

My daughter had just read the last chapter. "It reads more like science fiction than Bible interpretation. Isn't there anyplace in the Bible where the story of the future ages is told, so that you could refer to them step by step like you did with the past ages? What about Revelation?"

"Revelation is very complex and full of symbolism," I replied. "Some of the symbols are unmistakably astrological, for sure, like the 'four living creatures' who stand around the throne, and the woman 'clothed with the sun, with the moon under her feet, and on her head a crown of twelve stars.'[1] I have to study it more to see if I think it symbolizes each remaining age rather than just the final one. Many authors have already attempted to interpret Revelation--"

"Yes," Shannon interrupted, "I've read those Hal Lindsey books you've got, and the novel *The Seven Last Years* that was based on them."[2]

"In its own time, the Book of Revelation was probably taken to prophesy the fall of the Roman Empire, and this is how the translators of the *New American Bible* footnote much of the symbolism. The current trend of 'popular' interpretation definitely seems to be that the prophecies of Revelation will be fulfilled at least to the point of Christ's reappearance to establish rule over a thousand years of peace by around the end of this millenium."

"You don't think it will happen then, obviously."

"Obviously," I said with a smile, "after having just finished several thousand words to that effect! Maybe I'll try a book about Revelation some day. But it would take a whole book. There's just too much symbolism to handle in detail in this one. But just recently, when I had almost finished this book, I found a piece of scripture that fits so well that some people might think I found it first and then based my whole book on it. I am so impressed with its relevance to my work that I have decided to use it for the title."

"I suppose that means you're going to tell me about it."

"Of course I am! Here's one more chapter for you to read. Just think of the patience you've developed in your role as my literary device!"

"O.K. But please! Promise these will be your last words."

"I promise--for this book at least."

The Second Book of Esdras

The books of Esdras are from the Apocrypha. Apocrypha is derived from the Greek word *apokryphos*, which means "hidden." The name originally applied to writings that were esoteric and too important for general reading, meant only for the eyes of initiates.

Later the word came to be applied to a group of writings that were questionable, possibly heretical, and therefore secondary. Some Bibles do not contain them at all, while in others they are set apart into a special section.

The Catholic Bibles include most of them as canon and they are mixed in among the Old Testament books instead of set apart. 2 Esdras is included in the appendix of the *Catholic Vulgate*, and called Ezra 4; but it does not appear at all in the Catholic version of the *New American.* The translation that I paraphrase in this chapter is from the Oxford University Press *New English Bible.* The 2 Esdras is an apocalypse, probably written in the first century A.D. The Hebrew-Aramaic original has been lost, as well as most of the earliest Greek translation. The *New English Bible* translation is based on a Latin text, with reference to various critical editions of the Greek.[3]

E *sdras questioned God about many things, and in the course of many conversations with God's messenger angels, Esdras received explanations of the mysteries of human destiny. One of the questions was, "How long must we stay here? When will. . .we get our reward?" The answer: "As soon as the number of those like yourselves is complete. For the Lord has weighed the world in a balance, he has measured and numbered the ages; he will move nothing, alter nothing, until the appointed number is achieved."*[4]

Later, Esdras is told of the Judgment in a way that bears many similarities to the Revelation, but some details are different.

F *or those who are delivered from the evils of the ungodly, the Messiah and his companions will bring* **four hundred years** *of happiness. At the end of that time, the Messiah and all mortals will die and the world will return to its original silence for seven days as it was at the beginning of creation. "After seven days, the age which is not yet awake shall be roused and the age which is corruptible shall die."* **Then** *the judgment will take place and the Most High will appear as the Judge of all souls who once lived on Earth.*[5]

Now, 2 Esdras was written after the time of Christ

but well before the fall of the Roman Empire, which would have been looked upon as a true and tangible event to mark the passing away of the old order (age). Early Christians expected that Christ would return to destroy Rome, and then rule over the new age that would fulfill all their hopes for Utopia (a vision that is shared by those who look toward the end of **this** age).

Numbers in the Bible always have symbolic significance, but are usually not to be taken literally. Four hundred years could just as well mean four ages. If it does, then the four ages of the dispensation of the Messiah would be Pisces, Aquarius, Capricorn and Sagittarius. That leaves Scorpio for the Last Judgment!

In chapters 11 and 12, Esdras receives a dream--

A large eagle with twelve wings and three heads rose out of the sea and spread its wings over all the earth. Out of its wings, eight small and stunted wings sprouted. The eagle ruled over all the earth, meeting no resistance from any of its inhabitants. It told its wings not to wake up all at once, but to each wake up in turn. The heads were to remain still until the last.

*As Esdras watched, one wing rose and became ruler over all the earth; but after a time its reign came to an end, and it disappeared from sight. Then the next one arose and held its rule **for a long time.** Just as it was about to disappear, **a voice gave the message that none of its successors would reign so long.** Then the third wing arose, ruled and disappeared; and so each came to power in its turn.*

Some of the wings held power for only a short time and others arose but did not hold power. The little wings were active for short moments, attempting to seize kingship and then vanishing. In the end, the middle, largest head devoured two little wings and then got the whole world in its grasp, establishing an oppressive rule. But then the middle head vanished suddenly and the two heads remaining seized power over Earth, but as Esdras watched, the head on the right devoured the head on the left.

Then a lion appeared, roared and addressed the eagle in a human voice, announcing that he is speaking for the Most High. He asked the eagle if he is not the only survivor of the four beasts to which the Most High gave rule over the world, intending through them to bring the ages to an end. The lion then accused the eagle of holding the world in fear, with oppression, insolence and pride. He went on to say that the Most High has surveyed the periods he has fixed and they are now at an end. "So you, eagle, must now disappear--then all the earth will feel relief at its deliverance from your violence and look forward hopefully to the judgment and mercy of its Creator."

The one remaining head then disappeared and the two last little wings that had been sheltering themselves beneath it rose and ruled for a short and troubled period before the eagle's entire body burst into flames and Earth was struck with terror.

In fear, Esdras awakened, and prayed to the Lord to give him strength and to reveal to him the interpretation of his vision.

He was told that the eagle represented an empire ruled by twelve kings, one after another. The second would have the longest reign of the twelve. The voice at the close of the second reign meant that great conflicts would arise then that would bring the empire in danger of falling, but it would not fall at that time, but would be restored to its original strength.

The eight small wings meant that the empire would come under eight kings whose reigns would be trivial and short; two would come and go before the middle of the period, four would be kept back until nearer the end, and two until the end itself.

The three heads are interpreted to Esdras as three

*kings who would rule in the last years of the empire,.
They would restore much of its strength and rule more
oppressively than any before. They are the eagle's
heads because they will bring to a head a long series of
evil deeds. The largest head is a king who will die in
his bed in agony. One of the two who remain will kill
the other, but then, himself, will be murdered in the last
days. The last two little wings are short and troubled
kingdoms of the last days.*

*The lion is the Messiah whom the Most High has
kept back until the end. He will bring the kings to justice and destroy them, but will set God's people free.
That, then, is the interpretation of the vision as it was
told to Esdras by God's angel. The angel went on to tell
Esdras that this secret had been told only to him, and
that he should write it in a book and hide it and tell it
only to people whom he knew to be wise enough to
understand it and keep it safe.*[6]

For those of you who have read my entire book,
no explanation is necessary as to why I found this
vision of Esdras to be so striking. But for those of you
who, like my daughter, have skipped and skimmed and
read only some of the chapters, I shall interpret the
interpretation. The eagle is Scorpio, and as the symbol
of death, regeneration and rebirth, it is both the totality
and the last of the 12 ages. The twelve wings are, of
course, the twelve ages. The second age is Virgo, which
as the largest constellation, takes much longer than the
others. That makes the previous and first age Libra the
Balance, and as Esdras was told, "The Lord has
weighed the world in a balance."

The great conflicts at the close of the second reign
would involve the full flowering of the battle of opposites, as early woman-centered societies pass to the
patriarchy; and according to legend, a flood that nearly
destroyed all on earth would abate and the world would

be restored.

The eight kings could well be eight major civilizations that, great though they may be, would be trivial compared to the total empire (cycle).

The three heads who are three kings are a bit more of a puzzle, although they could be three great powers who will exist simultaneously in the final age. Or they could just be part of the symbolism of the three-in-one that is so much a part of our three-dimensional world. In this case the concept of three is blended with dualism, and the three heads are somewhat reminiscent of Satan, the Beast and his Prophet of the Hal Lindsey Revelation interpretations.

The Messiah returns as the lion, as Jesus was the descendant of Judah the Lion, who carried the banner of Leo within the twelve tribes of Israel.

The eagle was addressed as one of the four beasts who were, in biblical times, considered to symbolize the 'four corners of the world,' the cardinal cross of the equinox and solstice points. The eagle is clearly addressed as the final age.

When the angel explained earlier about the "four hundred years" after which the world would return to the silence as it was at the beginning of creation, it is said that after the silence a **new** age would awake. This seems a clear indication of a whole new cycle to be expected **after** the completion of the old. This is made even clearer in Chapter 14 of 2 Esdras, as the Lord again speaks to Esdras:

I revealed myself in the bush, and spoke to Moses, when my people Israel was in slavery in Egypt, and sent him to lead my people out of Egypt. I brought him up to Mount Sinai, and kept him with me for many days. I told him of many wonders, showing him the secrets of the ages and the end of time, and instructed him what to make known and what to conceal. So too I now give this order to you: commit to memory the signs I have shown you, the visions you have seen, and the explanations you have been given. You yourself are about to be taken away from the world of men, and thereafter you will remain with my son and with those like you, until the end of time. The world has lost its youth, and time is growing old. For the whole of time is in twelve divisions; nine divisions and half the tenth have already passed, and only two and a half still remain." [8]

Could this mean that the total number of Great Years for the experience of souls on Earth are twelve? Biblical times were halfway through the present Great Year. If this is the tenth cycle, then it represents a new beginning based on the maturation of a past cycle of evolution of consciousness that is symbolized by nine. The Last Judgment, then, if it is truly the end time for all humanity, would be two and a half cycles past our Age of Aries, or over 60,000 years into the future--only a fleeting moment of God's time. The past time for the evolution of humans would then be nine and a half Great Years, or about 483,570 years. That does sound just a wee bit more compatible with reason than the "scientific creationists" version of little more than 4000 years before Christ.

The great Jesuit philosopher, Teilhard de Chardin, wrote of the evolution in four stages: **Cosmogenesis,** the formation of the universe and Earth from the beginning; **Biogenesis,** the physical evolution of humanity; **Noogenesis,** the evolution of consciousness; and the last and final stage--**Christogenesis.**[9] Billions of years! Scarcely conceivable to our impatient souls. Perhaps the nine and a half Great Years before the time of Christ were the period of Noogenesis. Having achieved a level of consciousness able to comprehend the message of

Christ, will it take humanity another 60,000 years to be ready to live it? How little time we have left. How little we know!

But how foolish to look to the future with fears! We live in an exhilarating age where new mysteries continually open into realities. How very much more there is to learn!

May we all be raised upward on the wings of an eagle, and learn to shine like the Son! [10]

Endnotes

If I have quoted directly from the Bible, the endnote will cite the specific translation. If the endnote indicates chapter and verse only, then the passage is paraphrased from a composite reading of more than one Bible.

See publisher data in the following bibliography.

Introduction

1 **The New American Bible, Catholic Edition** (Nashville, Camden, New York: Thomas Nelson Publishers, 1971).

Chapter 1

1 **The New English Bible** (Oxford University Press, Cambridge University Press, 1970).

2 Here, in referring to the deity of the Creationists I emphasize the personification of God as male, and capitalize as they would. Later, in paraphrasing various Bible stories I refer to "the Lord" as "he" as it is written in the Bible. In all other cases I have avoided the use of personal pronouns to refer to the All-in-One. I believe that if one feels more comfort in visualizing a persona for God, it is equally valid to think of "Mother" as it is to think of "Father."

Chapter 2

The astronomical information in this chapter is found in many sources. The ones that I read prior to writing the chapter are listed in the bibliography.

1 The comparison of precession to a child's top is from **Stars and Men** by Stephen and Margaret Ionides.

2 The explanation of how the ancients observed the coming of a new age is from **Hamlet's Mill** by Giorgio de Santillana and Hertha von Dechend.

3 The astronomical list is found on page 49 of **Recent Advances in Natal Astrology** by Geoffrey Dean,

4 My thoughts about tropical vs. sidereal astrology

were clarified by Robert Hand's **Horoscope Symbols**.

5   The calendar information is from material presented at the "Master Class on Spherical Astronomy," Cape Cod Chapter, National Council for Geocosmic Research, in September of 1980.

6   James Trager, **The People's Chronology.**

7   The lecture cited was for a conference of National Council for Geocosmic Research in New York City, March 1982. Hand's **Essays On Astrology** is published by Para Research.

8   Robert Powell, lecture "World Chronology," American Federation of Astrologers Convention, Chicago, September 1982.

Chapter 3

1   **New English Bible.**

2   **New American Bible.**

3   **New American Bible.**

4   James Finley and Michael Pennock, **Your Faith and You**. During 1981-1984 (three school years) I taught confirmation classes for high school sophomores in a Catholic parish in Connecticut. This book was one of the textbooks used.

5   Ibid.

Chapter 4

1   The paraphrased Bible verses at the beginning of each "day" in the allegory are from *Genesis* Chapter 1, and are based on the King James Version.

2   The material on the Priestly-Yahwist sources is a composite of information I found in the Introduction to **The New American Bible** and from the **Encyclopedia Americana.**

3   The names for the triune God, Spirit, Mind and Individuality, are from the philosophy section of the biography of Edgar Cayce, **There Is A River**, by Thomas Sugrue. I could think of no words more appropriate than these.

4 *Exodus* 3 :14
5 *Exodus* 20:2-3
6 *John* 1:14, **The Holy Bible,** King James Version.

Chapter 5
1 The information on the "big bang" theories is from **The Creation of the Universe** by David E. Fisher.
2 Geraldine Thorston, **God Herself.**
3 My thoughts about positive/negative were strongly influenced by reading **Initiation** by Elisabeth Haich.
4 The quote here, from *Genesis* 1:1 is paraphrased, but the words earth, wind, waters, light, as stated, are typical of modern translations such as the **New American** and the **New English Bibles**.
5 Rabbi Joel Dobin, **To Rule Both Day and Night**.

Chapter 6
1 The details of my confrontation with religious fundamentalists can be found in my article, "Braving the Brimstone," in **Geocosmic News,** (National Council for Geocosmic Research, Winter 1982 issue).
2 The story of Adam and Eve is based on *Genesis,* chapters 2 and 3.

Chapter 7
1 Cain and Abel, *Genesis* 4.
2 *Genesis* 6:1-4.
3 Noah, *Genesis* 6,7,8 to 9:16.
4 *Genesis* 9:20-27.
5 Cayce Foundation, **The Hidden History of Reincarnation**.
6 **Mysteries of the Past** (Simon & Schuster, 1977).
7 Tower of Babel, *Genesis* 11:1-9.
8 Genealogy, *Genesis* 11:10-26.

Chapter 8
1 Abram's migration, *Genesis* 12:1-10.

2 **Mysteries of the Past**.

3 Peter Tompkins, **Secrets of the Great Pyramid**.

4 Colin Renfrew, **Before Civilization**.

5 *Genesis* 12:11-20.

6 *Genesis* 13 and 14.

7 The astrological interpretation of *Genesis* 15 is explained in Rabbi Dobin's **To Rule Both Day and Night**.

8 *Genesis* 15.

9 **New American Bible,** *Genesis* 10:15-16, and footnote 10, 1-32.

10 **Webster's New Twentieth Century Dictionary**,
2nd Edition gives Chaldean as "a semetic people related
to the Babylonians" and "an astrologer or sorcerer." The
footnote to Genesis 11:28 in the **New American Bible**
says that the term Chaldean is an anachronism
because the Chaldeans were not known to history until
about 1000 years after Abraham's time. Perhaps so, if
one only considers the historical Abraham. Why, then,
does the Bible (not just **New American**, but **King
James Version** and **New English**, as well), in referring
to Abraham's homeland, always say "Ur of the
Chaldeans?" (I used only "Ur" in some places in this
text, in keeping with various anthropology books I'd
read that traced the beginnings of *Homo sapiens* to Ur.
See page 23.) There must have been a reason why the
authors of *Genesis*--or perhaps ancient Greek transla-
tors--chose to link Abraham with the Chaldeans. I submit that this is one more example of the extensive
astrological content in the Bible.

11 *Genesis* 16.

Chapter 9

1   *Genesis* 17.

2   On circumcision: **The First Sex,** by Elizabeth Gould
Davies, states that circumcision is a survival of the
ancient goddess cult. The patriarchal declaration of circumcision as a covenant between man and God was an
attempt to rationalize a matriarchal custom that could

not be abolished.

3   On the Goldwater story: I was unable to locate the newspaper article that I'd read, but the rules to which it referred can be found in **The Complete Book of Jewish Observance** by Leo Trepp.

4   Dobin, **To Rule Both Day and Night.**

5   *Genesis* 18:1-15.

6   **New American Bible**, footnote 17,17 on page 16.

7   Destruction of Sodom and Gomorrah, *Genesis* 18:16-33 and 19:1-26.

8   *Genesis* 19:30-38.

9   *Genesis* 20.

10   *Genesis* 21:1-20.

11   Story of pact at Beer-sheba, *Genesis* 21:22-33.

12   The testing of Abraham, *Genesis* 22:1-18.

13   Sarah's death, *Genesis* 23.

Chapter 10

1   *Genesis* 24.

2   **New American Bible**, footnote 24,2, *Genesis* 24.

3   *Genesis* 25: 7-10.

4   My former student, Tom Canfield, who offered the information about Methuselah, says that he read it in the **Old Farmer's Almanac**. He doesn't remember which year. The arithmetic checks out correctly with the genealogy in *Genesis* 5 and the age of Noah at the time of the flood in *Genesis* 7:6!

5   *Galatians* 4:21-27.

6   The story of the origin of the Uncle Sam symbol can be found on pages 768-769 of **The People's Almanac** by David Wallenchensky and Irving Wallace.

7   Birth of Esau and Jacob: *Genesis* 25:10-34.

8   *Genesis* 26.

9   **New American Bible**, footnotes on page 26.

10   *Genesis* 26: 34-35.

11   Jacob's deception, *Genesis* 27.

12   **New American Bible**, footnote 27, 1-45, page 26.

13 Jacob acts to reconcile with Esau: *Genesis* 32:4:22.
14 Jacob wrestles with "some man" until dawn (symbolically, perhaps, dawn represents his own conscience)
"prevails," and is renamed Israel: *Genesis* 32:25-29.

Chapter 11
1 A few of the other books that discuss the twelve
tribes as zodiac symbols are: **To Rule Both Day and
Night**, Dobin; **Astrology's Pew in the Church**, Jacobs;
The Bible and The Stars, Heline; and **The Hidden
Wisdom in the Holy Bible**, Hodson.
2 *Genesis* 49:4.
3 *Genesis* 48:5-7.
4 *Genesis* 48:4, 7, and 26.
5 *Exodus* 1:1-5.
6 The actual birth order of Jacob's sons is in *Genesis*
29:31-35 and 30:1-24, except for the youngest
Benjamin, in 35:16-18.
7 *Deuteronomy* 33.
8 *Numbers* 2 (encampment--Judah gets the eastern,
sunrise position); *Numbers* 34; *Judges* 1 (Judah designated by the Lord to lead in battle); *2 Chronicles* .
9 The meanings for the names of Jacob's sons are
taken from the footnotes to *Genesis* 29, 30 and 35 in
The New American Bible.
10 *Numbers* 1.
11 *Deuteronomy* 33. The quote is from **The New
American Bible**.
12 The analysts referred to are Corinne Heline, **The
Bible and the Stars**, and Geoffrey Hodson, **The
Hidden Wisdom in the Holy Bible,Vol III**.
13 Don Jacobs, **Astrology's Pew in the Church**.
Reprints of this book are available through Experience
Astrology in San Francisco.
14 Dobin, **To Rule Both Day and Night**
15 *Numbers* 33:33; *Deuteronomy* 3:13; *Joshua* 1:12,
4:12, 13:7-8 and 13:29.
16 *Deuteronomy* 3:13.

17   *Genesis* 49:27.
18   *Genesis* 49:4.
19   *Genesis* 49:24.
20   Although there are many previous references to Aaron, brother of Moses, and his family, and to them as the priests, it is in *Numbers* 3 that the tribe of Levi is set apart to perform priestly functions.
21   *Deuteronomy* 33:7
22   The contrast between *Genesis* 49 and *Deuteronomy* 33.
23   *Genesis* 34.

Chapter 12
1   *Genesis* 37.

2   The Joseph story is covered in *Genesis* 39-50.

3   The information about ancient Egypt comes from many sources, some I can no longer identify.   More about Selket can be found in Thorston's **God Herself**. Haich's **Initiation** is a fascinating story about the training of an ancient Egyptian initiate. Although fictionalized, it contains a wealth of information on symbolism. More on the cult of the bull is in Chapter 11 of **Stars and Men** by the Ionideses.   **Secrets of the Great Pyramid** by Tompkins is must reading for those who are interested in the advanced knowledge possessed by the architects of the Pyramid at Giza.

Chapter 13
1   Ionides, **Stars and Men.**

2   Richard Cavendish, **The Great Religions**.

3   Amenhotep IV is mentioned in numerous sources. The new name that he took has variations: Akhenaton, Akhnaton, Ikhnaton. Details can be found in Chapter 4 of Ionides' **Stars and Men**, and in **Encyclopedia Americana,** Vol. 1, page 668.

4   **Atlas of the Bible**, (Readers Digest Assoc., Inc.).
5   Dobin, **To Rule Both Day and Night.**

6 The story of Moses to this point is found in *Exodus* 2 through 15:21.

7 *Exodus* 19:1 and 19:18-19.

8 *Exodus* 24:3-8.

9 *Exodus* 24: 15-18.

10 Ordination rites: Exodus 29.

11 *Exodus* 31:18.

12 *Exodus* 32.

13 *Exodus* 34.

14 The grumbling and the Lord's provision of water and manna is first mentioned in *Exodus* 15 and 16.

15 The incident at Kadesh is told in *Numbers* 20. The link with the "smitten by water" prediction is from **To Rule Both Day and Night**.

16 Tradition of hot cross buns: **Stars and Men.**

Chapter 14

1 The details about what the astrologers might have seen and done are based on the research of Don Jacobs for **Astrology's Pew in the Church**.

2 The nativity story is a composite of the versions in the gospels of *Matthew* and *Luke.*

3 The discussion on the origins and themes of the gospels was influenced by **The Jesus Book**, by Ronald Wilkins. This is another of the textbooks I used in teaching confirmation classes.

4 **New American Bible**, *John* 11:9-10.

5 **New American Bible**, footnote 11,10, John 11.

6 Much of the information in the historical sketch is repeated in a number of the sources in the following Bibliography as well as in others I've read and can no longer identify, therefore it is impossible to individually credit each thought. For more detail on church history, I recommend Cavendish's, **The Great Religions,** Louis de Wohl's **Founded on a Rock** and **The New Catholic Encyclopedia** (Catholic University of America, 1979).

7 This definition of Gnosticism is from **The New Catholic Encyclopedia**. For further study I suggest **The Gnostic Religion** by Hans Jonas.

8 For more detail on the library at Alexandria, see **Cosmos** by Carl Sagan.

9 The definition of *superstition* is from **The Random House Dictionary of the English Language**.

10 William J. Fielding, **Strange Superstitions and Magical Practices**.

11 **New Catholic Encyclopedia,** Vol. 1, *Astrology*.

12 Dobin, **To Rule Both Day and Night**

13 Jean-Louis Brau, Helen Weaver and Allan Edmands, **Larousse Encyclopedia of Astrology**.

14 **New Catholic Encyclopedia,** Vol. 1, *Astrology*.

15 The Rev. Laurence L. Cassidy, S.J., "The Believing Christian as a Dedicated Astrologer," **CAO Times**, 1978.

16 **New American Bible,** *John* 20:24-29.

17 The key words used for Sagittarius and Gemini are the same as those used by Marcia Moore and Mark Douglas in **Astrology: The Divine Science** .

18 Reference to "shadow": My thoughts that correlate astrological symbolism with Jung's psychology were first influenced by Liz Greene in **Relating**.

19 Readers Digest, **Atlas of the Bible**, page 26.

20 Brau, **Larousse Encyclopedia of Astrology**, pages 186-7.

21 Cavendish, **The Great Religions**.

22 *The Book of Jonah* is found in the Old Testament between *Obadiah* and *Micah*. This version is paraphrased from the **New American Bible**, with help from its footnotes.

23 East in astrology is the Ascendant--sunrise, a beginning. East, in the Bible, seems also to be associated with new ideas or beginnings. The Garden of Eden is in the east. Adam and Eve are settled to the east even after they are expelled from the garden. Abraham's family migrate from the east--the land of Ur of the

Chaldeans.   Much later, three astrologers (Chaldeans) from the east come to find the Messiah.

24 **New Catholic Encyclopedia**.

25 On Mary Magdalene: *John* 20:11-18.

26 For research on the idea that Jesus may have been married and had children, see **Holy Blood, Holy Grail**, Michael Baigent, Richard Leigh and Henry Lincoln.

27 Thorston, **God Herself**, p. 145.

28 Dobin, **To Rule Both Day and Night,** p. 43.

29 More information about the Goddess religions can be found in Thorston's **God Herself**, Merlin Stone's **When God Was a Woman**, and Barbara G. Walker's **The Women's Encyclopedia of Myths and Secrets**.

30 *Luke* 2:34-35.

31 Waverley translation, **Ptolemy's Tetrabiblos**.

32 The following discussion of astrological symbols, from this point to the end of the chapter, is influenced by Peter Lemesurier, **Gospel of the Stars**.

Chapter 15

1 My interpretation of numbers is developed from a composite of three primary sources, and from my own reasoning and meditation.   I do not agree in entirety with any of the three sources, but I recommend reading all of them: Haich's **Initiation**, Patrizia Norelli-Bachelet's **Symbols and the Question of Unity,** ; Faith Javane's and Dusty Bunker's **Numerology and The Divine Triangle**.

2 For a detailed explanation of Pythagoras and his solids, see Sagan's **Cosmos**.

3 **New American Bible**, *Mark* 8:18-21.

4 **Strange Superstitions**, page 77.

5 Hand, **Essays on Astrology**.

6 Greene, **Relating**.

Chapter 16

1 Aldous Huxley, **Brave New World**.

2 Morris West, **Clowns of God**.

3 The Four Horsemen of the Apocalypse are found in the New Testament in *Revelation* 6.

4 The four "living creatures": *Ezekiel 1 and 10, Revelation 4:6.*

5 Thorston, **God Herself**.

Chapter 17

1 *Revelation* 12:1.

2 Hal Lindsey, **The Late Great Planet Earth.**

3 The information of the apocrypha is from *Introduction to the Apocrypha* in **The New English Bible**, and from the **Encyclopedia Americana.**

4 **New English Bible**, *2 Esdras* 4:35-36.

5 Ibid, *2 Esdras* 7:26-36.

6 Ibid, *2 Esdras* 11 and 12.

7 Ibid, *2 Esdras* 14:2-13.

8 Pierre Teilhard de Chardin, **The Future of Man**.

9 The closing lines are based on a hymn by Michael Joncas (North American Liturgy Resources, Phoenix, AZ 85029). The verse: *"And he will raise you up on eagle's wings, bear you on the breath of dawn, make you shine like the sun ..."*

Bibliography

BIBLES: **The New American Bible**, Catholic Version,
Nashville, Camden, New York: Thomas
Nelson Pub., 1971.
The New English Bible, Oxford University
Press, Cambridge University Press,
1970.
**The Holy Bible, Authorized King James
Version,** Westport, Connecticut,
Trinity Publishing Co., Inc.

Baigent, Michael, Richard Leigh and Henry Lincoln,
Holy Blood, Holy Grail, New York: Dell
Publishing Co., 1982.

Bailey, Foster, **Spirit of Masonry**, London: Lucis Press,
1957.

Balizet, Carol, **The Seven Last Years**, New York:
Bantam Books, 1978.

Brau, Jean-Louis, Helen Weaver and Allan Edmands,
Larousse Encyclopedia of Astrology, McGraw-
Hill Book Co., 1980.

Cassidy, Laurence L., Ph.D, S.J., *"The Believing
Christian as a Dedicated Astrologer,"* **CAO
Times, Inc.**, 1978.

Cavendish, Richard, **The Great Religions**, New York:
Arco Publ., Inc., 1980.

Cayce Foundation, **The Hidden History of
Reincarnation**, Virginia Beach, Virginia: A.R.E.
Press, 1965

Davies, Elizabeth Gould, **The First Sex,** Baltimore:
Penguin, 1971.

Dean, Geoffrey, **Recent Advances In Natal Astrology**,
Bromley Kent, England: The Astrological
Association, 1977.

de Chardin, Pierre Teilhard, **The Future of Man**, New
York: Harper and Row, 1964.

de Santillana, Giorgio and Hertha von Dechend,
Hamlet's Mill, Boston: Gambit, Inc., 1969.

de Wohl, Louis, **Founded on a Rock**, Philadelphia and
New York: J. B. Lippincott Co., 1961.

Dobin, Rabbi Joel, **To Rule Both Day and Night**, New
York, Inner Traditions International, 1977.

Dobyns, Zipporah Pottenger, **The Zodiac as a Key to
History**, Los Angeles: TIA Publications, 1977.

Encyclopedia Americana, 1968.

Ferguson, Marilyn, **The Aquarian Conspiracy**, Los
Angeles: J.P. Tarcher, Inc., 1980.

Fielding, William J., **Strange Superstitions and
Magical Practices,** New York: Paperback Library,
Inc., 1966.

Finley, James and Michael Pennock, **Your Faith And
You**, Notre Dame, Indiana 46556: Ave Maria
Press, 1978.

Fisher, David E., **The Creation of the Universe**, New
York: Bobbs-Merrill, 1977.

Forman, Henry James, **The Story of Prophecy**, New
York: Tudor Publishing Co., 1936.

Greene, Liz, **Relating,** New York: Samuel Weiser, Inc.,
1978.

Haich, Elisabeth, **Initiation,** Garberville, CA: Seed
Center, 1965.

Hand, Robert, **Essays on Astrology**, Rockport, MA:
Para Research, 1982.

Hand, Robert, **Horoscope Symbols**, Rockport, MA:
Para Research, 1981.

Heline, Corinne, **The Bible and the Stars**, Los
Angeles: New Age Press, Inc., 1971.

Hodson, Geoffrey, **The Hidden Wisdom In The Holy
Bible**, Vol. III, Quest Edition, Wheaton, Illinois:
The Theosophical Publishing House, 1974.

Huxley, Aldous, **Brave New World**, New York;
Harper and Brothers, 1932.

Ionides, Stephen and Margaret, **Stars And Men**,
Indianapolis and New York: Bobbs-Merrill Co.,
1939.

Jacobs, Don, **Astrology's Pew in the Church,** 1136
    Union Mall, Honolulu, HI, 1979.

Javane, Faith and Dusty Bunker. **Numerology and
    The Divine Triangle**, Rockport, MA: Para
    Research, Inc., 1979.

Jonas, Hans, **The Gnostic Religion**, Boston: Beacon
    Press, 1958.

Jossick, Maria Simms, *"Braving the Brimstone,"*
    Geocosmic News, Vol. 8 Nos. 3 & 4, NCGR, 1982.

Kriyananda, Swami, **Your Sun Sign As A Spiritual
    Guide**, Nevada City, CA: Amanda Publications,
    1971.

Lemesurier, Peter, **Gospel of the Stars**, New York:
    Avon, 1977.

Lindsey, Hal, **The Late Great Planet Earth,** Grand
    Rapids, Michigan: Zondervan Publishing House,
    1970.

Martin, William, *"Waiting For The End,* " **The Atlantic
    Monthly** (June 1982).

Moore, Marcia and Mark Douglas, **Astrology: The
    Divine Science**, York Harbor, Maine: Arcane
    Publications, 03911, 1971.

Mysteries of the Past, Simon & Schuster, 1977.

National Geographic Society, **Great Religions of the
    World**, 1971.

The New Catholic Encyclopedia, Catholic University
    of America, 1979.

Norelli-Bachelet, Patrizia, **The Gnostic Circle**,
    Panorama City, CA: Aeon Books, Coreki Corp.,
    1975

Norelli-Bachelet, Patrizia, **Symbols and the Question
    of Unity**, Wassenaar, Holland: Servire Publishers,
    1974.

Old Farmer's Almanac, Dublin, NH 03444 (per note
    10-4).

Papon, Donald, **The Lure of the Heavens**, New York:
    Samuel Weiser, Inc., 1980.

Powell, Robert, Lecture, *"World Chronology,"* American Federation of Astrologers Convention. Chicago, September, 1982.

Powell, Robert and Peter Treadgold, **The Sidereal Zodiac,** London: Theosophical Publications, 1979.

The Random House Dictionary of the English Language, New York, 1967.

Readers Digest, **Atlas of the Bible**, Pleasantville, N.Y. & Montreal: Readers Digest Association, Inc., 1981.

Renfrew, Colin, **Before Civilization**, New York: Alfred A. Knopf, 1973.

Sagan, Carl, **Cosmos**, New York: Random House, 1980.

Simms, Maria Kay. See Maria Simms Jossick.

Stone, Merlin, **When God Was A Woman**, San Diego, New York, London: A Harvest/HBJ Book, 1976.

Sugure, Thomas, **There Is A River,** New York: Holt, Rinehart & Winston, Inc., pb edition, Dell Publishing Co., 1942.

Temple, Robert K.G., **The Sirius Mystery,** New York: St. Martin's Press, 1976.

Thorston, Geraldine, **God Herself**, New York: Avon Books, 1980.

Tompkins, Peter, **Secrets of the Great Pyramid**, New York, San Francisco, Evanston and London: Harper & Row, 1971.

Trager, James, **The People's Chronology**, New York: Holt, Rinehart & Winston, 1979.

Trepp, Leo, **The Complete Book Of Jewish Observance**, New York: Behrman House, Inc., Summit Books,1980.

Von Daniken, Erich, **Chariots of the Gods**, New York: Bantam, 1970.

Von Daniken, Erich, **In Search of Ancient Gods**, New York: Bantam, 1973.

Walker, Barbara G., **The Women's Encyclopedia of Myths and Secrets**, San Francisco: Harper &

Row, 1983.

Wallenchensky, David and Irving Wallace. **The People's Almanac**, New York: Doubleday & Co., Inc., 1975.

Waverley Translation: **Ptolemy's Tetrabiblos**, North Hollywood, CA: Symbols & Signs, 1976.

Webster's New Twentieth Century Dictionary, 2nd Edition, New York: Simon & Schuster 1983.

West, Morris, **Clowns of God,** New York: William Morrow, 1981.

Wilkins, Ronald J., **The Jesus Book**, Dubuque, Iowa: Wm. C. Brown Co., Publishers, 1979.

Index

Notes

Notes

INNER VISIONS SERIES

The Inner Visions Series explores inner realities and individual evolution. Some titles are biographical, while others describe methods of spiritual awakening. The purpose is to share with many the experiences of those whose vision of life reaches beyond limited realities to encompass a larger view of the universe.

Spirit Guides: We Are Not Alone
by Iris Belhayes
Channeled from Enid, whose message inspires hope, joy and reassurance.
ISBN 0-917086-80-5 $12.95

The Mystery of Personal Identity
by Michael Mayer
Psychology meets astrology in this exploration of that ancient question: "Who am I and what does my life mean?"
ISBN 0-917086-54-6 $9.95

Past Lives Future Growth
by Armand Marcotte and Ann Druffel
Amazing psychic Armand Marcotte is assisted in counseling by three guides from a former lifetime.
ISBN 0-917086-88-0 $12.95

Hands That Heal
by Echo Bodine Burns
This spiritual healer tells how you can utilize your own healing powers to help yourself and others.
ISBN 0-917086-76-7 $7.95

The Psychic and the Detective
by Ann Druffel with Armand Marcotte
Excitement and drama abound as Armand Marcotte assists police by using his psychic abilities to help solve crimes.
ISBN 0-917086-53-8 $7.95

A New Awareness
by Jack Nast
Channeled images of world changes that will catapult us from an era of fear and superstition into a consciousness of individual power and psychic knowing.
ISBN 0-917086-94-5 $9.95

Beyond the Veil
by Judy Laddon
Channeled information on the meaning of life, life after death, coming world changes and the necessity for a spiritual outlook for a fulfilled life.
IBSN 0-91708697-X $7.95

Order from
ACS Publications, Inc. Dept. TW288
PO Box 16430, San Diego, CA 92116-0430
Available at your local bookstore.
(Prices Subject to Change)

The best value in everything you need
to calculate and interpret charts
from
ACS Publications, Inc.
P.O. Box 16430, San Diego, CA 92116